Classical Hindu Thought

Classical Hindu Thought
An Introduction

Arvind Sharma

OXFORD
UNIVERSITY PRESS

OXFORD
UNIVERSITY PRESS

YMCA Library Building, Jai Singh Road, New Delhi 110 001

Oxford University Press is a department of the University of Oxford. It furthers the University's objective of excellence in research, scholarship, and education by publishing worldwide in

Oxford New York

Athens Auckland Bangkok Bogota Buenos Aires Calcutta Cape Town Chennai Dar es Salaam Delhi Florence Hong Kong Istanbul Karachi Kuala Lumpur Madrid Melbourne Mexico City Mumbai Nairobi Paris Sao Paulo Singapore Taipei Tokyo Toronto Warsaw

with associated companies in Berlin Ibadan

Published in India
By Oxford University Press, New Delhi

First published 2000

ISBN 019 564 4417

Typeset in Garamond
by Wordsmiths, Saraswati Vihar, Delhi 110 034
Printed by Rashtriya Printers, Delhi 110 032
Published by Manzar Khan, Oxford University Press
YMCA Library Building, Jai Singh Road, New Delhi 110 001

For

Dr (Mrs) Kapila Vatsyayan

Preface

Hinduism as a locution has become invested with heavy debate in recent times. In order to keep the present enterprise from getting embroiled in that debate I should begin by clarifying that I have here drawn upon the conventional rather than the controversial dimension of the word. Now, what do I mean by its 'conventional dimension'?

There are certain matters which are conventionally discussed under the rubric of 'Hinduism' in the western academia and this book is an attempt to engage in that discussion. If one went into a library and found one's way to that part of it which holds books on Hinduism, glanced at their contents, and then compared them with those of this book, one will find sufficient shared ground in the area of concern between those books and this book to admit that this book too belongs to the same population.

This book does not deal with classical Hinduism in its entirety. Religions are multidimensional and Hinduism is no exception. One popular taxonomy recognizes six such dimensions of religion: (1) doctrinal, (2) mythic, (3) ethical, (4) ritual, (5) experiential, and (6) social.[1]

In terms of these categories, this book sets out to explore the doctrinal dimension of classical Hinduism. None of the dimensions, of course, can be addressed in isolation in any religion, and particularly not in Hinduism, but they could certainly constitute the main focus of the discussion of a religion within a given historical period. In other words, this book is designed as an introduction to the essentials of classical Hindu thought. It will be helpful to identify three features

1. See Ninian Smart, *Worldviews: Crosscultural Explorations of Human Beliefs* (New York: Charles Scribner's Sons, 1983), pp. 7–9.

of the book to enable readers to use it to full advantage: (1) The first chapter constitutes the text of an oral presentation made at the Smithsonian Institution, designed to present classical Hindu thought in a concise and accessible manner. It should form a useful introduction to the conceptual framework of Hinduism, as the key ideas have deliberately been presented in a simple and direct manner. Their complexities and nuances are uncovered under the specific chapter headings. (2) The rest of the book may be viewed as a magnification of the first chapter, which is like a slender slide whose full details show up only when projected on the wide screen of the pages that follow it. (3) Among the essentials of classical Hindu thought, special and detailed consideration has been accorded to the concept of varṇa. This feature of the book, in my view, is as useful as it is unusual. The so-called caste system is perhaps the single most *misunderstood aspect* of Hinduism on which over six thousand books have been written! The corresponding concept of varṇa has therefore been presented in detail. An analogy is perhaps provided by the case of karma. This key concept of Hinduism was for decades confused with fatalism, until a whole generation of scholars rescued it from its dubious fate. If the discussion of varṇa occasionally seems to become apologetic, it is so in order to balance the apoplectic treatment it has sometimes received. Hopefully, as in the case of karma, the treatment of varṇa here will encourage a more accurate and adequate understanding of it, so that the study of classical Hinduism will be able to move beyond another bedevilling stereotype.

Why this stereotype arose and how it gained wide currency are questions which await full answers. Whatever the final answer might be, it might lie partly in the powerful paradox which characterized western culture when it entered into a phase of contact with India. The fact that the latter was an unequal partner must also have played its own role in the process. But the paradox which might have intensified, if not generated, the stereotype seems to have gone largely unnoticed. This paradox is symbolized in the person of Thomas Jefferson, who was *both* the author of the revolutionary dictum 'All men are created equal' and a slave-owner. His paradox symbolizes two opposite tendencies which have characterized modern western civilization—egalitarianism within and racism without, features which, in the opinion of some, continue to characterize it to this day.

The varṇa system involves them both. On the one hand, most

scholars maintain that the word varṇa means 'colour' even in the context of the caste system, and 'some, particularly towards the end of the nineteenth century, concluded that it referred to skin colour and therefore to racial categories similar to those found in modern European societies'.[2] On the other hand, the apparently hierarchical structure of the caste system provided the ideal counterpoint to the emergent egalitarianism of the West, a point which reaches its full maturity in the work of Louis Dumont.[3]

This *convergence* in the context of racism, and *contrast* in the context of egalitarianism, which the caste system offered in relation to the West, seems to have met the need for an intellectual justification of British rule over India admirably. As rulers of India, the British could justify their rule over India in terms of the inherent inegalitarianism of the caste system and claim that they were leavening India's society with humanity, while at the same time find in the racist origin of the caste system an Indian 'original sin' which, by the curious logic of feelings, exonerated them of their own. That the need for such justification is now greatly diminished by the historical developments in the second half of this century allows one to revisit the concept of varṇa, and associated concepts, in its fading years in a less loaded context.

2. Morton Klass, 'Varna and Jati', in Mircea Eliade, editor in chief, *The Encyclopedia of Religion* (New York: Macmillan Publishing Co., 1987), vol. 15, p. 189.

3. Louis Dumont, *Homo Hierarchicus: The Caste System and Its Implications* (Chicago: University of Chicago Press, 1980, complete revised English edition).

Acknowledgements

Permission to reproduce material from the following works by the concerned publishers is gratefully acknowledged: *A Dictionary of Hinduism*: Margaret and James Stutley (Routledge); *The Wonder That Was India*: A.L. Basham (Macmillan General Books); *Dancing with Siva: Hinduism's Contemporary Catechism:* Satguru Sivaya Subramuniya (Himalayan Academy); *Origins and Development of Classical Hinduism*: A.L. Basham (Beacon Press); and *Sanatana-Dharma*: Bhagavan Das (The Theosophical Publishing House).

Contents

Glossary of Sanskrit Words

ācārya	master, teacher
adharma	unrighteousness
ādhāva	mode of addressing a śūdra at a soma sacrifice
adhikāra	eligibility
ādiparva	the first book of the *Mahābhārata* epic
ādyā	the Original One
ādrava	mode of addressing a rājanya at the soma sacrifice
āgahi	mode of addressing a vaiśya at the soma sacrifice
āgamas	liturgical manuals
āgāmi	*see* karma
ahiṁsā	non-violence
aiśvarya	sovereignty
a-jīva	not living; matter
ākara grantha	*see* graṅtha
anādipravāhasattā	existence as a beginningless series
ānanda	bliss
ānandamaya kośa	*see* kośa
ananta	endless
anantya	infinity
annamaya-kośa	*see* kośa
anugraha	grace
āpaddharma	special rules governing conduct in times of crisis
apāna	one of the five categories of *prāṇa,* often associated with inhalation
apūrvam	unseen [stored] virtue or vice which will produce its due result
arūpavad	formless
ārya	a noble person; collectively the nobility
asam-bhāvanā	improbability
aṣara	imperishable

asita	black
āśrama	one of the four stages of life, into which Hinduism divides the life cycle
āśramadharma	duties incumbent on one passing through one of these stages
atyāśrama	an unconventional expression which appears in the *Śvetāśvatara Upaniṣad*, probably signifying the spiritually contingent character of *āśrama*-scheme
ātman	ultimate ground of one's being
avatāra	incarnation
avidyā	radical ignorance
āyāma	extension
baddha	bound
bādha	barred
bala	strength
bhagas	the six auspicious qualities possessed by God Viṣṇu: knowledge, strength, sovereignty, valour, power and splendour
bhagavān	popular name of God: the worshipful one
bhāgavata	related to or devoted to Bhagavān
bhakti	devotion
bhakti-yoga	the spiritual path of loving devotion
Bharata	name of a sage
bhavya	what will happen in the future; auspicious
bhūman	plenitude
bhūta-āśraya	material body as abode of the subtle body
bhūr	earth
bhuvaḥ	atmospheric region
brahmacārī	celibate; one going through the first stage of life
brahmaṇya	characterizing Brahman
brāhmaṇya	befitting a brāhmaṇa
brahmin	anglicized form for brāhmaṇa
Brahman	a designation of the ultimate reality in Hinduism
brāhmaṇa	social class consisting of priests, teachers, scholars, etc.
buddhi	intelligence
caṇḍāla	outcaste
cāndrāyaṇa	a penance
caryā	mode of life, especially devotional
cāturvarṇya	the order of the four varṇas

cit	consciousness
darśana	a philosophical school
dās	Sanskrit root: to give
dāsa	slave; sometimes contrasted with the Ārya
daśāvatāra	the ten representative incarnations of Viṣṇu
dāsa viśas	clans of Dāsas
dāsīputra	lit. 'son of a female slave' an abuse
dāsya	serving God as a slave serves a master
dāsyāḥ putraḥ	son of a slave-girl
deha	body
devī	the feminine principle as divine. It covers a wide spectrum of meanings, from the ultimate reality as the Goddess to any woman of distinction
dehabījāni-bhūta-dharma śūksmāṇi	subtle material elements which are the seed of the body
dharma	what makes a thing what it is, either descriptively or prescriptively or both; duty, righteousness
dharmabhūta-jñāna	attributive knowledge, as distinguished from jñāna as consciousness
dhyāna	meditation
dravya	substance
dvijāti	twice-born
ehi	mode of addressing a brāhmaṇa in the soma sacrifice
gaṇ	Sanskrit verb: 'to count or reckon'
gaṇa	troops
gaṇikā	courtesan
gāyatrī	sacred verse from the Vedas (*Ṛg Veda* III, 62. 10), which plays an important ritual and liturgical role in Hinduism
grantha	treatise. This could be on a specific topic (*prakaraṇa grantha)* or a general topic (*ākara grantha*)
guṇadharma	assignment of varṇa on the basis of quality rather than birth
guṇī	one possessing qualities, specially meritorious qualities
haviṣkṛt	one who offers an oblation
indriyāṇi	sense organs
Īśāna	name of God
Īśvara	Lord, God

itihāsa	epics
jāti	endogamous and commensal unit based on natal membership
jātyapakarṣa	downward mobility of a jāti
jātyutkarṣa	upward mobility of a jāti
jīva	living being
jīvanmukti	living liberation
jñāna	knowledge
jñāna-yoga	the spiritual path of liberative knowledge or wisdom
jīvātmā	the embodied ātman as undergoing rebirths
kaivalya	'onlyness', aloofness
kalpa	a period of 4320 million years, basic unit of computation of life of the universe in Hinduism
kalyāṇīvāk	auspicious speech
kānta	loving God as one spouse loves another
kāraṇa sarīra	causal body
karma	action, both as cause and effect, of all deeds performed by a person. It is classified, according to one common division, into the accumulated stock of karma which remains to be worked out (*sañcita*); which has begun to take effect (*kriyamāṇa*) and forthcoming karma (*āgāmi*)
karma-āśraya	karma-dependent
karma-indriyāṇi	organs of action
karmaṇā	by (ritual) action
karma-yoga	the spiritual path of action
karuṇā	compassion
kāyastha	a sub-caste
kena varṇāni	how are varṇas determined
kośa	on of the five sheaths which encase the ātman, as it were, and provide a description of the human personality as a layered entity, consisting of successive layers constituted by food, breath, mind, consciousness and bliss, called *annamaya*, *prāṇamaya*, *manomaya*, *vijñānamaya*, and *ānandamaya kośas*
kramamukti	gradual liberation
kṣatriya	social class consisting of warriors, public servants, etc.
kulapati	head of a family-based educational institution in ancient India

kūrma	tortoise
kūṭasthasattā	permanent being
līlā	sport
liṅgam	conical representation of Śiva, often considered phallic
liṅga-śarīra	another name for *sūkṣma-śarīra*
madhura	loving God as lovers love each other
mahādeva	the Great God; often specifically applied to Śiva
manana	reflection
manas	mind
manomaya-kośa	*see* kośa
mārga	a path, specially a spiritual path
matsya	fish; refers to the incarnation of Viṣṇu as a fish in the context of the avatāra doctrine
mokṣa	liberation from saṁsāra; the highest good
mukhya prāṇa	chief breath of life
mukta	liberated
mūladhāra cakra	one of a series of mystical circles, located at the root of the spine
muniśreṣṭha	best among the sages
mūrti	form, image
mūrti-traya	triple forms
naimittika dharma	periodic rites
nara-siṁha	man-lion
nididhyāsana	intensive meditation
niravayava	partless
nirguṇa Brahman	the ultimate reality as devoid of distinguishing attributes; Impersonal God
niṣāda	a tribe
niṣādādhipati	king of the niṣādas
nitya	eternal
nivṛtti	disengagement from active life in the world
pādakṛccha	a penance
palāśa	name of a tree from whose wood ceremonial staffs are made
pañca-janāḥ	lit. five peoples; the exact connotation of the term is uncertain
pañcakṛṣṭayaḥ	five tribes
parabrahma	supreme Brahman
pāraka	a penance
pāramārthikadṛṣṭi	transcendental perspective

pātaka	that which causes one to fall; a sin
paulkasa	subcategory among the lowest castes
phala	fruit, result
piṅgala	In the Hindu conception of the nervous system of the subtle body, *iḍā* and *piṅgalā* are two nerves which intertwine around the central *suṣumnā.*
pitṛkārya	*see* śrāddha
prājāpatya	a penance
prajñāna	consciousness
prakaraṇa grantha	*see* grantha
prakṛti	matter
prāṇa	life-breath
prāṇamaya-kośa	*see* kośa
prapatti	self-surrender to God
prārabdha	*see* karma
prasāda	grace; consecrated food
pravrajyā	life of mendicancy
pravṛtti	engagement in active life of the world
prāyaścitta	penance
prayojana	purpose
punarjanma	rebirth
purāṇa	ancient lore
purohita	chaplain; royal chaplain
puruṣa	person, soul
pūrvam	before
puruṣa	man
puruṣārthas	Hindu axiological doctrine which classifies the goals of human endeavour as dharma (righteousness); artha (wealth); kāṃa (sensuous pleasures) and ṃoksa (liberation)
rājadharma	royal code of conduct; duties appropriate for a king
rājanya	used a synonym for a kṣatriya
rājarṣi	royal sage
ṛṣis	seers or sages to whom the Vedas are revealed
ṛta	a word with three layers of meaning: natural order, moral order and ritual order
saccidānanda	the ultimate reality as the ultimate level of truth, awareness and bliss
śabda	Hindu analogue to the concept of revelation
ṣaḍdarśana	the six schools into which Hindu, and sometimes Indian philosophy is classified

sādhana	spiritual path
sādhāraṇa dharma	*see* sāmānya dharma
saguṇa Brahman	the ultimate reality as possessing distinguishing attributes; Personal God
sakhya	loving God as a friend loves a friend
śakti	the divine feminine principle as the locus of power; energy
śākta	worshipper of Śakti
sālokya	abiding in the same realm as God
samāna	one of the five categories of prāṇa, sometimes associated with the navel
sāmānya dharma	duties common to all human beings
sambandha	relation
saṁhāra	absorption
sāmīpya	divine proximity of God
sampradāya	sect
saṁsāra	the process of being continually reborn
saṁskāra	karmic traces; tendencies
samuccaya	co-ordinated
sannyāsa	the abandonment of worldliness either formally or attitudinally, or both
sannyāsī	renunciant
sannyāsin	variant of above
sañcita	*see* karma
śānta	loving God as a child loves a parent
sārṣṭi	empowerment like God
sārūpya	conforming to God
sarvadharma	possessing all attributes
sarvadharmabahiṣkṛta	excluded from all observances
sarvagata	omnipresent
sat	truth
satya	truth
sāyujya	being one with God
sita	white
smṛti	law books
soma	a sacred plant used in a sacrifice or that sacrifice itself
śrāddha	funeral ceremony performed periodically in honour of the departed
śravaṇa	audition
sṛṣṭi	creation

śruta	learning
śrutena	by hearing
sthāṇu	post
sthiti	duration
sthūla śarīra	gross or physical body
strīdharma	code of conduct specially applicable to women
śūdra	social class consisting of labourers, servants, etc.
sūdrāputra	son of a śūdra
sūdrayoni	birth as a śūdra
sūkṣma śarīra	subtle body
svadharma	one's inherent nature and/or duty
svaḥ	heaven or sky
śvapāka	lit. dog-eater; an outcaste
svarūpalakṣaṇa	what characterizes a thing as it is in itself, as distinguished from an external referent
śyāva	black
tāpasa	ascetic
tejas	splendour
tirobhāva	concealment
trimārga	the three paths of jñāna, bhakti and karma
trimūrti	the Hindu 'Trinity' comprising Brahmā Viṣṇu, and Śiva
triloka	the three worlds: the earth, atmosphere and heaven; or heaven, earth and hell, on a more pessimistic view
tri-vikrama	a reference to the three strides of Viṣṇu
udāna	one of the five categories of prāṇa, sometimes associated with, the throat
ugra	subcaste arising from miscegenation
upādhi	limitation
upāsanā	worship
vāhya	excluded
vaidehaka	a subcategory of the lowest castes
vaiśya	the social class consisting of agriculturists and merchants
vāmana	dwarf
vānaprastha	stage of life characterized by residence in a hermitage
varāha	boar
varṇa	the conceptual classes comprising Hinduism. These are: (1) brāhmaṇa; (2) kṣatriya; (3) vaiśya and (4) śūdra

varṇadharma	obligations arising from membership of one of the four social classes of Hinduism
varṇasaṅkara	admixture among the varṇas, a metaphor of social chaos
varṇāśrama	the combined duties incumbent on one as member of a social class at a particular stage in one's life
vātsalya	loving God as a parent loves a child
vedānta	school or schools of Hindu philosophy which draw their inspiration from those texts which constitute the concluding section of the Vedas
vibhūti	glory
vighneśvara	a name of Gaṇeśa, emphasizing his role as remover of obstacles
vijñānamaya-kośa	*see* kośa
vikalpa	option
vikśepa-śakti	power to generate unrest
viparīta-sambhāvanā	inveterate habits of thought
vīrya	valour
viś	clan
viṣaya	subject
viṣeśadharma	duties specific to one's station in life or stage of life
vrātya	one who loses caste through non-observance of purificatory rites
vṛṣala	a fallen kṣatriya
vyāvahārikadṛṣṭi	empirical perspective
vyāna	one of the five categories of *prāṇa*, one often viewed as pervading the body as a whole
yamas	rules of restraint for all, e.g. *ahiṁsa*
yajñas	rituals
yatidharma	code of conduct specially applicable to ascetics
yāvaka	a preparation of barley
yoga	spiritual discipline or path
yogasiddhi	perfection in yoga, occult powers so obtained

Introduction

Precognita

'With reference to the commencing of any scientific work, according to Hindu opinion, four questions present themselves:—(1) what qualifications are required to render one competent to enter upon the study?—(2) what is the subject-matter?—(3) what connection is there between the subject-matter and the book itself?—and (4) what inducement is there to enter upon the study at all? The answer to each of these questions is called an anubandha—a "bond of connection" or "cause"—because, unless a man knows what a book is about, and whether he is competent to understand it, and what good the knowledge will do him, he cannot be expected to apply himself to the study of the book, instead of employing himself otherwise' [*The Pandit*, July 1867, p. 48].[1]

It may not be a bad idea to commence this work by addressing the four questions technically known as *adhikāra*, *viṣaya*, *sambandha* and *prayojana*. These may be cast in a *modern* form to suit our convenience as follows: (1) What is the subject (viṣaya) and what is the organizing principle employed to deal with it? (2) How is it related to the broader context in which it is to be located (sambandha) in terms of its scope and limitations? (3) What is its emphatic purpose (prayojana)? (4) What constitutes its intended audience (adhikāra)?

The subject of this book is classical Hinduism, and it is organized in terms of its key concepts, such as Brahman, *karma, karma-yoga,* etc. While these terms are discussed in their logical connection here, they are discussed in the *context* of a period of Hinduism which is

1. Cited in Colonel G.A. Jacob, tr., *A Manual of Hindu Pantheism: The Vedāntasāra* (Varanasi: Bharat-Bharati, 1972 [fourth impression]), p. 24.

chronologically connected with those that precede and succeed it. These connections are most apparent in the discussion of varṇa, which has been deliberately extended beyond the purported period to generate a fuller understanding. The general discussion of the historical evolution of the key concepts in the second chapter also serves the same purpose, but to a limited context. This chronology needs to be clearly indicated.

The beginnings of Hinduism have been variously identified.[2] One may therefore initially prefer to deal with its history rather than etiology. One standard procedure, adopted here, is to broadly classify its history into four periods:

Vedic and pre-Vedic Hinduism:	third millennium to *circa* eighth century BCE
Classical Hinduism:	eighth century BCE to *circa* 1000 CE
Medieval Hinduism:	1000–1800 CE
Modern Hinduism:	1800–

The present book *relates to classical Hinduism* in terms of this periodization. In textual terms this covers the period from the Upaniṣads down to the late Purāṇas, and all that comes between them: the Smṛtis (law books), the Itihāsas (epics), the Purāṇas (ancient lore), the Āgamas (liturgical manuals) and Darśanas (philosophical literature), etc. The book covers the period of classical Hinduism and these texts, and the preceding and succeeding periods provide the limits, admittedly treated as somewhat porous at times. The period is distinct but there are limitations to the extent to which we may separate it from the succeeding and following ones if we wish to understand it. The interested reader constitutes its *audience*.

The *emphatic purpose* of this work is to synchronically and systematically present the governing concepts of classical Hinduism and their operation during this diachronically delimited period.

The Hindu scholarly tradition not only indicates that the book specify these four preliminary points, of subject, context, purpose and audience, but that it also distinguish between two kinds of treatises (*granthas*):[3] *prakaraṇa granthas* and the *ākara granthas*. The former deal

2. See Arvind Sharma, 'Hinduism', in Arvind Sharma, ed., *Our Religions* (San Francisco: Harper, 1993), p. 36.

3. Satguru Sivaya Subramuniyaswami, *Dancing with Śiva: Hinduism's Contemporary Catechism* (Concord, California: Himalayan Academy, 1993), p. 725.

with a part of the main topic, the latter with the whole of it. In terms of this classification, the present work will have to be considered a *prakaraṇa grantha*, that is, as a reference book rather than a general treatise or *ākara grantha*.

CHAPTER I

A Conceptual Introduction

Part One

I

It is perhaps best to commence a study of Hinduism by identifying the concept of Brahman. The word itself is of great antiquity; it occurs in the earliest sections of the Hindu scriptures and recurs throughout, undergoing semantic changes till it is firmly established as the Hindu designation for the ultimate reality. Just as Yahweh is the one ultimate reality in Judaism; God in Christianity; Allah in Islam; Nirvāṇa in Theravāda Buddhism; the Buddha in Mahāyāna Buddhism; Heaven in Confucianism and Tao in Taoism; Brahman is the one ultimate reality in Hinduism.

What, then, is this Brahman? Brahman, first of all, is one. That is to say, Brahman is the sole ultimate reality. There is no other ultimate reality beside it. Moreover, it is also ultimate. There is nothing beyond it. Just as one might first see the grass and the flowers in a garden, and then, raising one's vision, see the trees and then, moving further, see the clouds and the sky and the space that seems to extend far beyond it and then conclude, as a result, that there is nothing beyond space; similarly, with regard to the ultimate reality, one may go on ascending to higher and higher orders of reality till one comes to a stop at Brahman.

II

This Brahman, however, is viewed in Hinduism as possessing two aspects: and may therefore be referred to as *nirguṇa* Brahman and/or *saguṇa* Brahman. The word guṇa, which is common to the expressions nirguṇa and saguṇa, here means a distinguishing attribute or quality. A person possessing many good qualities or one particular quality in great measure is called a *guṇī*—one who possesses *guṇa* or quality. Nir means without; thus as Nirguṇa, Brahman does not possess *any* distinguishing attributes; in the other aspect as Saguṇa, Brahman possesses distinguishing attributes. How is this distinction between the two to be explained?

An example might help. At Mount Rushmore in the United States the faces of the four presidents have been carved out on the side of a rock. The other side, let us suppose, is bare. One could then say that the same mountain has two aspects to it: on one side it is sculpted, on the other side it is bare. Note that as bare it lacks or is at least not as rich in distinguishing attributes as the other side, embellished by the four faces of the presidents, each with its own distinguishing features. Another example might help. There exists, according to the Constitution of the United States, the position of the president of the country, called 'the presidency of the United States'. Note that the presidency, *per se*, is impersonal; howsoever different the individual presidents may have been from one another, as presidents they all partook of the same presidency. However, each president was and is an individual with a distinct personality. One may compare the concept of Brahman as Nirguṇa or impersonal with the presidency of the United States and Brahman as Saguṇa with the actual presidents of the United States. (One must avoid here the pitfall of regarding the presidency as a mere abstraction, though this is one of the criticisms levelled against the concept of Nirguṇa Brahman within the tradition.)

Crucial to the distinction between Nirguṇa and Saguṇa Brahman is the idea of personality. This idea involves the existence of distinguishing attributes. When we say that 'A' has a personality we mean that he or she has attributes which distinguish him or her in a prominent way; when we say that 'A' has a different personality from that of 'B', what we mean is that the attributes which distinguish 'A' are different from those which distinguish 'B'. Thus, when we say that Brahman possesses two aspects—nirguṇa and saguṇa—what is being said is that in one aspect it is impersonal, like a principle rather than a person, and that in another aspect it is like a person, rather than a mere principle.

Another way of developing the distinction would be to introduce the distinction of being with and without form. Water, for instance, possesses no visible form so long as it exists (pre-exists) only in the form of the gases hydrogen and oxygen. However, as water it may be said to possess form, albeit liquid form. Now when the same water is put in a freezer, it becomes ice, which possesses solid form. And the same water when heated becomes vapour and assumes a far more elusive form. In all these forms water may be seen as saguṇa; as H_2O it may be regarded as nirguṇa. It must not be forgotten that it is the same water which may be both formless or assume form; it is the same reality which possesses the two aspects of being formless and with form.

A lot of philosophical controversy in Hinduism centres on whether Brahman, the ultimate reality, is itself ultimately nirguṇa or saguṇa. Hardly any school denies that it possesses both these aspects; rather, the battle rages over the issue of which of the two is primary. Some of the schools which favour the view that Brahman is saguṇa—more like a personal God—interpret the term nirguṇa differently so as to accommodate it within their system. Then the word nirguṇa is understood not as meaning that Brahman possesses no attributes whatsoever but rather that it possesses no evil attributes. Or else the word nirguṇa is taken as representing the impersonal power of God, in the sense the president exercises the impersonal powers of the presidency. Similarly, scriptural passages which apparently seem to accord primacy to saguṇa Brahman are reinterpreted to represent a penultimate formulation by those who regard nirguṇa Brahman as supreme.

In this way we are led to the second step in charting Hinduism.

BRAHMAN

NIRGUṆA SAGUṆA

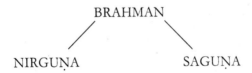

Again it should be borne in mind that nirguṇa and saguṇa are aspects of the same Brahman. To illustrate this, some scholars have suggested the following exercise. Take a strip of blank paper and draw a face or figure on one side. Leave the other blank. The blank side then represents nirguṇa Brahman and the side with the sketch represents saguṇa Brahman. Now fold the paper into a Mobius strip, that is, 'hold the bottom of the strip in your right hand and twist the top into a spiral'. You will see one aspect of Brahman change into the other. According to another scholar, water as H_2O is nirguṇa Brahman; water splashed on the face is saguṇa Brahman.

III

Let us develop the theme further. Brahman, when seen as possessing distinguishing characteristics—that is as saguṇa—can be depicted either as masculine or feminine. (The word Brahman by itself is neuter and this probably will go well with its nirguṇa aspect.) That is to say, if the ultimate reality, Brahman, is to be treated as a person, then it could be treated as either male or female. Thus, one could either end up with a masculine theology or a feminine theology, or both. The Western religious tradition, until recent times, seems to have opted for a masculine theology. Thus Yahweh, God and Allah, inasmuch as we can speak of them as persons in human terms, are masculine in their personality. The Hindu religious tradition has also, in the main, developed the concept of God along the lines of a masculine personality-type, but unlike the Western religious tradition it also contains a full-blown feminine theology, in which the saguṇa aspect of Brahman is identified not with a God but a Goddess, called Devī. When the saguṇa aspect of Brahman is identified with God or the masculine personality-type, saguṇa Brahman is referred to as Īśvara. This enables us to develop the next distinction:

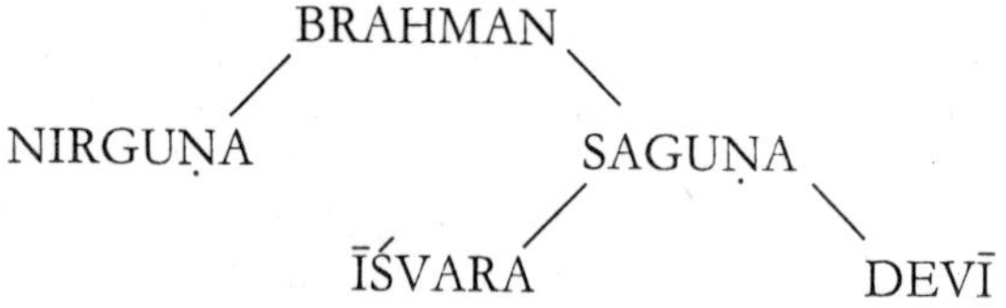

IV

The God principle as feminine is known not only as Devī but also as Śakti and there are those who worship Brahman as the ultimate reality in this way. The worshippers of Śakti are called Śāktas. Śakti means Power.

This feminine theology in Hinduism assumes two forms: (1) an independent feminine theology in which the Goddess is the supreme reality and all the gods are subject to her, and (2) one which is subordinate to the masculine theology, in which case various goddesses appear as the wives of the gods. At this stage in the presentation of Hindu concepts, it should suffice to say that there does exist in Hinduism an independent feminine theology. One may now revert to a more detailed consideration of saguṇa Brahman as it is elaborated along masculine lines—the major line of development in Hindu theology.

V

Saguṇa Brahman, then, as Īśvara is God, and is analogous to the God of the Western religious traditions in that he plays three fundamental roles in relation to the cosmos: He brings it into being, He sustains it and in the end He terminates it. He is thus the creator, the preserver and the destroyer of the universe. God as playing each of these roles has been individualized within the Hindu tradition. As the creator He is known as Brahmā, as the preserver, Viṣṇu and as the destroyer, Śiva. Thus each role model has been differentiated, generating what is sometimes called the Hindu trinity. So we are led to the next stage in the charting of Hinduism:

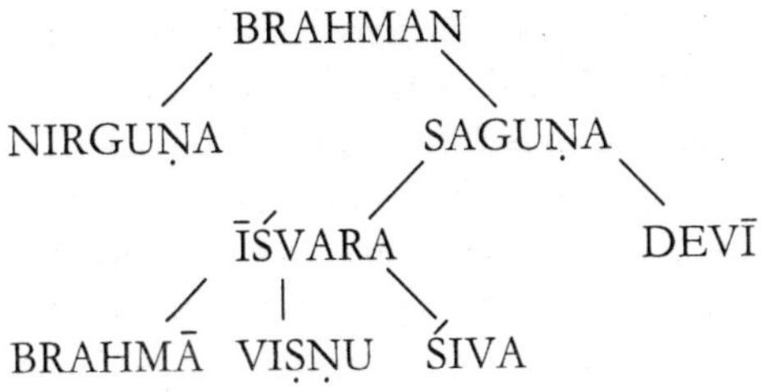

VI

As Brahmā, God brings the world into being, but the exact nature of this process has to be carefully understood and distinguished from the common understanding of it in a western religious context. Two points especially need to be borne in mind. The first is that whereas in the main western religions the universe comes into being once and goes out of existence once, the situation within Hinduism is different. Almost all schools of Hindu thought accept a cyclical as opposed to a linear cosmology. That is to say, in Hinduism, the universe has come into being several times and gone out of existence several times and this process has been going on from beginningless time and will go on forever. So, *creatio ex nihilo*, or creation out of nothing, is a concept not particularly congenial to most of Hindu thought. This brings us to the second point, that matter in some form or the other never ceases to exist. What actually happens, according to the Hindu view, is that it undergoes a change of form. Thus there is really no creation, only a manifestation, and really no destruction at the end, only a dissolution. Just as pots may be made out of clay and when broken dissolve back into clay, so it is with the universe. God, then, as giving form to the universe as we see it now, is called the 'creator'. The exact nature of the relationship between God and this everlasting matter is a point of much controversy in Hindu philosophy.

Once the universe has come into being it is supposed to last for trillions of years before it comes to an end and one cycle of manifestation and dissolution is completed. It is the responsibility of God as Viṣṇu to ensure that the universe does not undergo premature dissolution for whatever reason. This is what is meant by Viṣṇu's role as the preserver of the universe. In the course of carrying out this responsibility, Viṣṇu sometimes has to intervene in order to ensure the continued existence of the universe or of the cosmic order on which its continued existence depends; that is, Viṣṇu has to descend into the universe to preserve it. Such a descent is known as *avatāra*, or incarnation, as this is what Viṣṇu has to do to save the universe—to appear in person. Hindu mythology records numerous occasions when this has happened and confidently predicts that such occasions will also continue to arise. Out of these occasions, it selects ten for special attention. This, in brief, is the doctrine of the ten incarnations of Viṣṇu (*daśāvatāra*). According to this doctrine, Viṣṇu successively assumed the forms of (1) a fish, (2) a tortoise, (3) a boar, (4) a man-lion, (5) a dwarf, (6) Paraśurāma (Rāma with the axe), (7) Rāma (with the bow, to distinguish him from the former), (8) Kṛṣṇa, and (9) the Buddha. These nine incarnations have already taken place, while the one as Kalkī, the tenth one, will take place at the end of the present degenerate age. From the Hindu point of view, the most important incarnations are those of Rāma and Kṛṣṇa. When the time comes for the universe to be dissolved then Śiva puts an end to the current cycle.

The following chart recapitulates the discussion so far:

BRAHMAN

NIRGUṆA SAGUṆA

ĪŚVARA DEVĪ

BRAHMĀ VIṢṆU ŚIVA

Fish
Tortoise
Boar
Man-Lion
Dwarf
Paraśurāma
Rāma
Kṛṣṇa
Buddha
Kalkī

Part Two

Let us now turn to a consideration of the nature of a human being according to Hindu thought. Each well-defined ideology has some concept of a human being. Thus, if we asked a scientific materialist 'What comprises a human being?', she would probably respond by saying that a human being is a psycho-physical organism. She may elaborate the point further by stating that the 'psychic' or mental component of a human being is not only intimately linked to the physical but may even be a by-product of it. Consciousness, though itself not physical, is generated by the coming together of the various physical and chemical components of the body. Should it be asked 'How can that which lacks consciousness, namely physical and chemical elements, generate consciousness?', the answer would perhaps be that the whole is greater than the sum of its parts. Just as the two gases of hydrogen and oxygen produce water by coming together, which possesses the property of wetness, a property which the gases themselves do not possess, so do the physical and chemical elements, though themselves without it, produce consciousness by coming together.

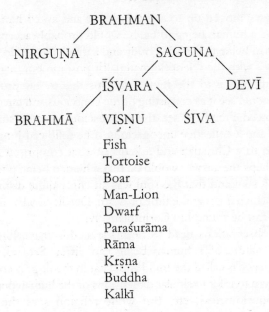

If next we moved on to a psychologist and asked him what he understood a human being to be, he would probably accept the fact that a human being possesses a body and a mind. He would probably not disagree with the scientific-materialist position but might attach greater importance to the mind (perhaps due to his professional bias). He would see it as consisting of the conscious and unconscious, if he followed Freud, or see the unconscious as consisting of an individual and a collective unconscious, if he followed Jung. If now one turned to a Christian and asked her what comprised a human being, perhaps the answer would be that a human being possessed a body and a soul and that the soul was an entity quite distinct from the body, which it left at the time of death. Details of what happened thereafter can be found in I Corinthians XV.

A few observations need to be made at this stage. First, views about the nature of a human being can differ. Second, what in modern science is called the mind and what in theology is considered the soul seem to refer to similar dimensions of the human personality, that is consciousness, etc. But while religion sees the soul as something distinguishable and separable from the body, science sees the mind as something distinguishable but not separable from the body. With this in the background, let us now ask the question: What, according to Hinduism, constitutes a human being?

According to Hindu thought, a human being possesses three 'bodies'. Although in the course of normal living we do not distinguish among them and separate them, they are both distinguishable and separable. They are: (1) the gross or physical body, (2) the subtle body, and (3) the causal body. Just as water appears to be a single substance but upon being subjected to chemical analysis turns out to consist of two gases, so too, although we appear to be one person, when subjected to analysis, we turn out to be three-in-one: all the three bodies collapsed into one. The physical body is identified with our physical body as we know it; the subtle body is identified with our psychological drives, thoughts and emotions, and the causal body is what causes us to possess such body and mind that we possess. Here, an illustration might help. The food that we eat relates to the physical body. But why do we eat? Because we feel hungry—this relates to the subtle body. But why do we feel hungry? Because we want to exist—this relates to the causal body.

The picture is not yet complete. Over and above, or underlying these, is what the Hindus call the *ātman.* It is (unlike the bodies which are subject to change) that element in the human personality which is not subject to change. This permanent substratum in our personality, the ātman, is the very core of our being. While it can exist without the three bodies, the bodies cannot exist without it.

Hindus use the word *jīva* to describe a living being in the normal sense. It is this jīva which possesses the three bodies in association with the ātman; hence, in Hinduism people like us are described as *jīvātmans* in philosophical terms. All of us are so many jīvātmans. At this point a clarification is vital regarding the use of the English word *soul.* This word is sometimes used to describe the subtle body, or the subtle and causal bodies together, and sometimes to translate the word ātman. Confusion can result if the two uses are not clearly distinguished. For instance, as is well known, Hindus believe in reincarnation; that is, they believe that upon dying the subtle-cum-causal bodies leave the physical body and go on to inhabit another physical body. This process is sometimes described as the soul passing on from one body to another, but strictly speaking this would apply only to the subtle-cum-causal body. What about the ātman? Does it move around too?

Here, another clarification is required. One should begin by noting that the ātman is the ultimate reality about us. All things about us change but it does not. For anything to be ultimate it must either be indivisibly minute or all-embracingly pervasive. The atom (prior to the rise of sub-atomic physics) would illustrate the former case and space the latter. Thus, ultimacy implies either atomicity or all-pervasiveness. Accordingly, some schools of Hindu thought regard the ātman as atomic in size, others as all-pervasive. All, however, speak of jīvātmans as migrating from one body to another.

We are so many jīvātmans being born, dying and being reborn in this universe. The process of rebirth is known as *punarjanma* (literally, rebirth). The overall scenario of the involvement of the jīvātman in the process of punarjanma is called *saṁsāra.*

One might like to ask the question: Why are we in saṁsāra? In other words, why are we here? What are we doing in this universe, dying and being born again? As we just saw, the question: Why are we in saṁsāra? reduces itself to the question: Why are we reborn?

The fundamental Hindu answer to this question is: We are here because we want to be here. We are reborn because we want to be reborn. One might counter by saying: No, I do not want to be reborn. Well, then, let me ask you: Do you want to be rich? Do you want to marry a handsome man or a beautiful girl? Do you want to excel professionally? The point of this line of interrogation is that at some point we will find ourselves saying yes to some such question and a positive answer would mean that we have desires. We are reborn because at the time of dying we have unfulfilled desires.

The idea of dying and being reborn may be usefully compared to the daily experience of going to bed at night and then getting up in the morning. One life is like a day; death is like sleep and waking up the next day is like being born into another life. Just as we start the next day at the point we left off the previous day, so is it with life. Just as what we do today or what happens to us today is connected with what we did yesterday or what happened to us yesterday, so does what happened to us in a previous life connect with our present life. And just as what we do today will affect what happens to us tomorrow, so will what we do in this life influence what happens to us in the next.

Once this continuity is recognized, interconnections also become clear. This interconnectedness of happenings or events is one way of looking at the complex concept of karma.

First of all, one should recognize that *karma* and *reincarnation* are two distinct concepts. There are so-called primitive societies, for instance, which believe in reincarnation but not in karma—that is to say, they believe in reincarnation but not in the idea that there is a moral order connecting these reincarnations. There are also religions which believe in karma but not in rebirth. It may seem a bit forced but one could argue that religions which believe in only one life here on earth and then an afterlife in heaven or hell believe in the idea of karma. Karma connotes moral justice. If we go to heaven for being virtuous and to hell for being vicious, then this basic conceptualization is being recognized, though in a way very different from the one in Hinduism. One might say that the western interpretation of karma in this sense is spatial and the Hindu concept temporal. In the Hindu view you go on moving forward in time and the results of your deeds catch up with you. Or, perhaps more appropriately, one might say that the western concept of karma is vertical and the Hindu concept horizontal.

HEAVEN

PREVIOUS LIFE — ———————— —NEXT LIFE
B D

HELL

Thus, the concept of karma as such can be detached from that of rebirth but in Hindu thought both are regarded as logical corollaries—the idea of karma is especially seen as implying rebirth. If something good or bad happens to us for which no obvious cause is traceable in this life then in Hinduism it is explained in terms of an effect of some action performed by us in a past life. Similarly, if no visible results are produced in this life by actions performed by us now, then the results, it is argued, will manifest in future lives.

Karma is a very general concept. It includes both action as well as the result of action; and such action and reaction can take place at the physical, verbal and mental levels. In brief, what it suggests is that the kinds of situations we create for ourselves in life tend to repeat themselves and that the kinds of situations we create for others are the kinds of situations we will find ourselves in.

If we leave matters as they are and do not interfere in any way then this is what lies in store for us. We will go on dying continually and being reborn in various states as human beings or as gods or animals or even plants, in accordance with our karma. This is a process—and this process of saṁsāra, involving continual punarjanma, has been going on from beginningless time and will go on forever. This is the normal scenario.

But, one might ask: Is this all? Does Hinduism just describe the situation and leave it at that? The answer, of course, is that there is more to it. For although the process of saṁsāra, as a general process, is eternal in the sense of being without a beginning or an end, an individual's involvement in it, though without a beginning, can be brought to an end. When this happens, the individual, the jīva, is said to have become liberated. The jīva then achieves liberation, *mukti*, the Hindu counterpart of salvation.

Part Three

When the idea of liberation is thus introduced into the picture, several questions naturally arise: What is liberation? Why would one want to become liberated? How does one become liberated? And, what happens when one becomes liberated?

What is liberation is in one sense a very complex question, but let us take the easy way out by saying that liberation is the cessation of rebirth, or—which comes to the same thing—the cessation of the involvement of the jīva in the process of saṁsāra. The real question to be faced at this stage is: Why should we want to become liberated?

To this, the Hindu religious tradition offers two answers—a blunt one and a courteous one. The blunt answer is that if you do not want to become liberated then you should not want to become liberated and could not be liberated and therefore would not be liberated. That is to say, if your life as you lead it is fully or even reasonably satisfactory for you, and you feel no kind of dissatisfaction or uneasiness about it, then this aspect of the Hindu worldview is not meant for you. Somewhat arrogantly you might even be told that you are not ready for it. The point is this. Life as we know it and live it does not offer us permanent and perfect happiness. It has its ups and downs and if one feels that this is the way things are and one should not be too concerned about this state of affairs then one is not yet in a mental state conducive to liberation. It must be made perfectly clear at this stage that there is *per se* no reason why one should be led to a quest for liberation by the vicissitudes of life. One could take the Taoist view, for example, that the right thing to do is to roll with the punches and rise with the crests—if one may mix pugilistic and oceanic metaphors. But Hindu thought makes the claim that it is possible to achieve a state of being which is entirely blissful, should one want to achieve such a state; however, this state of perfect and permanent happiness can never be achieved in saṁsāra. There is a structural flaw in the world of saṁsāra which makes it impossible to achieve perfect and permanent happiness within it—the flaw is that it is subject to constant change. And if everything is constantly changing—and that includes us as well as the universe—then there might be moments or even years when we are in a state of happy alignment with the universe. But even as we are in this state we may be moving out of line, as everything is changing. Perhaps for a while all things change in the same direction and such a dynamic alignment may last for quite a long time, but in the end, inevitably, things must go 'out of focus'. Thus, perfect and permanent happiness is not to be had so long as one is in saṁsāra.

One could, of course, maintain, however implausible it might appear, that one is interested not in happiness but in truth, that what brings us to the study of a religion like Hinduism—or any other—is a quest not for happiness but truth, if one is blessed with a sufficiently stoic disposition. It is here that Hindu thought scores its next point—that breaking away from the world of saṁsāra involves a direct encounter with Reality. It constitutes an encounter with Truth. If one does not bite at the bait of either bliss or truth then Hindu thought pulls out another carrot—what we now fashionably call altered states of consciousness or awareness. It makes the point that the ultimate reality is such as to provide the ultimate in expanded awareness. It is for this reason that Brahman, the ultimate reality, is often referred to in terms of truth, awareness and bliss, or as *sat*, *cit* and *ānanda*, the three being considered inseparable like wetness, liquidity and transparency in the case of water. This enables us to elaborate our chart further (see next page).

In this chart, a line demarcates the two worlds so to say, the noumenal world and the phenomenal world, and there are two points at which they seem to meet: when God incarnates himself or *descends* into the world and when the jīva realizes his or her true nature and *ascends* to the realization that he or she is really the ātman and not the three bodies. But we are getting ahead of the story. The answer to the question—why should liberation be sought?—is found in the prospect of perfect and permanent happiness or, alternatively, in an expanded awareness or in the encounter with ultimate truth, all of which are involved in the attainment of liberation. That is the carrot. The stick is that our life is shot through with suffering. Hindu sages have marvelled at the obstinate perversity of human beings, who refuse to budge notwithstanding the carrot of liberation and the stick of suffering.

Let us suppose that someone from amongst us becomes motivated towards encountering Brahman instead of wallowing forever in saṁsāra. It is worthwhile to speculate on how this might happen. It could actually happen in a rather paradoxical way: through the experience of either great suffering or great joy in the world. So long as our life presents a tolerable blend of the good and the bad we continue to function in a kind of a psychologically steady state, in which a movement in one direction is immediately balanced by a movement in the opposite direction through the alternation of joy

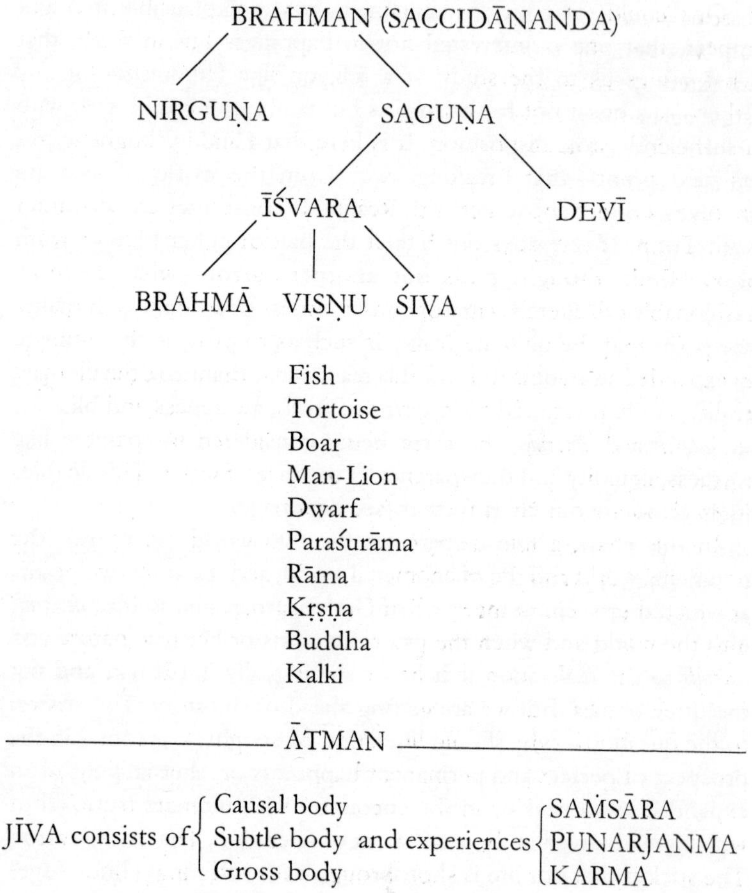

and sorrow. Let us suppose that we encounter extreme grief. The athlete who loses the use of her legs when the Olympic medal is within her reach; the mother who loses a child of many prayers; the father who loses the mother; the child who loses both. And so on. One should note, however, that the impact of a tragic event cannot be dissociated from the sensitivity of the person involved. Even a major tragedy may leave a less sensitive person unshaken; while a minor tragedy may change the course of life of a sensitive one. The mere prospect of a tragedy may have on the very sensitive the effect that an actual tragedy has on the less sensitive, as represented by the case of Buddha. Suppose one undergoes an experience which makes one's present life seem empty or vain or simply visibly vulnerable to an extent one had not noticed earlier. Now, put such a psychological state against what the realization of Brahman has to offer, namely its very antithesis. This is the dialectical movement which might turn us towards Brahman.

Or let us take a very different case. This person has all he or she wants in life. He or she was born in a rich family, has gone to the right schools, has the right job, has married the right girl or boy and has even read the right books but then feels: am I missing out on something? He or she applies what may be called the Huxley criterion to life. Aldous Huxley says that he turned to the study of Vedānta (a form of philosophical Hinduism) because after having seen the paintings of Michelangelo and heard the music of Beethoven and read Shakespeare he asked himself: is this all? Is this all, or is there a yet higher level of felicity which can be experienced? This may be called the superlative motive as opposed to the dialectical one. Here, one is not reacting to the negative experiences of life; rather, one wants to enhance the positive experiences one has had. Hinduism recognizes both these motives.

Part Four

For whatever reason, then, let us suppose that the jīva, moving on from birth to death to rebirth in his or her own cycle within this larger cycle of saṁsāra, 'the wheel within the wheel', becomes dissatisfied with the status quo. What must he or she do?

A simple example might help here. Suppose you are living in a city. You have been living in it for a number of years and now you want to leave it. You may want to leave it because you had a terribly unpleasant experience there or you may want to leave it because it has nothing more to offer. But you want to leave it, so what do you do? You find out about other cities, get their maps, ask your friends or visit a few of them and try to find out what suits you best. Similarly, you are now disappointed with the *saṁsāric* worldview and you are now looking for another worldview. Let us suppose you attend a course on Hinduism, read a book on Vedānta or meet a Swami from India and somehow this new worldview—the outline of which was presented in the preceding pages—begins to appeal to you. In other words, you wish to move from saṁsāra towards Brahman. The question naturally arises: From where do I start? If I ask you where you are going to go after this class, you might tell me, 'To the library.' Where do you start from when you want to go to the library? You start from right where you are. The same is the case in turning towards Brahman—you start right from where you are. The trick, of course, is to find out where you are!

The whole idea is to move from where you are to where you want to go. Such a move involves taking a path from where you are to where you want to go. The connection established by the path between the two points helps explain why any technique which enables you to reach Brahman from where you are is called yoga. An alternative word for yoga is mārga or path. The word yoga is derived from a root, *yuj*, meaning to join, which is evident in the English word 'yoke'. The word yoke can be used in at least two senses: (1) to join, as when oxen are yoked to the plough, and (2) to discipline, as when India was under the British yoke. Hence, a method of discipline which enables one to join, to attain union with Brahman, is called yoga.

Let us try to understand this idea a little more clearly. Suppose that you, all of you, decide to go to New York from Washington, right now. Although each of you will go by car, or by train or by air (and some may even walk), and share these means of transport, you will discover, if you observe closely, that none of you will follow exactly the same path. To begin with, your starting points are different. All of you are sitting on different chairs and each of you will start from a different point. That is why it is said that there are as many yogas or mārgas as there are people. But, although you all may not follow exactly the same path, most of you will be going by the same pathway. And, one can safely say that one of three modes of transportation and the paths associated with them will be used. Most will go by road (car or bus) or train or air. This is what is meant when it is said that there are three main yogas through which Brahman or God can be approached: those of *jñāna*, the yoga or path of knowledge; *bhakti*, the yoga or path of devotion; and karma, the yoga or path of action. Further, just as you may go part of the way by car or bus, part of the way by train and part by air, you can also combine the three yogas, which are no more exclusive than the paths. Moreover, note that your choice of path will depend on the mode of transport most easily available to you. If, for instance, you have a car, you will prefer to drive. Similarly, which yoga you adopt will depend on what you have, that is, what kind of temperament you have. Knowing, feeling and striving are common to all, but personalities reflect these traits in varying degrees. Indeed, perhaps one can identify a personality type on the basis of which of these traits predominates. If one is the knowing type, one will gravitate towards Jñāna-yoga. If one is the feeling type, one will gravitate towards Bhakti-yoga. If one is the striving type, one will gravitate towards Karma-yoga.

Each of these yogas can, in turn, be connected with one of the two aspects of Brahman, the saguṇa and the nirguṇa. It is to be remembered that these are not separate realities but distinct aspects of the same reality.

Those who espouse Jñāna-yoga believe that it enables them to experience nirguṇa Brahman. We must now carefully understand what they mean by jñāna. The word jñāna means knowledge and knowledge can be of two kinds: mediate and immediate. If I read in a book that mango is sweet, it is mediate knowledge. When I taste it, it is immediate or experiential knowledge. Knowledge of Brahman is the second type of knowing, though the first type may be of some help too. But it is the realization of Brahman that is the goal of Jñāna-yoga. By experience, then, is meant direct experience. But this experience is unlike any other experience we normally have. In all of normal experience outside of deep sleep there is a distinction between the knower and the known. I have thoughts; there is the 'I', there are the 'thoughts' and there is the 'having' of thoughts. So also with feeling, perceptions, etc. I see a chair. There is the 'I', there is the 'chair' and there is the 'seeing'. Now, notice that in deep sleep the situation is different. Can you ever consciously say 'I am asleep?' The affirmation that one is asleep constitutes the denial thereof. In deep sleep the distinction between the subject and the object vanishes. You can never use the present tense in relation to sleep. You can say 'I have slept', you can say 'I will sleep' but you can't say 'I am asleep'. So it is with the experience of Brahman. It cannot be articulated while it is being had but, like sleep, can be recollected in moments of tranquillity.

We now have to talk of nirguṇa Brahman, but the question is: can we talk about it? For, this aspect of Brahman has no distinctions whatsoever. It is said that there are three kinds of distinctions. A car is different from a tree—this is one kind of distinction. One car is different from another—this is another kind of distinction. Then you have distinctions within a car—tyres, wheels, seats, engines, etc. The first kind of distinction is between one class and another, as between car and tree. The second is between members of the same class—between one car and another. The third is within a member of the class—the wheel, tyres, etc. of a car. It is said that nirguṇa Brahman does not possess any distinction of any kind. If it does not possess any distinction of any kind then it can't even be described, for in order to describe it you need someone who describes and something which is described and a distinction has already arisen. It is the kind of problem one has in talking of sleep when asleep. But though Brahman as it is, is inaccessible to words, it is not inaccessible to experience, for the range of our experience exceeds the range of our thoughts and words. We can't grasp the moon with a hand but we can point to it with a finger. The role of language in relation to Brahman is similar.

The followers of Jñāna-yoga claim that once Brahman is realized, one becomes one with it—for if there is only distinctionless Brahman, how can one remain apart from it? And yet this is not *quite* correct, for one is never *not* different from it in everyday reality. How, then, can one become one with it? This calls for some explanation. If one reads the Hindu scriptures where these ideas are discussed one finds that the spiritual seekers of those days pursued a dual line of investigation into the nature of reality. One approach they took was to look at the external world and search for its ultimate ground. It is obvious that a category which is more encompassing than another must be regarded as more fundamental and ultimate than the less encompassing one. They went through various tentative formulations—the earth, the sky which includes the earth, space which includes both earth and sky, and so on—until they came up with Brahman as the ultimate ground of the universe. The other line of inquiry was to seek the ultimate ground of one's own being. We do so many things, perform so many actions. What is common to all of them—breath, life, or food without which there may be neither breath nor life? Ultimately they hit upon the ātman as the ultimate ground of the human personality. Then they made the revolutionary discovery that ātman and Brahman were the same—they were identical. The ultimate ground of our being was identical with the ultimate ground of the universe. One must be very careful here. It is not said that ātman becomes Brahman; what is said is that ātman *is* Brahman or vice versa. An illustration from the world of astronomy will help drive home the point. For a long time astronomers thought that there were two stars—the morning star and the evening star—until it was discovered that both were in fact Venus. What happened when this discovery was made? Did the morning star become the evening star? Did the evening star merge into the morning star? Neither. They were always one and the same.

A person becomes liberated the moment this identity is realized. All his accumulated karma is destroyed. He does not acquire any fresh karma. The karma which gave rise to the present physical body runs its course and ends when the person dies. Do note that the person does not die at the moment of realization. He returns to the world and sees chairs and tables and you and me. But it is said that although he sees them as different, he knows them to be one—just as someone with double vision sees the moon as two but knows it to be one. The person's existence between realization and physical death has been compared to the continuing motion of the potter's wheel after the potter has stopped rotating it and before it comes to a complete stop.

One may well ask whether such a Brahman really exists and is not a mere abstraction. An analogy might help. If we do not look up at the sky but keep our vision restricted to the earth we will always see space filled with some object. We might well ask: Can there be objectless space? We have to look up at the sky to realize that perhaps there is such a thing as pure space, which has now been confirmed by space flights. Similarly, we might ask: Can there be contentless consciousness, pure consciousness, as jñāna-yoga claims Brahman to be? Those who follow the path of bhakti argue that pure consciousness is an abstraction, a fiction, since we know from our experience that consciousness is always consciousness of something. Therefore, when we speak of knowledge, of spiritual knowledge, what we really mean is knowledge of God. But this knowledge of God is no abstract knowledge; it is knowledge of his auspicious attributes, his graciousness, to which a human being responds with devotion. This then is the other path, the other yoga, of devotion. Just as the yoga of jñāna or knowledge connects with the nirguṇa aspect of Brahman, the yoga of devotion is linked with the saguṇa aspect of Brahman. We have seen that as saguṇa, Brahman can be personalized in various ways. How are our personalities distinguished in this world? As noted earlier, it is the difference among persons which defines a person and gives him a personality. If all persons were alike, no one would have a personality. It is our difference from others which defines us, just as their difference from us defines them. The same applies in the realm of Brahman once it is regarded as possessing personality. Its personality can be conceived of in multiple ways.

For instance, we can look at Brahman as just a person; as possessing a personality without defining it any further, as when we say: 'He has a personality'. We mean to say that he stands out in striking contrast against his background. What is the cosmic background? There is this entire universe, a vast astronomical universe and as against this someone stands out as its creator, its sustainer, its consummator, and that is God or Īśvara. Our adoration can then be directed towards him and from him grace will flow in our direction. The majesty of this God is overwhelming.

Or we may choose to look upon God as personal in his aspect of the creator of the universe. Then he would be adored and worshipped as Brahmā. In talking of Brahmā, however, there is need for caution. For one, the worship of Brahmā is not as common in present-day India as the worship of the other gods—Viṣṇu and Śiva. It seems likely that at one time the worship of Brahmā was fairly widespread but for various reasons it went out of vogue. Hence, one finds very few votaries of Brahmā today, which is odd because it is Brahmā who, at the beginning of each age, proclaims the revealed scriptures of the Hindus and for that reason alone one would expect him to occupy an important position in the pantheon. The other need for caution is suggested by his role as creator. In the Western religious tradition, creation has meant creation out of nothing, *creatio ex nihilo*. This idea is not generally accepted in Hinduism on account of a rather strong commitment to the view that nothing can come out of nothing. The matter out of which the universe is made pre-exists in some form. In this sense it might be more correct to call Brahmā the architect rather than the creator of the universe. Indeed, Brahmā is sometimes called Viśvakarmā which suggests his being the architect of the universe rather than its creator.

Another way in which Brahman can be conceived in personal terms is as Viṣṇu. In this mode of personalization the role of God as the sustainer of the universe is pre-eminent. It is also in this role that God incarnates himself in various ways and makes himself accessible to his devotees, at the same time helping the good and chastising the wicked. Sometimes it is an incarnation of Viṣṇu which is worshipped rather than Viṣṇu himself. The two most favoured incarnations are those of Rāma and Kṛṣṇa.

A third way in which Brahman can be personalized is as the destroyer of the universe—that is, as Śiva. The word *destroyer* has a pejorative connotation of which it must be purged in order to understand the personality of Śiva fully. It has even been suggested that the word Śiva is an attempt to do just that, for the word Śiva means *auspicious* and destroying is inauspicious. It has also been suggested that the word is apotropaic, just as we try to placate a powerful person by being complimentary to him though in reality we fear his power. A more philosophical explanation may also be in order. It is good to destroy certain things, such as illness, misfortune, evil proclivities, death or even rebirth. Here, destruction is redemption. Then the old must be destroyed to make way for the new. It is in this kind of a role that Śiva is cast.

But suppose we wish to personalize Brahman not in masculine but in feminine terms? Here, the tradition of Devī, also called Śakti, becomes relevant. It should be kept in mind here that those who worship Devī regard her as the supreme Goddess who is subordinate to none and to whom all gods are subordinate.

This brings us to the amalgamation of personality traits. We saw earlier how we could choose to concentrate on the transcendent majesty of God and personalize Brahman only as Īśvara or God. We also saw how we might distinguish the various cosmic functions of God as creator, sustainer and consummator and personalize Brahman in each of these ways. It is also possible to personalize the three gods in their different roles as a unity rather than a collectivity, which was the case with Īśvara or God. God collectively personalized in this role is known as Trimūrti or God with three forms. In some ways, this parallels the triune concept of God in Christianity. If Īśvara in this context may be seen as the one-in-three, then the Trimūrti is three-in-one. Worship of the Trimūrti is not as popular as that of its individual members; nevertheless its adoration is not unknown.

Since the worship of Brahmā is less popular than that of Viṣṇu and Śiva, the tendency to amalgamate the personalities sometimes takes the form of the dual divinity of Viṣṇu and Śiva known as Harihara.

The results are much more dramatic if one combines the masculine and feminine forms of anatomy and personality, perhaps as a tribute to the psychophysical truth that no one is pure male or female but only so on account of the predominance of those elements. This has typically taken the form of the amalgamation of Śiva with Śakti rather than, for example, Īśvara with Devī. The situation may be understood thus: typically the male and the female come together not in the same body but as separate bodies united in marriage. The three major gods acquired wives—one mode of personality amalgamation, for nothing is said to be as effective an agent of personality modification as marriage. But there were problems. Brahmā, the creator God, was too ascetically inclined to be enthusiastic about having a wife and when he finally did acquire one she turned out to be rather philosophically inclined herself. Then, he fell in love with his daughter and this is the traditional explanation of why he fell from grace. Viṣṇu acquired not one wife but two in the course of time and during his various incarnations had to oblige many other women. In his incarnation as Kṛṣṇa he provided the most convincing testimony in favour of marriage, espousing over 16,000 wives! Śiva had too forbidding a lifestyle for anyone to marry him but he too was finally married to one who turned out to be a match for him. He represents power at its highest point, a point, unfortunately, at which it often takes on destructive force. He obtained a wife potentially as formidable as him in her form as the female principle of power, Śakti. They have even been anatomically unified as Ardhanārīśvara, a form already known to a Syrian Christian author of the second century! These gods have children and even household pets and are often worshipped with their families.

Brahman thus personalized could be worshipped with devotion. This is Bhakti-yoga. Devotion here means intense longing for God and since what we long for we constantly remember, devotion is also defined as a constant remembrance of God. The intensity of a devotee's love for God has been compared to the passionate attachment of a man and a woman and to the attachment of a miser for his wealth. The first of these examples illustrates how human relationships can be used as a model for the divine relationship. Just as Brahman can be personalized in several ways, it can also be related to as with a person, in several personal ways: the way a servant is devoted to a master, a friend to a friend, a child to a parent, a parent to a child, a spouse to a spouse, a lover to a beloved, and so on. In Bhakti, human relationships thus become paradigms of relating to the Divine.

Devotion finally leads to salvation. At this point a major soteriological difference surfaces between the paths of Jñāna and Bhakti. The practice of Jñāna-yoga can (though not necessarily) lead to salvation in this life. Salvation, however, is accepted as a post-mortem state in Bhakti-yoga. After death one repairs to the realm of the god one worshipped—for example Vaikuṇṭha in the case of Viṣṇu, and Śivaloka ('the residence of Śiva') in the case of Śiva. There is even a connection made between the modes of salvation, devotion and religious practices. The exact details might vary with the system but the following pattern can be taken as representative.

Type of Practice	Mode of Devotion	Nature of Salvation
(1) External acts of worship	Servant in relation to God	Residence in the realm of God (*sālokya*)
(2) Acts of intimate service to God	Good son in relation to God	Nearness to God (*sāmīpya*)
(3) Contemplation and internal worship	Friend in relation to God	Gaining the form of God (*sārūpya*)
(4) Direct knowledge of God	God as truth	'Union' with God (*sāyujya*)

A few clarifications may be offered here. The word sāyujya (from the same root found in the Sanskrit word yoga and the English yoke) is sometimes used in Hindu non-dualism to represent the identity of ātman and Brahman. It has no such connotation here, for even in the state of salvation, the soul is entitatively different from God. Sometimes another word, *sārṣti*, is enumerated as a form of salvation. It denotes having the same power as God and is usually subsumed under sāyujya in the fourfold schema of the kind outlined above, the significance of which may be explained with the help of an example.

Let us take the case of a student who has been admitted to the university of his choice. The university has a vice-chancellor who is like god on the campus. In such a situation, just being on the campus would correspond to sālokya; being close to the vice-chancellor to sāmīpya; being able to wear the same insignia as he does to sārūpya; being able to exercise his powers to sarṣṭi; and being his close confidante and in constant communion with him to sāyujya.

The presence of these distinctions in salvation is interesting for it contrasts with the absence of any such distinction in Hindu monism. Thus, distinctions as a philosophical principle are very important to the theistic systems of Hinduism and seem to find their way into the post-mortem eschatology of these systems. By contrast, distinctions among human beings as devotees in the pre-mortem state are minimized, as all are seen to be equal in the eyes of God. Somewhat ironically, Hindu monism is said to be more inclined to uphold social distinctions, although it asserts their complete annulment in the state of salvation.

It was stated earlier that theoretically there are as many yogas as there are individuals; that three yogas are more commonly employed than others, namely the yogas of knowledge (jñāna), devotion (bhakti) and works (karma); that these three yogas are not mutually exclusive and that they are also called mārgas or paths—a metaphor in terms of which they can be discussed with some clarity. Having discussed the path of knowledge (Jñāna-yoga) and the path of devotion (Bhakti-yoga), it remains for us to discuss the path of action (Karma-yoga).

If we examine the implications of following the path of jñāna or bhakti in relation to our daily living in the ordinary course of life, we are likely to discover that these are not very comforting. Suppose one did become convinced that by following the path of knowledge one would gain enlightenment. This path, however, has traditionally involved the acceptance of a lifestyle inconsistent with our normal mode of living. On this view, seeking salvation is a full-time job. In order to become single-minded in the pursuit of Realization we must give up our mentally porous existence and the various cares and anxieties that fracture our concentration. If we examine life closely we will find that most of these distractions stem from two sources: (1) job and (2) marriage. The followers of the path of knowledge recommend a highly radical procedure for preventing these from interfering with the single-minded pursuit of ultimate verities; they recommend complete abandonment of them or what is called *sannyāsa* in Hinduism. However, to abandon one's professional and marital existence in order to grapple with Brahman alone is not everyone's cup of tea. Hence, tradition has found it simpler to recommend faith in God and carrying on with one's life. But, a full-fledged faith in God can be no less disruptive of normal life. Faith here does not mean the token faith of visiting church on Sundays, but the faith that God alone counts in life. The kind of problems such devotional enthusiasm can create in ordinary day-to-day living is illustrated by the life of Mīrā Bāī, a poet-saint of medieval times. She was married but cared little for marriage. Her husband regarded her as a religious nut.

While it is true that the path of devotion is better suited to ordinary life than the path of knowledge, especially if the expression of this devotion is kept as a part of life and does not become the whole of it, Hinduism evolved another form of yoga called Karma-yoga which is not only fully consistent with ordinary life but makes the point that salvation can be achieved through action. How marvellous! One can go on doing whatever one is doing, and also attain salvation. But, as one might have guessed, there is a catch. The basic principle of Karma-yoga is that it is not what one does but how one does it that counts and if one has the know-how in this sense, one can become liberated by doing whatever it is one does. 'God cares not for the verb but the adverb.'

In a sense one is playing with fire here, for if what is done becomes secondary to how it is done, one could do anything and literally get away with murder. This is exactly what Kṛṣṇa tells Arjuna in the *Bhagavadgītā*. Many find this interpretation of Karma-yoga alarming—and with good reason. But one should be very careful in interpreting such doctrines. As Paul says, that Jesus Christ died for our sins does not give us carte blanche to continue sinning. The doctrine of Karma-yoga can cut in two different directions with equal ease—perhaps one should say it is a double-edged sword. If how you do something and not what you do is the key, then, you might say, 'Well I can *do* anything and it does not matter', or, 'Well I don't need to do anything special, and can go on doing what I am doing for it does not matter'. Sociologically, there is a world of difference between the two interpretations. The first approach can be used to disturb the existing social order, while the second one can be used to reinforce the status quo. When the direction of the first interpretation is hinted at it is also suggested that such an interpretation might lead to social chaos. It is in fact the second one which became the dominant interpretation and has remained so. Let us examine this version of Karma-yoga and see its implications for modern living.

One may begin by making a few clarifications. Earlier in the chapter we talked about the doctrine of karma; in this part we are talking of Karma-yoga. These should not be confused. Karma is action in general, Karma-yoga is the use of action as an instrument of God-realization. In a sense, Karma-yoga is used to overcome karma: that is, if one is successful in practising Karma-yoga then one is able to transcend the cycle of saṁsāra characterized by the operation of the 'law' of karma. The other clarification relates to the concept of *dharma* in relation to karma. As already mentioned, if it is not what you do which matters but how you do it then you are left with the existential question: 'What then should I do?', that is, the theoretical possibility of being able to do anything becomes an acute embarrassment of riches. At this point Hinduism, which in a sense gives rise to the question, also provides the answer. It is clear, concise and direct: do your dharma or duty.

But how do I know what my duty is? The Hindu religious tradition answers this with considerable precision. It asks you two questions to provide you with an answer. The first is: What does your father do? Is he a priest, a warrior, a trader or a labourer? All professions in Hindu sociology can ultimately be comprehended under these categories. You follow the occupation of your father—that is your dharma or duty. This kind of duty is called *varṇadharma* because the four possible professional categories are called varṇas. The names assigned to them in that order are Brāhmaṇa, Kṣatriya, Vaiśya, Śūdra. The second question is: What is your age? If you are under twenty-five then you should be a celibate student. That is your dharma. If you are between the ages of twenty-five and fifty then you should be leading a married life, the life of a householder. If you are between the ages of fifty and seventy-five then you should be living in a forest and detaching yourself from the world. If over seventy-five, you should be leading the life of a wandering ascetic. These four stages of life—a celibate student, a householder, a forest-dweller and a renunciant—are called *āśramas*. The names assigned to them in the tradition are: *brahmacarya*, *gārhasthya*, *vānaprasthya* and *sannyāsa*. The duties associated with them are called *āśramadharmas*. And Hinduism has often described itself as *varṇāśrama* dharma: in other words, that religion which is distinguished from all other religions by the institutions of varṇa and āśrama.

The foregoing is a simplified picture but it serves to identify the basic pattern. However, in understanding classical Hinduism today a few salient facts must be kept in mind. First, no one is quite sure whether the kind of system just described ever actually operated, at least with full force. It is an 'ideal type', but inasmuch as ideas or ideal types exert their own influence independently of the extent to which they are actualized, the model has been quite influential. Second, the system of varṇa duties is one aspect of the caste system that is closely associated with Hinduism. These were supposed to refer to one's natal occupation, inherited from one's parents, but this ceased to be the case long ago. In present-day India, traders by caste are professors by vocation (meant for Brahmins). Brahmins are in the army (meant for Kṣatriyas or warriors); warriors by caste are field-labourers (meant for Śūdras or labourers), and so on. In ancient India Śūdras have even been kings. Yet such is the longevity of 'archetypes' that the Hindu tradition in some sense retains it and perceives its distinctness in terms of varṇāśrama dharma.

Very broadly, then, the path of action enjoins performing one's duty consistent with one's station in life. This may be identified as the core of the message. The Hindu religious tradition also provides a way of determining what these duties are, but the ideal construct does not seem to have worked all that well. Rather, the trend within modern Hinduism is to either reject it or accept a modified or rarefied form of it. In the Western world the message could be paraphrased, perhaps at the risk of trivializing it, in terms of 'doing your own thing', provided one takes the saying earnestly and not casually. The concept of duty in the Hindu religious tradition is highly contextual.

You may be beginning to wonder whether something is not being held back from you—for I have not yet said *how* things are to be done, how actions to be performed, so that even the ordinary round of daily living acquires a salvific potency. The *Bhagavadgītā* proclaims: Perform your actions without any sense of attachment to the results. This message, again, like so many things in Hinduism and perhaps in any religion, has to be understood with caution. When it is said that one should remain detached towards the fruits of one's actions it is *not* implied (*a*) either that one should give them up or (*b*) become indifferent to achieving them. Option (*a*) is barred by the statement that non-attachment to result does not imply inaction. Or, as is often said, renunciation *in* action is implied, not renunciation *of* action. What then is renounced? The fruits of action; but one might argue that renunciation *of* the fruits of action weakens the will to act by stripping action of the motivation for it. To this the reply that is given is: performing action for its own sake is the only proper motivation. Option (*b*) is thus barred by emphasizing that action should not only be detached, it should also be efficient.

We need to inquire now how karma leads to salvation. We have said how jñāna links up with nirguṇa Brahman and bhakti with saguṇa Brahman. But what does karma link up with? The standard explanation here is that Karma-yoga serves to purify one's heart and mind in such a way that only the mind which has been thus cleansed can reach Brahman through either jñāna or bhakti. It is stated that when one acts without regard for the result of action one does not in effect act, for only egocentric action is spiritually binding. Such a state of non-action leads to the realization of nirguṇa Brahman. Alternatively, when one acts without regard for result one may take the view that it is not oneself who is acting but God acting through one. This leads to the realization of saguṇa Brahman.

The chart on the next page represents our discussion of Hinduism at a glance, up to this point.

In the traditional Hindu formulation, what you should do—your *svadharma*—may be determined by reference to the next two diagrams. The first depicts the varṇas, the second the āśramas (p. 30). The division of the āśramas into segments of twenty-five years is suggestive rather than definitive.

Part Five

At this point one might feel inclined to ask: All this is fine, but where are these ideas coming from? Who thought them up? When? Why? How?

Before answering these questions it might be useful to establish a parallel. Suppose I were to ask a Christian to expound his view of life. I would probably be told that on account of disobedience, humanity was alienated from God and that this great barrier was

HINDUISM AT A GLANCE

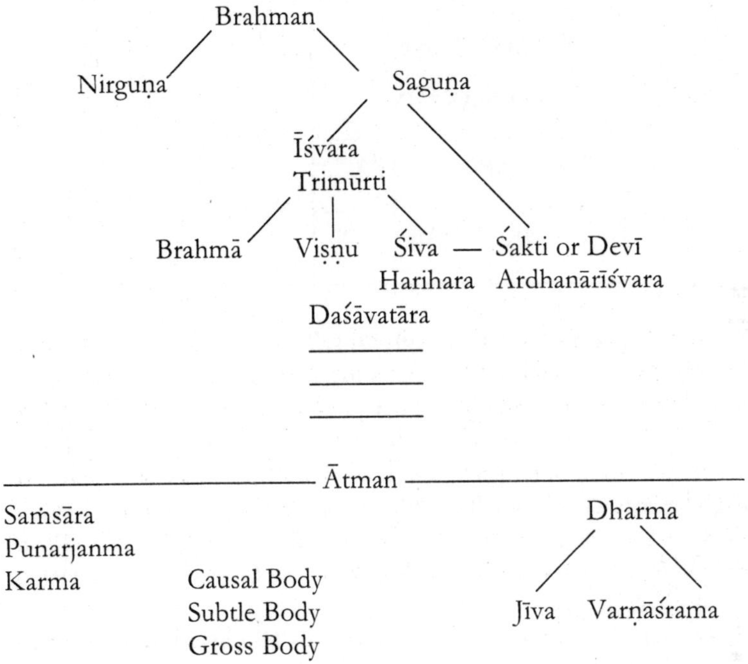

VARṆA

BRĀHMAṆA
KṢATRIYA
VAIŚYA
ŚŪDRA

ĀŚRAMA

BRAHMACARYA	
	YEAR 25
GĀRHASTHYA	
	YEAR 50
VĀNAPRASTHYA	
	YEAR 75
SANNYĀSA	

removed by Jesus Christ through his self-sacrifice. I would probably be told how according to Christianity a human being is born once and dies once and is judged once, and how after death he will be resurrected at the end of time (an idea one must not confuse with the resuscitation of corpses), and how all the believers will be gathered together into everlasting life. 'What a marvellous worldview!', I would exclaim and then ask: 'But where does all this come from?' 'From the Bible, of course', one would say; or the Gospels, if one wished to be more precise.

A similar question could be asked of the Hindu worldview: Where does it come from? The Hindu answer would be: 'From the Vedas, of course'; or the Upaniṣads if one wished to be more precise. When one refers to the Bible or the Gospels, most people know what is meant; unfortunately, this is usually not the case with the words Vedas and Upaniṣads. The plural is used because the Vedas are four in number and the Upaniṣads many more. The word Veda is also sometimes used in the singular to refer collectively to all the four Vedas.

Just as it makes more sense to talk first of the Bible and then locate the Gospels in it, it makes more sense to first talk of the Vedas and locate the Upaniṣads within them. The Vedas are the sacred and revealed scriptures of the Hindus. But, this being said, it must immediately be pointed out that the Vedas differ in several ways from the Bible. First, the Bible consists of two parts: the Old Testament and the New Testament. This distinction helps in understanding the Vedas as well, as we shall soon see. But, here another point needs to be made. The Bible virtually incorporates the sacred scriptures of another religion—Judaism—and claims them as its own. Such is not the case with the Vedas. The corpus is not shared by another religion. Second, the Vedas are much larger in size and would fill a good-sized bookshelf. Third, the Vedas, unlike the Bible, were never definitively 'closed'. Fourth, even to call the Vedas a scripture is a misnomer, for they were transmitted orally for centuries before being *written* down. Fifth, the Vedas are unilingual, although their language naturally exhibits development in such a vast corpus. Thus the Vedas are in archaic Sanskrit as distinguished from the Bible, which is in Hebrew, Aramaic and Koine Greek in the original. Yet, notwithstanding these differences, it can be asserted that the Vedas bear the same relation to Hinduism as the Bible does to Christianity—they constitute scriptural authority within the tradition.

But, how did the Vedas come into being? Here, there are two accounts to deal with—the traditional and the historical. According to the traditional account, the Vedas are revealed at the time of creation. They are given, as it were, with the world and *in toto*. They are not composed by anyone but verbally revealed to *ṛṣis* or seers, who are so called because they 'see' the Vedas. Actually, they hear them. It is a divine audition. On this view (1) the entire body of literature is revealed—not an iota of it is composed by human beings; (2) it is revealed *in toto* at a stroke, and (3) it is revealed *in toto* at the very beginning of creation. A parallel here would be Moses receiving the entire Pentateuch at Sinai. But modern scholarship views the Pentateuch differently.

The same is true of the Vedas. The reconstructed scenario goes somewhat as follows. It begins around 2000 BCE with the Indo-European tribes inhabiting what are now called the Russian steppes. They are called Indo-European because the language which they are supposed to have spoken was the precursor of some of the main languages which are now spoken in India (Indo-) and Europe (-European). For reasons that are not too clear, these tribes started spilling over into the areas on their borders along a wide arc extending from Asia Minor to Afghanistan. They moved into Greece, made an impact on the Middle East, moved into what is now Iran and Pakistan. When they moved into the Indian subcontinent they did something they did not do elsewhere. They started keeping a record of their religious experience in India—from 1500 BCE onwards, when they are generally believed to have entered India. This record is known as the Veda and it was kept by the Aryans, which is what the Indo-Europeans called themselves.

This body of literature can now be briefly described. Although the Vedas are four in number, in the present context it is the division of each of these into four layers which is far more significant. Attention shall therefore be confined to this fourfold division.

Each Veda is divided into four layers. The first layer is called Mantra or Saṁhitā and is in the nature of an anthology of hymns. This is followed by the Brāhmaṇas. The word brāhmaṇa here means the authoritative utterance of a priest and is not to be mistaken for the Hindu 'caste' known by exactly the same name. These texts deal with the application of the hymns in ritual, along with elaborations and explanations. The third layer is called the Āraṇyakas, and means forest-books. These texts were composed in forests by hermits who had retired there to reflect on the meaning of sacrificial ritual. The fourth layer consists of the Upaniṣads. The word *sad* in Upaniṣad is related to the English word 'sit' and refers to teachings which were revealed when the students sat *up* close (*upa, ni*) to the masters.

The important thing to remember about these four layers is that each layer represents a phase in the development of the religious consciousness of the Aryan people. In the beginning the people were content with singing hymns to the gods. That was in the Saṁhitā period. But then ritual developed and became increasingly elaborate, giving rise to the Brāhmaṇa period. Centuries of obsession with ritual were followed by reflection on ritual. These are embodied in the Arāṇyakas. Finally, reflection was no longer kept confined within the bounds of ritual but extended into a questioning of the meaning of life, nature, the universe and God. Speculations on these topics comprise the Upaniṣads, along with vestigial material from the earlier periods.

Once the Upaniṣads appeared, the Vedic canon was considered closed. As pointed out earlier, there was no formal procedure by which this was achieved. An informal consensus emerged in the tradition that the answers to the questions with which the Aryans had wrestled were to be found here. They represented the 'end' of the search—it was here that the 'conclusions' were to be found. This conviction on the part of the tradition is represented by the other word used to designate the Upaniṣads, namely Vedānta, or the end of the Vedas.

Veda or Vedas

Ṛg Veda	*Yajur Veda*	*Sāma Veda*	*Atharva Veda*
Mantra or Saṁhitā			1500–1200 BCE
Brāhmaṇa			1200–1000 BCE
Āraṇyaka			1000–800 BCE
Upaniṣad	VEDĀNTA		800–600 BCE –

The chart above sums up the conclusions of this section. The worldview described in the foregoing is the worldview that emerges from a study of the Vedānta.

Part Six

According to both traditional and historical accounts, the seers or ṛṣis were participants in the process by which the Vedas were revealed. The Vedas were, moreover, not revealed in the sense that the Bible and Qur'ān were revealed—by God—but were revealed in the sense that the law of gravity was revealed to Newton and the law of relativity to Einstein. In other words, the Vedas are valuable because they constitute verifiable records of the religious experience of a segment of humanity and their main value consists in facilitating that experience. They possess, in this sense, not intrinsic but only instrumental value, and are meant to be discarded if they come in the way of the discovery of truth. As a scriptural text says: 'Leave aside all scriptures and seek truth alone.' As a Hindu, one's primary loyalty is not to the Vedas, and not even to Hinduism; it is to truth. To say that the Vedas are revealed means that religious experience is possible.

If one thus feels stirred by the Hindu call for the search for the Real, one might be inclined to ask: 'How will one know that one has "arrived"?' Indeed, with so many paths and so many vistas of salvation, how will we know that we have made it? The Hindu answer to this question is at one level highly poetic and at another somewhat pedestrian. The poetic answer is that by 'its bliss ye shall know it!' Or, to paraphrase it in less ecstatic terms, one knows it of one's own accord. When we grew from children into adults, by what criterion did we come to realize that we had indeed become adults? Stations of life are traversed not by information but transformation. The process of our transformation from childhood to adulthood also provided the criteria by which we judged that transformation. This is not as strange as it sounds, for it is only in the light of the sun itself that we see the sun.

When in the end one enters the City of God one will know it. I use the word city here to suggest that, according to the Hindu view, religion represents a realm of spiritual experience and all people in that realm may not experience it similarly, but that does not mean that they are not part of the same realm. I arrived in Washington yesterday. I arrived at the National airport and not at the Dulles. But did I not land in Washington? And did not those who arrived through the Dulles? Did they not land in Washington? Similarly, residents of Washington can pass their entire lives without visiting certain parts of the city. Does this mean that they are not residents of Washington? Even a person who has never been inside the Smithsonian Institution can be a resident of Washington. You may deplore his taste or criticize his judgement but you cannot refute the fact that both of you live in the same city—the same realm. All those who live in Washington qualify as residents of Washington, though each may experience it in his own way. In similar fashion, the spiritual dimension of life is a realm—a city of God.

Recommended Reading

Klaus K. Klostermaier, *A Survey of Hinduism* (Albany, NY: State University of New York Press, 1994), p. 715.

A recent, up-to-date, comprehensive, well-organized, compact, sensitive and systematic survey of Hinduism by a leading modern scholar of Hinduism.

T.M.P. Mahadevan, *Outlines of Hinduism* (Bombay: Chetana Ltd, 1971), p. 312.

A lucid and comprehensive account of Hinduism, which presupposes some prior familiarity with Hinduism.

S. Radhakrishnan, *The Hindu View of Life* (New York: The Macmillan Co., 1927).

A classic and concise statement of Hinduism by a major intellectual spokesman of our times.

Louis Renou, ed., *Hinduism* (New York: George Braziller, 1962), p. 225.

An excellent introduction to Hinduism, less technical than Mahadevan's and more detailed than Radhakrishnan's, put together by a renowned French savant.

Arvind Sharma, 'Hinduism', in Arvind Sharma, ed., *Our Religions* (San Francisco: Harper, 1993), pp. 3–67.

CHAPTER II

A Historical Survey

In the previous chapter the architectonics of classical Hindu thought was disclosed with the help of the key building blocks it employs and the way they are arranged. Such a presentation may be called synchronic. That is to say, it presented the constellation of concepts associated with classical Hindu thought ahistorically.

Classical Hindu thought, however, did not suddenly emerge fully fashioned in every respect, like a mansion in a dream. Even within the classical period the key concepts underwent change or at least refinement and realignment. Indeed, this arrangement of ideas may be compared to the arrangement of elements within a kaleidoscope. By shifting the position of the kaleidoscope the elements themselves are not altered but the pattern in which they are arranged does undergo an alteration, thereby generating a set of new relationships, and thus a new perspective. In the case of the kaleidoscope these elements are simultaneously present, but in the case of classical Hinduism its constituent elements emerged in a certain order—a chronological order, as they achieved a certain logical order. It is interesting to consider how the sequence in which the concepts emerged might have influenced the way in which they were combined to provide classical Hinduism with its characteristic contours. It might be equally if not more interesting to speculate on how the concepts may have constellated differently—and how the relations among them might have differed—if the sequence had been different. All this must be left to the reader's imagination. In this chapter we attempt the task of historically surveying the emergence of the various key concepts of classical Hinduism and shift from a synchronic into a diachronic gear, as it were.

One of the earliest concepts to emerge was that of the gods or *devas*, which is prominent in the *Ṛg Veda* (*c.* 1500 BCE). According to the traditional Hindu understanding, gods were already perceived as manifestations of one single supreme god or Īśvara. This is said to be the view of Yāska, one of the earliest Hindu exegetes of the *Ṛg Veda*, who is usually placed in the seventh century BCE. This view has been described as 'pantheistic monotheism'.[1] Modern western scholars ascribe the emergence of the concept of monotheism to a later period; although already in the *Ṛg Veda* there is a tendency on the part of god Indra, to whom the largest number of hymns are devoted, to absorb the attributes of the other gods[2] and he is even referred to as the one god or *eko devaḥ*.[3] However, although this trend to enthrone one god as supreme persists through the Brāhmaṇas, it is in an early, perhaps the earliest Upaniṣad, the *Bṛhad-āraṇyaka* (eighth century BCE) that we find an unequivocal and unmistakable assertion of monotheism.

1. Then Vidagdha Śākalya questioned him. 'How many gods are there, Yājñavalkya?'

He answered in accord with the following *Nivid* (invocationary formula): 'As many as are mentioned in the *Nivid* of the Hymn to all the Gods, namely, three hundred and three, and three thousand and three [=3306].'

'Yes,' said he, 'but just how many gods are there, Yājñavalkya?'
'Thirty-three.'
'Yes,' said he, 'but just how many gods are there, Yājñavalkya?'
'Six.'
'Yes,' said he, 'but just how many gods are there, Yājñavalkya?'
'Three.'
'Yes,' said he, 'but just how many gods are there, Yājñavalkya?'
'Two.'
'Yes,' said he, 'but just how many gods are there, Yājñavalkya?'
'One and a half.'
'Yes,' said he, 'but just how many gods are there, Yājñavalkya?'
'One.'[4]

1. See Vasudeva Sharana Agrawala, 'Yāska and Pāṇini' in *The Cultural Heritage of India* (Calcutta: Ramakrishna Mission Institute of Culture, 1958), vol. I, p. 301.

2. Thomas J. Hopkins, *The Hindu Religious Tradition* (Encino, California and Belmont, California: Dickenson Publishing Co., Inc., 1971), p. 17.

3. Ainslie T. Embree, ed., *Sources of Indian Tradition* (second edition) (New York: Columbia University Press, 1988), p. 6.

4. Robert Ernest Hume, tr., *The Thirteen Principal Upanishads* (second edition) (London: Oxford University Press, 1968), pp. 119–20.

In the same text, the *Bṛhadāraṇyaka Upaniṣad*, we also find passages which the theism of classical Hinduism explicitly applies to Īśvara or the Supreme Lord,[5] as well as the first hints of distinction between two types of Brahman, paving the way for its formalization in saguṇa and nirguṇa Brahman. This text also seems to assert the primacy of nirguṇa brahman. Thus the classical Hindu concepts of Brahman saguṇa and nirguṇa, along with the concept of Īśvara, seem to have been in place by the eighth century BCE. The concept of a supreme god is clearly evidenced and sometimes the word Īśvara is associated with it as in one of the four Vedas (*Atharva Veda* XIX.6.4) and *other* words with the same verbal root such as *Īśāna*, are also clearly connected with it (*Bṛhadāraṇyaka Upaniṣad* IV.4.15). It is, however, after the beginning of the Common Era that the word Īśvara (as distinguished from the concept) gains currency in classical Hinduism.[6]

While the word jīva is not found in the *Bṛhadāraṇyaka Upaniṣad* and the concept is (IV.4.5–6), it is found in the *Chāndogya Upaniṣad* (VI.3.2), which is usually assigned to the same period as the *Brhād-araṇyaka.* However, it is used therein with a different nuance. The word jīva (as distinguished from the concept) also gains currency subsequently, during the period of the 'Verse' Upaniṣads (*Kaṭha*, *Muṇḍaka*, *Śvetāśvatara*, etc.) which are usually placed between 500 BCE and 200 BCE.[7] It is also during this period that the three main gods of classical Hinduism emerge, each being associated with a verse Upaniṣad: Brahmā with *Muṇḍaka*, Viṣṇu with *Kaṭha* and Śiva with *Śvetāśvatara.* Brahmā can be traced to an even earlier period through the *Kauṣītakī Upaniṣad* (*c.* 500 BCE).[8]

All of them as trimūrti begin to be emerge in the *Maitrī Upaniṣad* (V.1), which is placed between 200 BCE and 200 CE.[9] But as Klaus K. Klostermaier points out:

> Hindu texts do indeed speak of the triad of Brahmā as creator, Viṣṇu as preserver, and Śiva as destroyer, fulfilling the functions of the One God, but all these texts belong to one of the traditions in which the Supreme is identical

5. S. Radhakrishnan, ed., *The Principal Upaniṣads* (London: George Allen & Unwin Ltd, 1953), p. 224ff.

6. Margaret and James Stutley, *A Dictionary of Hinduism* (London: Routledge & Kegan Paul, 1977), p. 120.

7. Thomas J. Hopkins, *The Hindu Religious Tradition*, p. 141.

8. S. Radhakrishnan, ed., *The Principal Upaniṣads*, p. 755ff.

9. Thomas J. Hopkins, *The Hindu Religious Tradition*, p. 141.

with one of those names and the three separate names are but different aspects of the same being. Some of the famous trimūrtis are quite clearly recognizable as artistic expressions of different modalities of one and the same Īśvara.'[10]

Even when in the fourth century the doctrine is celebrated in a famous verse by Kālidāsa, some scholars note: 'From the context it is clear that Kālidāsa's hymn to the Trimūrti is really addressed to Brahmā here looked on as the high god.'[11] A certain fluidity is thus seen to characterize the doctrine, which may explain in part why it did not create the theological difficulties of trinitarian Christianity, as it 'did not abolish the belief in the exclusive supremacy of these gods, taken separately.'[12]

This seems to apply to the concept of goddess as well. The goddess figure is mentioned even in the earliest available text of Hinduism, the Vedas[13]; and female divinities[14] are also present, Vāc[15] being prominent among them. Female divinities also appear in the early Upaniṣads (*Kena Upaniṣad* I.3.12) but in a secondary rather than primary role. It is in the period of the Verse Upaniṣads rather than the Prose Upaniṣads that the female divinities appear distinctly and even more so in the period of what have been called the Late Upaniṣads. The striking feature to be reckoned with historically here is that the goddess as an ultimate principle makes a full-fledged appearance sometime towards of the end of the Gupta period (sixth century).[16] It is interesting that the concepts of the goddess, the trinity and *puruṣārtha* (as well become apparent later) appear in their developed version during or around the political heyday of classical Hinduism.

History suggests that in the earliest stratum, going back to the eighth–seventh century BCE, the religious ideas in place were those

10. Klaus K. Klostermaier, *A Survey of Hinduism* (Albany, NY: State University of New York Press, 1989), p. 133.

11. A.L. Basham, *The Wonder That Was India* (third revised edition) (London: Sedgwick & Jackson, 1988), p. 311.

12. M. Hiriyanna, *The Essentials of Indian Philosophy* (London: George Allen & Unwin Ltd, 1949) , p. 176.

13. See K.M. Sen, *Hinduism* (Harmondsworth: Penguin Books, 1963), p. 23.

14. Louis Renou, *Vedic India* (tr. Philip Spratt) (Calcutta: Sushil Gupta [India] Pvt. Ltd, 1957), pp. 71–2.

15 Thomas J. Hopkins, *The Hindu Religious Tradition*, pp. 20–1.

16 Thomas B. Coburn, *Encountering the Goddess: A Translation of the Devī-Māhātmya and a Study of its Interpretations* (Albany, NY: State University of New York, 1991), p. 13.

of Brahman and its dual classification, jīva, karma and rebirth, and mokṣa (e.g. *Bṛhadāraṇyaka Upaniṣad* IV.4.7).[17] Such is the situation during the period of the so-called Prose Upaniṣads. In the period of the Verse Upaniṣads (*c.* 500–200 BCE) the gods Brahmā, Viṣṇu and Śiva emerge clearly. It is also during this period that the ideas of saṁsāra and *māyā* find a clear expression as also the idea of bhakti (*Śvetāśvatara* VI.16; I.10; VI.23), which is somewhat different from the devotion shown to Ṛg Vedic gods.

Between 200 BCE and 200 CE, another set of developments takes place—basically resulting in a trinitization of Brahmā, Viṣṇu and Śiva as gods and of jñāna, bhakti and karma as paths, especially when the *Bhagavadgītā* and the *Manusmṛti*[18] are kept in mind.

One may now turn to the other set of ideas represented by terms like varṇa, āśrama and puruṣārtha. By the time of the Prose Upaniṣads the four varṇas were well known (*Bṛhadāraṇyaka Upaniṣad* I.4.11–13) and their connection with the doctrine of karma was in the process of being established (*Chāndogya Upaniṣad* V.10.8). The āśramas are not mentioned as such but P.V. Kane thinks that their outlines had emerged by this time with a fair degree of clarity, as is clear from the *Āpastamba Dharmasūtra* (800–400 BCE).[19]

By the time of the Verse Upaniṣads (500 BCE–200 BCE), the doctrines have crystallized further. The *Śvetāśvatara Upaniṣad* does not speak of the four varṇas, although it does speak of varṇas (IV.1) in a different sense; however, it uses the expression *atyāśrama* (VI.21) which, when taken either in the sense of one who is firmly established in an āśrama or has transcended the scheme, confirms it as firmly established as a concept. We know that already during the Brāhmaṇa period (*c.* 800 BCE) distinctions based on varṇa were being taken into consideration in determining the heights of burial mounds (*Śatapatha Brāhmaṇa* XIII.8.3.11) even though it is not certain whether or not the link between varṇa and karma had been forged by this time. This tendency becomes apparent in the Prose Upaniṣads

17. On these doctrinal developments, so significant for classical Hinduism, see A.L. Basham, *The Origins and Development of Classical Hinduism* (ed. Kenneth G. Zysk) (Boston: Beacon Press, 1989), Chapter Three.

18. K. Satchidananda Murty, *Vedic Hermeneutics* (Delhi: Motilal Banarsidass, 1993), pp. 39–41.

19. P.V. Kane, *History of Dharmaśāstra* (Poona: Bhandarkar Oriental Research Institute, 1962), vol. II, pp. 416–17; vol. IV, p. ix; vol. V, pt II, p. 1643.

though, interestingly, the Verse Upaniṣads do not provide any striking confirmation of it.

Such evidence, though indirect, surfaces among the Late Upaniṣads (200 BCE–200 CE) as when the *Maitrī Upaniṣad* talks negatively of śūdras learned in the Śāstras or scriptural texts (VII.8). It is, however, in the *Manusmṛti* (second century), preceded by the Dharmasūtras, that caste distinctions are codified. In the earlier periods the situation, at least on the basis of the Upaniṣadic evidence, is more fluid, as is clear from the encounter of Raikva and Jānaśruti in the *Chāndogya* (IV.3.1–8) as well as of Satyakāma with Hāridrumata Gautama (IV.4.1–5). It also points to the possibility that traces of untouchability might have existed prior to the emergence of the caste system, as the reference to the varṇas here is more fluid than the reference to the caṇḍālas in the *Chāndogya* (V.10.7).[20] It is a matter of some interest that classical Hinduism, although it debarred śūdras from the access to Vedic study and ritual, could not suppress evidence to the contrary even within that period.[21]

The doctrine of the four puruṣārthas can be read back even into early classical Hinduism but its formal recognition belongs to the later phase of the classical period, and by the time of the *Manusmṛti* (second century) it seems to be well in place.[22] The *Mahābhārata*, whose evolution is usually said to cover the period 400 BCE–400 CE, in a celebrated verse (XVIII.5.38), prides itself as a veritable encyclopaedia of the puruṣārthas.

This survey of the main items of classical Hindu thought may be concluded with a reference to the position of the Vedas. The historical relationship of the Vedas to classical Hinduism is rich and complex. First, classical Hinduism alone is considered by some scholars as constituting Hinduism. These scholars describe the previous phase in the religious history of India as Vedism and consider Hinduism, Buddhism and Jainism as arising equally out of the ashes of the collapse of the Vedic sacrificial worldview. According to this view, Hinduism differs from the other two in treating itself as a genetically identifiable lineal descendantof Vedism. Second, in classical Hinduism

20. This possibility, however, does not seem to have been entertained by R.S. Sharma, *Śūdras in Ancient India* (Delhi: Motilal Banarsidass, 1980), see pp. 52, 75–6, 89.

21. K. Satchidananda Murty, *Vedic Hermeneutics*, pp. 14–17.

22. P.V. Kane, *History of Dharmaśāstra*, vol. V, pt II, pp. 1510–15.

the Vedas functioned both as religious authority and as symbolic of it. And they functioned as the ultimate source of religious authority with regard to two referents: morality (dharma) and reality (Brahman or what it confers, namely mokṣa). All those schools of Indian thought which accepted Vedic authority in matters of dharma came to be deemed orthodox, while those which accepted it as authoritative in terms of the disclosure of reality, namely, the schools of Mīmāṁsa and Vedānta, even more so. As symbolic of religious authority, the concept of Veda was extended to figuratively embrace other bodies of literature sacred to classical Hinduism. Thus

> [the] Hindu tradition (i) regards the *Mahābhārata* as the fifth Veda, the *Bhagavadgītā* as the 'nectar milked from the Upaniṣadic cows', (ii) considers that through Vālmīkī the Veda actually became the *Rāmāyaṇa* when the Supreme Person knowable by it was born as Daśaratha's son, and (iii) conceived the *Bhāgavata* [*Purāṇa*] to be the ripe delicious fruit which dropped from the wish-fulfilling Vedic tree.... One who was [sic] seriously and sincerely studied and pondered over these books for long and grasped the core of their teaching would not scoff at this tradition.[23]

Third, although classical Hinduism is firmly committed to the tradition of the oral transmission of the Vedas, the accounts of some of the incarnations such as the fish (*matsya*) in which God rescued Manu (like Noah) from the Deluge, 'he also saved the Vedas from the flood'.[24] This strongly suggests that the Vedas were in some sense a tangible entity. Fourth, the tradition, while accepting Vedic authority, had different views regarding its basis. One view was that it was authoritative because it was the word of God. However, the view which gained wider currency was the view that the Vedas were authoritative *per se* and were eternal. This eternality itself was interpreted in one of two ways: that the Vedas were eternal in the sense that the truths conveyed by them were eternal; or that they were literally eternal. Although the view that the Vedas are eternal principially and not literally is echoed by the grammarian Patañjali (second century BCE)[25] and later by Vācaspati Miśra[26] (ninth

23. K. Satchidananda Murty, *Vedic Hermeneutics*, p. 13 note.

24. A.L. Basham, *The Wonder That Was India*, p. 302.

25. M. Hiriyanna, *Outlines of Indian Philosophy* (London: George Allen & Unwin, 1932) p. 313.

26. K. Satchidananda Murty, *Revelation and Reason in Advaita Vedānta* (New York: Columbia University Press, 1959), pp. 41–2.

century), the view which gained greater currency, especially through the efforts of the Mīmāṁsā school, was the latter—that the text was literally eternal. Does such a stance represent a hardening of the otherwise vague reverence in which the Vedas were held by classical Hinduism in the face of the attacks on it by Buddhists, Jainas and Indian Materialists?[27]

27. For earlier attempts at a survey of this kind, see Franklin Edgerton, *The Beginnings of Indian Philosophy* (Cambridge: Harvard University Press, 1965). For a more recent attempt, see A.L. Basham, *The Origins and Development of Classical Hinduism.*

CHAPTER III

Brahman: Nirguṇa and Saguṇa

One of the clearest enunciations of the Hindu concept of God is found in the *Taittirīya Upaniṣad* II.1: *Satyam jñānam anantam brahma.*[1]

It is commonplace in the discussion of Hindu philosophy, however, to maintain that Brahman may be taken to mean either saguṇa or nirguṇa Brahman,[2] although the two are not clearly mutually exclusive but represent two standpoints of viewing the same reality.[3] How this description of the selfsame Brahman is understood in a dual sense will be demonstrated in this chapter. That the description of the *Taittirīya Upaniṣad* applies to Brahman alone is clearly stated in the *Brahmasūtra*. Thus Hajime Nakamura notes:

> Nearly all the characters which can be supposed to the absolute are ascribed to this *Brahman*. *Brahman* has unlimited extension (*āyāma*) in terms of space; it is omnipresent (*sarvagata*, III, 2, 37). It is endless (*ananta*, III, 2, 26), and is called 'plenitude' (*bhūman*, 1, 3, 8). It is without parts (*niravayava*, II, 1, 26), and without form (*arūpavad*, III, 2, 33). It is eternal, and is called imperishable (*akṣara*, I, 3, 10; III, 3, 1). *Brahman* in itself is undifferentiated (III, 2, 11). There occurs no increase or diminution of its qualities (III, 3, 12). It is difficult to describe it positively in terms of words; it can be expressed only negatively (III, 2, 12).

1. It is not without interest that *Taittirīya* is one of the earliest Upaniṣads; see Hajime Nakamura, *A History of Early Vedānta Philosophy* (Delhi: Motilal Banarsidass, 1983), vol. I, pp. 10, 42.

2. Thomas J. Hopkins, *The Hindu Religious Tradition* (Belmont, California: Dickenson Publishing Co., Inc., 1971), p. 119; T.M.P. Mahadevan, *Outlines of Hinduism* (Bombay: Chetana Ltd, 1971), p. 150.

3. Satishchandra Chatterjee and Dhirendramohan Datta, *An Introduction to Indian Philosophy* (University of Calcutta, 1968: first published 1939), p. 367.

On the other hand, *Brahman* is at the same time the world-cause, and it is said that all the attributes (*sarvadharma*) of the world-cause can be applied to *Brahman* (II, 1, 37). The characteristics of 'truth, knowledge and endlessness,' set forth in the *Taittirīya Upaniṣad*, II, 1, can be applied only to Brahman (I, 1, 15) [italics mine].[4]

We shall therefore now examine how this description applies to nirguṇa and saguṇa Brahman respectively.[5]

II

The description of Brahman in its nirguṇa aspect as *satya*, *jñāna* and *ananta* can be interpreted in two ways. If Brahman is regarded as utterly ineffable then, following Śaṅkara's gloss on *Taittirīya* II, 1, one would have to state that Brahman, in this absolutely transcendent aspect,

cannot be described at all and it is, therefore, called indeterminate or characterless or nirguṇa. The description of Brahman even as infinite, real, consciousness, though more accurate than accidental descriptions, cannot directly convey the idea of Brahman. It only serves to direct the mind towards Brahman by denying of it finiteness, unreality and unconsciousness.[6]

However, there might be some room for compromise, especially

4. Hajime Nakamura, *A History of Early Vedānta Philosophy*, vol. 1, p. 485, emphasis added. The citations are from the *Brahmasūtra*, an aphoristic summary of the teachings of the Upaniṣads.

5. Some scholars have argued that the description in the *Taittirīya Upaniṣad* can be applied only to nirguṇa Brahman. Thus it is said: 'Similarly, the description of God as conscious, real, infinite (*satyam, jñānam, anantam Brahman*) is an attempt to describe his essence (*svarūpa*) whereas the description of Him as Creator, Sustainer and Destroyer of the world, or by any other characteristic connected with the world, is a mere accidental description and it holds good only from the point of view of the world (vyāvahārikadṛṣṭi). As we can regard the actor on the stage from a point of view other than that of the stage, so we can look at God also from a non-worldly point of view (pāramārthikadṛṣṭi) and try to dissociate Him from the characters which we ascribe to Him from the point of view of the world. God in this aspect of what He really is, without any reference to the world, is called by Śaṅkara, Paramabrahma or the Supreme God.' (Satishchandra Chatterjee and Dhirendramohan Datta, *An Introduction to Indian Philosophy*, p. 389). But this only represents the Advaitic point of view, as will be shown later. For more on *svarūpalakṣaṇa* see Swami Madhavananda, tr., *Vedānta-Paribhāṣā of Dharmarāja Adhvarīndra* (Howrah: Belur Math, 1972), pp. 150ff.

6. Satishchandra Chatterjee and Dhirendramohan Datta, *An Introduction to Indian Philosophy*, p. 391.

if we read *ananda* for ananta here, as suggested by Deussen.[7] For, then, satya, jñana and ananda become virtually interchangeable with *saccidānanda* and the comment by Hiriyanna on that epithet can virtually be transferred to *Taittirīya* II, 1. Hiriyanna writes:

The spiritual and unitary character of this absolute reality is very well expressed by the classical phrase *saccidānanda.* As a single term defining its nature, it is met with only in the latter Upanishads; but its three elements—*sat, cit* and *ānanda*—are used of Brahman, singly and in pairs, even in the earliest of them. *Sat,* which means 'being', points to the positive character of Brahman distinguishing it from all non-being. But positive entities, to judge from our experience, may be spiritual or not. The next epithet *cit,* which means 'sentience,' shows that it is spiritual. The last epithet *ānanda,* which stands for 'peace,' indicates its unitary and all-embracing character, inasmuch as variety is the source of all trouble and restlessness. 'Fear arises from the other,' as a famous Upaniṣadic saying has it. Thus the three epithets together signify that Brahman is the sole spiritual reality of the Absolute, which comprehends not only all being (*sat*) but also all thought (*cit*) so that whatever partakes of the character of either must eventually be traced to it.[8]

It is clear then that *Taittirīya* II, 1 can be taken to describe Brahman either in its ineffable aspect or as an undifferentiated unity. Śaṅkara's gloss on *Brahmasūtra* I, 7, 15 seems to support Hiriyanna's interpretation, although his gloss on the Upaniṣadic passage appears to emphasize the ineffability of Brahman. Part of his gloss on *Brahmasūtra* I, 7, 15 runs thus:

The Self, consisting of joy, is the highest Brahman for the following reason also. On the introductory words 'he who knows Brahman attains the highest' (Taitt. Up. II, 1), there follows a mantra proclaiming that Brahman, which forms the general topic of the chapter, possesses the qualities of true existence, intelligence, infinity; after that it is said that from Brahman there sprang at first the ether and then all other moving and non-moving things, and that, entering into the beings which it had emitted, Brahman stays in the recess, inmost of all; thereupon, for its better comprehension, the series of the different Selfs ('different from this is the inner Self,' &c.) are enumerated, and then finally the same Brahman which the mantra had proclaimed, is again proclaimed in the passage under discussion, 'different from this is the other inner Self, which consists of bliss.'

To assume that a mantra and the Brāhmaṇa passage belonging to it have the

7. Paul Deussen, *The Philosophy of the Upanishads* (Edinburgh: T. & T. Clark, 1908), pp. 126–8.

8. M. Hiriyanna, *The Essentials of Indian Philosophy* (London: George Allen & Unwin, 1948), p. 22.

same sense is only proper, on account of the absence of contradiction (which results therefrom); for otherwise we should be driven to the unwelcome inference that the text drops the topic once started, and turns to an altogether new subject.[9]

III

So, the word most often used to denote the ultimate reality in Hindu thought is Brahman.[10] The word is of neuter gender but may be used to denote the ultimate reality in either of two senses, impersonally or as a person, that is nirguṇa Brahman or saguṇa Brahman. In the rest of the discussion the word 'Brahman' will be used in the sense of saguṇa Brahman or God unless otherwise specified. The words 'Īśvara' and 'Bhagvān' also denote God in Hinduism. The significance of these terms will become apparent in the course of this chapter.

What, then, is Brahman or God? The question can be answered in at least three ways: (1) God as he is by Himself *per se*; (2) God as the possessor of various attributes; and (3) God as the performer of various cosmic functions.

For a definition of God as it is by itself, most Hindus turn to that famous passage in one of the Upaniṣads: *satyam jñānam anantam Brahma* (*Taittirīya Upaniṣad* II, 1). The passage, which can be interpreted both theistically and monistically, translates simply as: 'Truth, knowledge and infinity (is) Brahman.' We shall here follow the interpretation of the great theist Rāmānuja (1017–1137) as summarized by S. Radhakrishnan:

> 'Truth, knowledge and infinity is Brahman,' says the Upaniṣad. These several terms refer to the one supreme reality and declare that the absolute Brahman is unchangeable perfection, and possesses intelligence which is ever uncontracted, while the intelligence of released souls was for some time in a contracted condition. It is infinite (anantam), since its nature is free from all limitations of place, time and substance, and different in kind from all things. Infinity characterises the qualities as well as the nature of Brahman, which is not the case with regard to the souls called eternal (nitya). It is first without a second, since there is no other God than God.[11]

9. George Thibaut, tr., *The Vedānta-Sūtras with the Commentary by Śankarāchārya* (Oxford: Clarendon Press, 1890), pt I, p. 68.

10. See Jan Gonda, *Notes on Brahman* (Utrecht: J.L. Byers, 1950); R.C. Zaehner, *Hinduism* (London: Oxford University Press, 1966), Chapter 2.

11. S. Radhakrishnan, *Indian Philosophy*, vol. II (London: George Allen & Unwin,

God as Being (sat)

How does the God of Rāmānuja compare with the 'God of Abraham, the God of Isaac and the God of Jacob'? By taking a closer look at the Judeo-Christian concept of God, we learn that:

> God then, according to Judaism and Christianity, is or has unlimited being, and the various divine 'attributes' or characteristics are so many ways in which the infinite divine reality *is* or exists, or has being.
>
> First among these attributes we may place what the scholastics called *aseity* (from the Latin *a se esse*, being from oneself), usually translated as 'self-existence'. The concept of self-existence, as it occurs in the work of the great theologians, contains two elements.
>
> 1. God is not dependent either for existence or for characteristics upon any other reality. God has not been created by any higher being. There is nothing capable either of constituting or of destroying God. God just *is*, in infinite richness and plenitude of being as the ultimate, unconditioned, all-conditioning reality. In abstract terms, God has absolute ontological independence.
>
> 2. It follows from this that God is eternal, without beginning or end. If God had a beginning, there would have to be a prior reality to bring God into being; and in order for God's existence to be terminated, there would have to be some reality capable of effecting this. Each of these ideas is excluded by God's absolute ontological independence.[12]

So far the parallel holds. God, both in Judaism and Christianity as well as in Hinduism, shares these features. This is indeed what is meant by saying that God is *sat*. However, although eternal, God is not the sole eternal in Hindu thought, but possesses co-eternals. The idea of souls and matter as co-eternals of God goes at least as far back as the *Śvetāśvatara Upaniṣad* and is upheld in the Nyāya system and the theistic versions of Vedānta. In other words, just as the concept of God in the Western philosophy of religion is grounded in the biblical God who is Who He Is, so is the concept of God in Hindu philosophy grounded in Upaniṣadic theism. The *Śvetāśvatara Upaniṣad* is representative of such theism:

> There are, according to the *Śvetāśvatara*, three 'unborn ones': the Lord, knowing and all-powerful; the individual *ātman*, unknowing and powerless; and Nature, Prakṛiti, made up of primary matter. In terms of relationships, this triad can be described as the Mover or Impeller (the Lord), the enjoyer (the individual self),

---

1927), p. 687. For Rāmānuja's own gloss on the Upanisadic passage, see J.B. Carman, *The Theology of Rāmānuja* (New Haven: Yale University Press, 1974), p. 102.

12. John H. Hick, *Philosophy of Religion* (third edition) (Englewood Cliffs, New Jersey: Prentice-Hall Inc., 1990), p. 8.

and the object of enjoyment (Nature, or primary matter). Brahman, the infinite Self, encompasses these three aspects but is itself inactive.

Salvation for the individual self occurs by a change in the relationships within the triad.[13]

This system left an indelible stamp on subsequent Hindu theism with the result that in Hindu theism all three—God, Matter and Souls—are eternal. Wherein, then, does God's superiority consist of? It has been variously suggested as consisting in consciousness being his eternal attribute, whereas it is not so of the souls; or in his being totally beyond the trammels of saṁsāra or the spatio-temporal realm unlike the other souls; or in the utter dependence of matter and souls on him for their existence. This last point raises the interesting possibility that God may withdraw his sustaining support, but it is maintained that this is 'a mere possibility that never even from the metaphysical point of view, can mature into actuality'.[14] Even when the world is not manifest, the souls and matter continue to exist in a subtle form. It has been suggested that 'creation and dissolution are not to be taken as events in time but are to be interpreted as signifying logical dependence on the one Supreme'.[15]

God as Knowledge (jñāna)

A qualitative distinction is drawn between the knowledge of God and of souls, just as a qualitative distinction is drawn between the nature of God's existence and that of souls and matter. The specific form this distinction takes depends on the philosophical system. But as Rāmānuja himself explains in the context in which the term appears: 'The word "knowledge" or "consciousness" (*jñāna*) describes the state of permanently uncontracted knowledge, thus distinguishing (Him) from released souls, whose knowledge was at one time contracted.'[16] More light is shed on the relationship of the souls and God by the realization that the

soul (*jīva*) is of the essence of spirit. It *is* and *has* knowledge. The soul as knowledge does not change; but as having knowledge it changes. Knowledge as an attribute is called *dharmabhūta-jñāna*; it characterizes both soul and God.

13. Thomas J. Hopkins, *The Hindu Religious Tradition*, p. 70.

14. Charles A. Moore, ed., *The Indian Mind* (Honolulu: University of Hawaii Press, 1967), p. 307.

15. S. Radhakrishnan, *Indian Philosophy*, vol. II, p. 686.

16. See J.B. Carman, *The Theology of Rāmānuja*, p. 102.

As an attribute, it is inseparable from them. It is also a substance (*dravya*) in the sense that it is capable of contradiction and expansion, and is the substrate of change. The soul's attributive knowledge expands to its fullest extent in the state of release; there is nothing then that the soul cannot know. In the state of bondage, however, the soul's attributive knowledge is more or less contracted.[17]

God's 'cognitive activity is one and eternal' as this alone is consistent with his cosmic role.

God as Infinity (anantam)

In order to see the specific significance of infinity it may be recalled here that in Rāmānuja's system the souls are infinite in number, and of three kinds: '(1) The eternal (*nitya*) *jīvas* which have never been in bondage, (2) the freed (*mukta*) souls which have already achieved their salvation, and (3) the bound (*baddha*) souls which are caught up in the vortex of *saṁsāra*.'[18] This shows how Rāmānuja has used the definitional element of *sat* or being in relation to God as representing unconditional being so as to distinguish God from (a) matter and (b) souls, conditioned by being involved in matter. He has used jñāna or knowledge to distinguish God from those souls who are now released but whose knowledge was at one time contracted. He is now using the definitional element of infinity in God to distinguish him from the souls who are ever free, for they do not share the attribute of his infinity: they may 'have always enjoyed God's transcendental realm' but 'do not, in the strict sense, share Brahman's essential attribute of infinity'.[19]

It has been shown, even at the risk of occasionally having had to become technical, that the doctrine of God in Hindu theism proceeds in consideration of the co-eternals, souls and matter. This does not seem to be the case with Judeo-Christian theism. But lest one not see the wood for the trees, another description of God, even more popular than the one cited earlier, is Saccidānanda—or God as being the embodiment of Truth, Consciousness and Bliss. In the theistic interpretation,

the qualities of being (*sat*), consciousness (*cit*) and bliss (*ānanda*) give to Brahman a character and personality. Brahman's knowledge is immediate, and is not dependent on the organs of sense. He is all knowing and has direct intuition of

17. T.M.P. Mahadevan, *Outlines of Hinduism*, p. 153.
18. Ibid.
19. J.B. Carman, *The Theology of Rāmānuja*, p. 102.

all. Brahman is the supreme personality, while the individuals are personal in an imperfect way. Personality implies the power to plan and realize one's purposes. God is perfect personality, since he contains all experience within himself and is dependent on nothing external to him. The most prominent qualities of God are knowledge, power and love (*karuṇā*).[20]

God as the possessor of various auspicious attributes is known as *Bhagavān*, a term which, according to tradition, refers to God as the possessor of six *bhāgas* or auspicious qualities.[21] J.B. Carman notes: 'Rāmānuja frequently refers to the six qualities as the examples of the entire ocean or treasure of the auspicious qualities of the Divine nature, but he never defines them.'[22] On the reasonable assumption that the understanding of the term in later tradition reflects Rāmānuja's own, the following comments can be made:

> The six qualities are defined as follows. Jñāna (knowledge) is direct and simultaneous knowledge of all things. Bala (strength) is the capacity to support everything without ever being fatigued (or, by His will). Aiśvarya (sovereignty or lordship) is unchallenged rule over all. Vīrya (valor) is the quality of immutability in spite of being the material cause of the mutable creation (vīrya may alternatively be given the above definition of bala). Śakti (power) is given two alternative meanings: (1) the power of being the material cause of all, or (2) the power to make possible what is impossible for others. Tejas (splendor) likewise has been given two definitions: (1) self-sufficiency, not requiring any external aid, or (2) the quality of over-powering others by His splendor.[23]

This depiction of God as the abode of auspicious qualities was meant to create room for discussing those aspects of God with which He is associated in the Judeo-Christian context, in a Hindu

20. S. Radhakrishnan, *Indian Philosophy*, vol. II, p. 683.

21. J.B. Carman, *The Theology of Rāmānuja*, p. 162. There are also other explanations of the word *bhagavān* offered within the tradition (see K. Srinivasan, *Monotheism of Hindu Religion* [Tirupati: Tirumala Tirupati Devasthanam, 1977], p. 10).

22. J.B. Carman, *The Theology of Rāmānuja*, p. 162.

23. Ibid., p. 163. Bharatan Kumarappa argues that Rāmānuja's 'enumeration of six qualities—glory, strength, dominion, wisdom, energy and power—as belonging to Brahman ... has no warrant in the Upanisads' (*The Hindu Conception of Deity as Culminating in Rāmānuja* [London: Luzac & Co., 1934], p. 186). But elsewhere he admits that even in the Upaniṣads, at 'a later stage ... Brahman ... came also to be regarded as possessing many transcendent qualities as well as several perfections' (ibid., p. 25). It is true that the classic Upaniṣads do not list the six qualities as such but a perusal of section 1 of Chapter III should suffice to show how several of these qualities are associated with rulership.

setting. Such a discussion may now be carried out under the headings of (1) Monotheism and (2) God as infinite, Self-existent.[24]

Monotheism

One can distinguish among many attitudes towards the ultimate reality, especially when it is conceived as God. Words like atheism, agnosticism, scepticism, naturalism, deism, theism, polytheism, henotheism, pantheism and monotheism, etc. come to mind to describe these attitudes.[25] From among these the Western religious tradition has chosen to crystallize its thinking about the ultimate around the idea of monotheism—'the belief that there is but one supreme Being, who is personal and moral and who seeks a total and unqualified response from human creatures'.[26]

In the context of Hindu thought, primary consideration needs to be given to the concept of polytheism,[27] henotheism and monotheism. Most scholars, Western and Indian, have tended to accept the successive application of these terms to the Vedic pantheon as a correct depiction of the way in which Vedic thinking evolved, though not without some reservations and elaborations.[28] This, however, calls for further comment. The situation which gave rise to henotheism, that is belief in *one* God as distinguished from monotheism or belief in *one* only God',[29] needs to be examined. The Vedic poet-seers showed a tendency to address hymns to a particular god as if he were the only one, either without denying the existence of

24. See John H. Hick, *Philosophy of Religion*, Chapter One.

25. Ibid., pp. 5–6. Almost all of these positions or positions analogous to them are represented within the Indian religious traditions; see Satishchandra Chatterjee and Dhirendramohan Datta, *An Introduction to Indian Philosophy*, pp. 63, 209, 212, 253, 315, 352, 366, etc. For agnosticism and scepticism, see Haridass Bhattacharyya, ed., *The Cultural Heritage of India*, vol. III (Calcutta: The Ramakrishna Mission Institute of Culture, 1963 [first published 1937]), Chapter 8. For more on pantheism, see M. Hiriyanna, *Outlines of Indian Philosophy* (London: George Allen & Unwin, 1964 [first published 1932]), p. 41; etc.

26. John H. Hick, *Philosophy of Religion*, p. 6.

27. It should not be confused with polynominalism. See Jan Gonda, *Notes on the Names and the Name of God in Ancient India* (Amsterdam: North Holland Publishing Co., 1970).

28. M. Hiriyanna, *Outlines of Indian Philosophy*, p. 39; S. Radhakrishnan and Charles A. Moore, eds, *A Source Book of Indian Philosophy* (Princeton, New Jersey: Princeton University Press, 1957), Chapter I, etc.

29. M. Hiriyanna, *Outlines of Indian Philosophy*, p. 39.

other gods or bringing them in some kind of relationship with this one god. 'Max Müller then had to invent a new term (actually he borrowed it from elsewhere) "henotheism" to describe the tendency in the Vedas to elevate a god who normally occupied no higher position than that of one among many to the position of the supreme being.'[30] When this observation is coupled with another, that Vedic Hindus not only did not develop the Judaic concept of monotheism but seemed equally prone to monism,[31] it is easy to see how it appeared that the 'Hindus got stuck at a half-way house position so to say',[32] from the point of view of the monotheists.

Pratima Bowes has suggested that henotheism is not a 'confused halfway house between polytheism and monotheism proper. It is an expression of the attitude of mind which is prepared to use either of these languages and switch from one to the other according to need'.[33] This point needs to be elaborated. It should be recognized, first, that 'the same god may be treated either polytheistically or monotheistically';[34] second, that it is not necessary for a god to 'belong exclusively either to a polytheistic complex or to a monotheistic one';[35] third, that in classical Hinduism no else than in Vedic Hinduism, polytheism and monotheism are 'not treated as illogical incompatibles; they embody two different outlooks on the divine, one sees the many in one, while the other sees the one in many';[36] fourth, that 'it is not so much the case that there are polytheistic and monotheistic gods, there are polytheistic and monotheistic attitudes to divine reality and accordingly two kinds of language in respect of it'[37] and, finally, that the two languages 'are adopted from different points of view, and serve different purposes'.[38] In the polytheistic view the 'gods belong to a specific complex of belief and attitudes to life and they must be conceived to be close to man in order to

30. Pratima Bowes, *The Hindu Religious Tradition: A Philosophical Approach* (London: Routledge & Kegan Paul, 1977), p. 103.

31. M. Hiriyanna, *The Essentials of Indian Philosophy*, pp. 14–16.

32. Pratima Bowes, *The Hindu Religious Tradition*, p. 103.

33. Ibid., p. 105.

34. Ibid., p. 102.

35. Ibid.

36. Ibid., p. 103.

37. Ibid., p. 107.

38. Ibid., p. 105.

fulfil their function',[39] as the 'polytheistic approach to the divine is rooted in man's involvement with the objects of his immediate concern, or with life in its everyday setting'.[40] The monotheistic approach, on the other hand, may be seen as one of ultimate concern. It could then be said that:

> Insofar as polytheism is a version of theism, a suitable description for it is not deification of a lot of ordinary things of this world mistakenly believed to be divinities by the primitive mind, it is seeing that divine essence—that which is the source of all value and existence—is manifested in things that men are immediately concerned with and which they value as fulfilling the possibilities of life on earth. So god-language can be a shorthand expression for this perception which is given concrete embodiment in the personalities of gods. It need not be thought to be a product of exaggerated fancy coupled with lack of 'information' about the one true God.[41]

It is suggested that if such an understanding of polytheism is accepted in the philosophy of religion then several otherwise mystifying aspects of Hinduism are clarified. It is often pointed out, for instance, that God in Hinduism is both immanent as well as transcendent,[42] while in Christianity it is transcendent.[43] What difference does this fact generate between the two traditions? At least a partial answer is now possible. It facilitates the simultaneous existence of polytheistic and monotheistic worldviews within the Hindu religious tradition. Observers of the Hindu scene are baffled by the fact, for instance, that Kṛṣṇa can dally with the milkmaids on the one hand (as in the *Bhāgavata Purāṇa*) and on the other identify himself with the supreme Brahman (as in the *Bhagavadgītā*). A possible solution to this riddle is suggested by the above discussion. A Muslim observer of the Hindu scene pointed out centuries ago that the Hindus are not shocked by stories which depict their gods behaving in a very human, not to say licentious, manner.[44] But if the 'belonging together of gods and men in one world, and the perception of life that goes

39. Ibid.
40. Ibid.
41. Ibid., p. 109.
42. M. Hiriyanna, *The Essentials of Indian Philosophy*, p. 16.
43. John H. Hick, *Philosophy of Religion*, p. 9.
44. Ainslie T. Embree, ed., *Alberuni's India* (New York: W.W. Norton & Co., Inc., 1971), p. 39.

with it, is the impulse behind polytheism',[45] then the abovementioned situation becomes more comprehensible.

Such an understanding of polytheism may enhance our understanding of western monotheism as well. For, in the light of the above, one arrives at an enhanced philosophical appreciation of the following observations of John H. Hick:

> The difficulty involved in maintaining such a faith in practice, even within a culture that has been permeated for centuries by monotheistic teaching, is evidenced by the polytheistic and henotheistic elements in our own life. A religiously sensitive visitor from another planet would doubtless report that we divide our energies in the service of many deities—the god of money, of a business corporation, of success, and of power, the status gods, and (for a brief period once a week) the God of Judeo-Christian faith. When we rise above this practical polytheism, it is generally into a henotheistic devotion to the nation, or to the American way of life, in order to enjoy our solidarity with an in-group against the out-group.[46]

Not only polytheism but monotheism too requires a revised understanding when applied in the Hindu philosophical context. Two points are important here. First, monotheism in Hinduism is found alongside monism, which is hardly the case in the Judeo-Christian tradition.[47] This has important philosophical implications, for the 'main issue which was debated by the Vedāntins who came after Śaṅkara'—a celebrated eighth-century exponent of non-dualistic philosophy—'was whether Brahman is *nirguṇa* or *saguṇa*'.[48] That is to say: is the ultimate reality ultimately Impersonal or Personal. This was rarely an issue in the West.[49] The second point relates to the nature of monotheism itself.

> Indian monotheism in its living forms, from the Vedic age till now, has believed *rather in the unity of the gods in God, than the denial of gods for God.* Hence, Indian monotheism has a peculiarity which distinguishes it from the Christian or the Mohamedan. This is a persistent feature of orthodox Indian faith throughout, not a mere passing phase of Vedic times.[50]

45. Pratima Bowes, *The Hindu Religions Tradition*, p. 106.

46. John H. Hick, *Philosophy of Religion*, p. 7.

47. Donald Johnson and Jean Johnson, *God and Gods in Hinduism* (New Delhi: Arnold-Heinemann India, 1972), p. 26.

48. T.M.P. Mahadevan, *Outlines of Hinduism*, p. 150.

49. See Geoffrey Parrinder, *Upanishads, Gita and Bible* (New York: Harper & Row, 1962), Chapter 3.

50. Satishchandra Chatterjee and Dhirendramohan Datta, *An Introduction to Indian Philosophy*, pp. 352–3.

Infinite, Self-existent

The self-existent aspect of God may be considered first from the Hindu point of view. This aspect of God is described in the Hindu religious tradition by referring to God as sat.[51] The concept of sat may now be related to the discussion of the nature of God's existence in the philosophy of religion, where two conclusions are usually drawn when God is described as self-existent: (1) 'God is not dependent either for existence or for characteristics upon any other reality'[52] and (2) that 'God is eternal, without beginning or end.' Indeed, 'divine eternity means more, however, than simply that God exists without beginning or end,'[53] for, as Anselm states, God is 'absolutely outside all time'.[54]

The first conclusion need not detain us long, as God's independent existence is not a matter of controversy in Hinduism any more than it is in Christianity. An extract from the *Śvetāśvatara Upaniṣad* should confirm the point:

The beginning, the efficient cause of the conjoining [of soul and matter]
Seen as beyond the three times (past, present, and future), without parts too.
Worship him who takes on all forms, becomes becoming.
The adorable God who dwells in your own thoughts, primeval.
Higher and other than the [world-] tree, time, and form.
Is he from whom this compounded world proceeds.
Righteousness (*dharma*) he brings, rejecting evil, he, the Lord of good fortune.[55]

It is the second of the two conclusions which needs to be examined carefully in the Hindu context, for typically in Hindu thought the cosmos is 'beginningless and endless in time as well as space',[56] and the human soul is eternal as well. But the eternality of both the cosmos and the soul must be distinguished from that of Brahman or God. The universe is eternal but eternally changing; Brahman or God 'insofar as, at its deepest level, it has its being outside time, but it is distinct' from Brahman or God 'in that it does not share its creative activity in time. In western terminology, it

51. See J.A.B. van Buitenen, *Rāmānuja's Vedārthasangraha* (Poona: Deccan College Monograph Series 16, 1956), Introduction.

52. John H. Hick, *Philosophy of Religion*, p. 8.

53. Ibid.

54. Ibid.

55. R.C. Zaehner, *Hindu Scriptures*, pp. 81–2.

56. Ibid., p. 62.

partakes of Absolute Being, but is not for that reason God.'[57] In Indian terminology, we may contrast the eternal existence of God and the universe thus: '[God] is the eternal or rock-seated being, *kūṭasthasattā* while the world is only timeless, endless existence, *anādipravāhasattā*.'[58]

After discussing God's aseity, we can turn to a discussion of his infinity. Infinity belongs to God as much in the Hindu religious tradition as in the Judaeo-Christian. When the vision of God is vouchsafed to Arjuna, Arjuna exclaims in the *Bhagavadgītā* (XI.19):

> Without beginning, middle, or end, of infinite power,
> Of infinite arms, whose eyes are the moon and sun,
> I see Thee, whose face is flaming fire,
> Burning this whole universe with Thy radiance.[59]

A more philosophical rather than experiential recognition of God's infinity will proceed along these lines: God's infinity is really an expression of his power and intelligence. For who but one with infinite power could generate an infinite universe and who but one with infinite intelligence could sustain it.[60]

We may next examine the typically Hindu ways in which these concepts of God's self-existence and infinity operate.

The concept of sat or existence in relation to God ramifies through Hindu ontology, epistemology and axiology. Its ontological and epistemological implications can be seen in a single line of the *Ṛg Veda*—perhaps the most quoted and best known single line from that corpus, which has virtually replaced in certain circles, in popularity, the traditional *Gāyatrī*, the knowledge of which made one a 'twice born' in ancient India.[61] The line under discussion is contained in X.164.46 and translates as follows: The Real is One; sages speak (of it) variously.[62]

57. Ibid., p. 55.

58. S. Radhakrishnan, *Indian Philosophy*, vol. I, p. 534.

59. Franklin Edgerton, tr., *The Bhagavad Gītā*, Part I (Cambridge, Massachusetts: Harvard University Press, 1946), p. 111.

60. P.N. Srinivasachari, *The Philosophy of Viśiṣṭādvaita* (Adyar, Madras: The Adyar Library and Research Center, 1970 [first printed 1943]), pp. 120–1.

61. *Ṛg Veda* III.62.10; see P.V. Kane, *History of Dharmaśāstra*, vol. II, pt I (Poona: Bhandarkar Oriental Research Institute, 1974), pp. 304ff.

62. See R.C. Zaehner, *Hindu Scriptures*, p. 19; Satishchandra Chatterjee and Dhirendramohan Datta, *An Introduction to Indian Philosophy*, p. 352; S. Radhakrishnan, *Indian Philosophy*, vol. I (cited in part); Charles A. Moore, ed., *The Indian Mind*, p. 17;

It has been pointed out by Pratima Bowes that in this statement

> The term 'truth' has two meanings, one ontological and the other epistemological, that is it means both Being and statements about it. The Sanskrit for Being is 'Sat', and a derivative of it, 'Satya', may mean either Being (ontological) or a valid understanding of it expressed in language (epistemological). As far as the ontological category of Being or Truth (Sat or Satya) is concerned, which refers to what I have labelled 'religious reality', it is being claimed that there is only one Truth, but with infinite aspects that may be approached in diverse ways and this means that there may be many truths about it when truth means an epistemological category which applies to the expression of our understanding of it.[63]

Apart from these ontological and epistemological implications, the description of God as sat has axiological implications too. To see this, one needs to turn from the *Ṛg Veda* to the *Bhagavadgītā* (XVII.226): Sat—This is used in the same sense of 'real' and in the sense of 'good'.

From the context it is clear that the referent of sat here is Brahman. Although one commentator feels that the word sat is not applicable to Brahman in the sense of 'goodness'[64]—and one wonders why—he goes on to add: 'but in the realm of ethics, goodness is reality, and evil its negation'.[65] Another commentator is more forthcoming: 'The Real and the Good are interchangeable words. It is somehow gratifying to find the *Gītā* making this thoroughly Thomistic statement some two thousand years before the appearance of Aquinas.'[66]

T.M.P. Mahadevan, *Outlines of Hinduism*, pp. 10, 17; M. Hiriyanna, *Outlines of Indian Philosophy*, p. 39.

63. Pratima Bowes, *The Hindu Religions Tradition*, p. 269.

64. W. Douglas P. Hill, *The Bhagavadgītā* (second edition) (London: Oxford University Press, 1966), p. 300, fn. 3.

65. Ibid.

66. R.C. Zaehner, *The Bhagavadgītā* (London: Oxford University Press, 1969), p. 382. The axiological implication of the term *sat* is also apparent from the following (ibid., p. 383. In what follows 'Ch.U.' is an abbreviation for the *Chāndogya Upaniṣad*): 'In Sanskrit *sat* and *satya* mean both "reality" and "truth"—truth in every sense of the word, not just "absolute" truth, but truthfulness in general. By telling a lie you deny that 'You are that,' and you thereby destroy the reality, the truth, that is within you: you simply cease to exist. Hence the famous sequence in Ch.U. 6.8–16, the refrain of which is "That *you* are", after explaining in parables how this is to be understood, finishes up by a devastating application of the doctrine to practical life:

> Again, my dear boy, people bring in a man handcuffed (to face the ordeal), crying out, 'He has committed a robbery, he has stolen, heat the axe for him!' If he is

In the theistic system of Rāmānuja, which is often taken as a major representative of Hindu theism, this equation applies *a fortiori*, because for Rāmānuja God is the abode of auspicious qualities, and totally free from evil. Bharatan Kumarappa articulates the contribution of Rāmānuja:

Another point is also noticeable, though it cannot be said to be peculiarly Vaiṣṇava, for, as we have seen, it is not lacking entirely even in the Upaniṣads—the view, namely that the Deity is a Perfect being, in whom there is no evil. But while in the Upaniṣads this doctrine is never clearly or consistently formulated, the Śri Bhāṣya passages we have cited show Rāmānuja consistently maintaining that Brahman has only auspicious qualities, and that He is entirely free from evil qualities. It is significant that the passages from the Viṣṇu Purāṇa which he selects to support his view also make it very clear that Brahman is free from all defects, and that nothing but auspicious qualities constitute His nature. So central in Rāmānuja's view of the Deity is the doctrine that Brahman is altogether perfect and excludes everything that is evil, that he introduces this teaching wherever possible, even for example when he is discussing passages which by no stretch of imagination can be thought to imply it.[67]

The infinity (*anantatva*) of God also plays an important role in Hindu thought. It has often been noted how God can possess innumerable attributes; we must now note that God himself is infinite.[68] However, we must at the same time also note that so are the selves or souls. 'This is important, as it is because the self of man is infinite in all systems Hindu, theistic or monistic, that a realization of the Infinite and Absolute Reality, whether called God or Brahman, can happen to man.'[69] But wherein, then, does God's

---

guilty, he makes himself out to be what he is not, speaks untruly, clothes (himself) in untruth. He takes hold of the red-hot axe and is burnt. Then he is killed.

If, however, he is innocent, he shows himself to be what he is, speaks the truth, clothes (him)self in truth. He takes hold of the red-hot axe and is not burnt. Then he is released.

So, just as such a man is not burnt (because he embodied Truth), so does this whole universe have this (truth) as its Self. That is the Truth: (That is the Real:) That is the Self: That *you* are.'

67. Bharatan Kumarappa, *The Hindu Conception of Deity as Culminating in Rāmānuja*, pp. 188–9. Vaiṣṇava means pertaining to Viṣṇu or to his followers. Śrī Bhāṣya is the name of Rāmānuja's commentary on the *Brahmasūtra*. The *Viṣṇu Puraṇa* is one of the eighteen sectarian devotional texts called the *Purāṇas*.

68. J.B. Carman, *The Theology of Rāmānuja*, pp. 55, 77–81, 93, 101–3.

69. Pratima Bowes, *The Hindu Religious Traditions: A Philosophical Approach*, p. 198. Also see p. 292.

superiority lie? In this: that He has never lost that infinity while the souls lose it by getting bound in matter and then regain it.[70]

The infinity of Brahman, however, cuts in two ways, depending on whether an absolutistic or a theistic stance is adopted. From an absolutistic point of view, even to describe Brahman as infinity is to compromise its transcendence. As it was noted earlier, 'the description of Brahman even as *infinite*, real, consciousness though more accurate than accidental descriptions, cannot directly convey the idea of Brahman. It only serves to direct the mind towards Brahman by denying of it *finiteness*, unreality and unconsciousness.'[71] On the theistic interpretation, God is infinite in the sense that finitude is the attribute of matter and bound souls.[72] There is another implication of infinity on which the absolutistic and the theistic interpretations diverge. The theistic tradition associated with Rāmānuja dismisses the alleged 'philosophical' meanings of the term *infinite*.[73] It is argued, for instance, that the 'term "infinite" in the philosophy of religion corrects the tendency of thought to abstract itself from the thinking process'[74] and 'gives a positive meaning to the infinite as actual and determinate. This meaning is defined by the idea of "inner plan and purpose" for which it is employed.'[75] This is explained by stating that 'the infinity of space-time has a positive meaning'[76] compared to the other senses of infinity:

Space is a totality and is real; time is a real process and is not an appearance, and the infinity of space-time is an ordered and orderly plan of creation, whose purpose is to arouse the sense of sublimity and wonder; and it has its own value in the religious consciousness. Scientific imagination is overwhelmed by the immensity of the cosmos with its vast stretch of space extending beyond the starry heavens and the Milky Way and by the immense sweep of time and the idea that the relation between a point on the blackboard and the known universe is the ratio between the known and the unknown universe crushes the conceit of man and inspires humility and reverence. This is strengthened by the

70. P.N. Srinivasachari, *The Philosophy of Viśiṣṭādvaita*, pp. 31–2.

71. Satishchandra Chatterjee and Dhirendramohan Datta, *An Introduction to Indian Philosophy*, p. 391, emphasis added. By accidental description is meant referring to Brahman as the creator, etc. of the universe (ibid., p. 388).

72. *Viśiṣṭādvaita Philosophy and Religion* (Madras: Rāmānuja Research Society, 1974), pp. 117–18.

73. P.N. Srinivasachari, *The Philosophy of Viśiṣṭādvaita*, pp. 117–18.

74. Ibid., p. 118.

75. Ibid.

76. Ibid., p. 119.

Purāṇic theory of endless Brahman-s and their age in terms of aeons and *yuga-s*. The cosmic consciousness of Arjuna brings out the spiritual significance of the infinity of space-time as a partial expression of the wonderful māyā of Īśvara.[77]

There are further implications of infinity which flow along the absolutistic–theistic divide in Hindu thought. In absolutistic philosophy, the infinity of Brahman could easily carry the implication that it is beyond good and evil. It could be argued, for instance, that Brahman is beyond sat and *asat* in both its meaning of reality and goodness as *empirically* understood,[78] and that even when it is described as infinity the implication is that any such duality between finitude and infinity must also be transcended.[79] Or, alternatively, in its infinity Brahman must encompass all, good as well as evil,[80] as in the case of unity and diversity. 'To cite an illustration as old as the Upaniṣads: It is like the sun which explains the phenomena of day and night, but at the same time transcends them in that it knows no nights, nor even day in our sense of the term'.[81] One must be fair to the absolutist position here though. Brahman could still be associated with good rather than evil, just as if we had to associate the sun with either night or day, we would associate it with day—but the association is at one remove, and a step lower. The implication of the infinity of God in Hindu theism moves in a very different direction and is in a way quite similar to the Christian:

77. Ibid. Even some absolutist thinkers have moved towards such a stance, though from an opposite direction. Here, P.N. Srinivasachari seems to maintain that the infinity associated with God reflects his glory; Ānandagiri explains the word *vibhūti* ('glory', 'power', 'lordship') as applied to God in the tenth chapter of the *Bhagavadgītā* as denoting God's 'infiniteness and the fact that great seers ... possessed their power and wisdom insofar as they partook of a very small portion of this power and wisdom.' (W. Douglas P. Hill, *The Bhagavadgītā*, p. 148, fn. 4).

78. Eliot Deutsch, *Advaita Vedānta: A Philosophical Reconstruction* (Honolulu, East-West Center Press, 1969), pp. 99–100; Eliot Deutsch and J.A.B. van Buitenen, *A Source Book of Advaita Vedānta* (Honolulu: University Press of Hawaii, 1971), pp. 48, 270.

79. Śaṅkara on *Taittirīya Upaniṣad* II.1. His logic can be applied to 'infinity' as it is applied to 'reality' in relation to Brahman; see K. Satchidananda Murty, *Revelation and Reason in Advaita Vedānta* (New York: Columbia University Press, 1959), pp. 58–67. For the argument that infinity may allow for coexistence of contradictory qualities even in God, see N.K. Devaraja, *Hinduism and Christianity* (New Delhi: Asia Publishing House, 1969), p. 51.

80. S. Radhakrishnan, *Indian Philosophy*, vol. II, pp. 621–2.

The thought that Righteousness is so all-important that the Deity considers even His infinitude of little account when righteousness needs to be established is a remarkable contribution which the Gita makes to the conception of the Divine. Instead of Thought or Consciousness, which was the chief attribute of the Supreme Being in the Upaniṣads, Righteousness seems here to become His essential attribute. The author of the Gītā was evidently too much of an eclectic to set this view in opposition to the view of the Upaniṣads, and accordingly, the new thought of the Deity here implied does not gain the pointedness and clarity of expression which it deserves. Nevertheless it is clearly a contribution of very great significance.[82]

Brahman continues to be the rope in the tug-of-war between the exponents of its saguṇa and nirguṇa aspects in Hindu philosophical[83] and mythological studies.[84]

81. M. Hiriyanna, *The Essentials of Indian Philosophy*, p. 154.

82. Bharatan Kumarappa, *The Hindu Conception of Deity as Culminating in Rāmānuja*, p. 60. One must also be fair to the Gītā, however. As Bharatan Kumarappa observes in a footnote (ibid.), 'Passages occur which appear to teach that the Deity is beyond good and evil. These will be considered in the sequel. It would, of course, be easy to explain them as Upaniṣadic teaching retained inconsistently by the author of the *Gītā*. But such a method of interpretation should not, it seems to us, be adopted except when other ways of explaining them fail.'

83. John Grimes, *Problems and Perspectives in Religious Discourse: Advaita Vedānta Implications* (Albany, NY: State University of New York Press, 1994), *passim*.

84. Deborah A. Soifer, *The Myths of Narasiṁha and Vāmana: Two Avatārs in Cosmological Perspective* (Albany, NY: State University of New York Press, 1991), p. 95.

CHAPTER IV

Īśvara

As stated earlier, the one ultimate reality can be visualized either in personal or impersonal terms. However, the chronological order of priority of Brahman (neuter) and Brahman (masculine) cannot be determined with certainty.[1] In fact, it is quite possible that the Hindus did not consciously distinguish between the two and that may be why, according to M. Hiriyanna, we find monotheism and monism 'often mixed up with each other'[2] in the Brāhmaṇa period. After identifying the monistic element in the Brāhmaṇa period, Hiriyanna writes:

> This current of thought, as already stated, is often found blended with the other one of monotheism. The reason for it is that the supreme God, as conceived in the period, is not always identified with the other gods alone, but also with the whole universe of which he is the creator. 'He is all and everything' is what, for example, is said in one place of Prajāpati. That is, the supreme God is regarded not merely as a creator, externally related to the world, but also as constituting its very substance, as the monistic principle does. It is now usual to represent the monism of the later mantras and the Brāhmaṇas as pantheistic; but it is not correct to do so, since the term as applicable to this teaching connotes the idea not merely of immanence but also of transcendence. Thus, for instance, what is known as the Hymn of Man declares 'Having covered the world on all sides, it extended beyond it the length of ten fingers.' The primal principle, no doubt, is immanent in the world which emerges from it, but is certainly not exhausted by it.[3]

1. J. Gonda, *Notes on Brahman* (Utrecht: J.L. Beyers 1950), p. 62.
2. M. Hiriyanna, *The Essentials of Indian Philosophy* (London: George Allen & Unwin, 1948), p. 14.
3. Ibid., p. 16.

Another illustration is provided by a passage from the *Śatapatha Brāhmaṇa* (II, 2, 3, 1–3):

In the beginning *brahma* was this [universe]. Then it emitted the gods, and having emitted them it caused them to ascend into these worlds—Agni into this world, Vayu into the atmosphere and Sūrya into the sky.

Now, there are higher worlds and there are higher divinities. He (*sa*) made these divinities ascend into these [higher] worlds. Just as these [three] worlds and these [three] divinities are manifest, so are these [higher] worlds and these [higher] divinities manifest. These [higher] divinities he made ascend into these [higher] worlds.

Then *brahma* went to the remote sphere. Having gone up to the remote sphere it thought, 'How can I descend into these worlds'. Then he descended with these two, with name and form ...[4]

Greg Bailey remarks pertinently after citing this passage:

Making clear distinction between personal and impersonal in relation to a concept like *brahma* was not the Indian way of doing things. It is more accurate to say that in some 'idealistic' circles *brahma* was completely divested of any personal attributes; whereas in other circles (represented in many passages of the oldest Upaniṣads) personal portrayals of *brahma* were interwoven with impersonal ones.[5]

Therefore, this study of monotheism as represented by Īśvara is in full awareness of the aforementioned situation. Saguṇa Brahman directly points to the concept of Īśvara.

The qualified Brahman, if personified, becomes the God or Īśvara. ... Like it, God also may be represented as the cosmic parallel to the finite individual self, the distinction between them being entirely one of adjuncts. The consequence of this distinction is that God remains untouched by any of the evil consequences of association with a finite adjunct, such as narrow love and hate. It is attachment which implies preferences and exclusions; but God, being equally attached to all, is really detached. There is a Sanskrit verse which says: 'One should give up attachment; but if that be not possible, one might cultivate it, but it should be equal attachment for all.' In the language of popular religion, God is represented as the creator of the universe, and Māyā as the power (*śakti*) that helps him in creating it. In this form, he becomes the material as well as the efficient cause of the universe and is sometimes spoken of as the great Magician who brings forth out of himself the [whole] spectacle of the universe. The point of the comparison with a magician is that he is in no way deluded by that spectacle as

4. See Greg Bailey, *The Mythology of Brahmā* (Delhi: Oxford University Press, 1983), p. 6.

5. Ibid.

6. M. Hiriyanna, *The Essentials of Indian Philosophy*, p. 164.

others are, for there is in his case a never-failing realization of its actual character; and this is the reason why, as we stated above, evil does not touch him.[6]

It is worth noting that one could theoretically develop a viable philosophical system with saguṇa Brahman alone, without involving its personalization.[7] Such, however, is *not* the case in Hinduism.[8]

A popular word by which God is known in this more personal and intimate manner to the Hindu is *Bhagavān*.

Quite probably Hinduism's most famous and widely encountered epithet for divinity conceived as ceaselessly and actively solicitous of human welfare is *Bhāgavat* ('having shares'). *Bhagavān* (the more commonly cited first-person nominative form of the word) occurs as early as the *Ṛgveda*; the term expressly refers to Rudra-Śiva in the *Śvetāśvatara Upaniṣad* (5.4), and is the common honorific of the Buddha in the Pali texts. *Bhagavān* doubtless is most familiar, however, in reference to Viṣṇu-Nārāyaṇa/Vāsudeva-Kṛṣṇa. And, indeed, *bhāgavata* ('related to or devoted to *Bhagavān*') may be the most common, even earliest, general designation of a devotee of Viṣṇu.[9]

II

Depending on how the Hindus began to look (1) upon God; (2) upon God's relationship to the world; and (3) upon God's relationship with the cosmos provides a clue to an understanding of the theistic variation within Hinduism, consistently with monotheism.

By the eighth century the various cultic divinities which had begun to flourish under the umbrella of Hindu monotheism began to lend themselves to systematization, by being brought into connection with the divine attributes of God. In the most popular form of Hindu theism these are 'knowledge, lordship, potency, strength, virility and splendour (*jñāna, aiśvarya, śakti, bala, vīrya* and *tejas*)',[10] qualities which God possesses in his transcendent form (with his other forms to be discussed subsequently). The famous Hindu thinker

7. Eliot Deutsch, *Advaita Vedānta: A Philosophical Reconstruction* (Honolulu: East-West Center Press, 1969), p. 43.

8. Arvind Sharma, *A Hindu Perspective on the Philosophy of Religion* (London: Macmillan, 1990), pp. 103–4.

9. G.R. Welbon, 'Vaiṣṇavism: Bhāgavats', in Mircea Eliade, Editor-in-Chief, *The Encyclopedia of Religion* (New York: Macmillan, 1987) vol. 15, p. 172.

10. T.M.P. Mahadevan, *Outlines of Hinduism* (Bombay: Chetana Ltd, 1971), pp. 147, 192.

Śaṅkara, 'in his commentary on the *Gītā* speaks of the six attributes of God that correspond to the six Gods, Śiva, Viṣṇu, Śakti, Sūrya, Gaṇapati [or Gaṇeśa] and Kumāra'[11] or Kārttikeya. This is known as the *Saṇmata* tradition. According to the tradition, Śaṅkara 'revived and gave stability to six alternate ways of worship, the *śaṇmata-s*'.

Śiva: 'The auspicious, gracious or kindly one.' Supreme Being of the Śaivite religion. God Śiva is All and in all, simultaneously the creator and the creation, both immanent and transcendent. As personal Deity, He is creator, preserver and destroyer. He is a one being, perhaps best understood in three perfections: Parameśvara (Primal Soul), Parāśakti (Pure Consciousness) and Paraśiva (Absolute Reality).

Viṣṇu: 'All-pervasive.' Supreme Deity of the Vaishṇavite religion. God as personal Lord and Creator, the All-Loving Divine Personality, who periodically incarnates and lives a fully human life to reestablish *dharma* whenever necessary. In Śaivism, Vishṇu is Śiva's aspect as Preserver.

Śakti: Within the Śākta religion, the worship of the Goddess is paramount, in Her many fierce and benign forms. Śakti is the Divine Mother of manifest creation, visualized as a female form, and Śiva is specifically the Unmanifest Absolute. The fierce or black (*asita*) forms of the Goddess include Kālī, Durgā, Chaṇḍī, Chāmuṇḍī, Bhadrakālī and Bhairavī. The benign or white (*sita*) forms include Umā, Gaurī, Ambikā, Pārvatī, Maheśvarī, Lalitā and Annapūrṇā. As Rājarājeśvari ('divine queen of kings'), She is the presiding Deity of the Śrī Chakra *yantra*. She is also worshipped as the ten Mahavidyās, manifestations of the highest knowledge—Kālī, Tārā, Shoḍaśī, Bhuvaneśvarī, Chinnamasta, Bhairavī, Dhūmāvatī, Bagatā, Mātaṅgī and Kamalā. While some Śāktas view these as individual beings, most revere them as manifestations of the singular Devī. There are also numerous minor Goddess forms, in the category of *grāmadevatā* ('village Deity'). These include Piṭāri, 'snake-catcher' (usually represented by a simple stone), and Mariyamman, 'smallpox Goddess.'

Sūrya: 'Sun.' One of the principal Divinities of the *Vedas*, also prominent in the epics and *Purāṇas*. Śaivites revere Sūrya, the Sun God each morning as Śiva Sūrya. Smārtas and Vaishṇavas revere the golden orb as Sūrya Nārāyaṇa. As the source of light, the sun is the most readily apparent image of Divinity available to man. As the giver of life, Sūrya is worshipped during harvest festivals everywhere. Esoterically, the sun represents the point where the manifest and unmanifest worlds meet or unite. In *yoga*, the sun represents the masculine force, *piṅgala*. Sūrya also signifies the Self within. In the Vedic description of the course of souls after death, the 'path of the sun' leads liberated souls to the realm of Brahman; while the path of the moon leads back to physical birth.

11. William Cenkner, *A Tradition of Teachers: Saṅkara and the Jagadguru Today* (Delhi: Motilal Banarsidass, 1983), p. 116.

Gaṇeśa: 'Lord of Categories.' (From *gaṇ*, 'to count or reckon,' and *Īśa*, 'lord.') Or: 'Lord of attendants (*gaṇa*),' synonymous with *Gaṇapati*. Gaṇeśa is a Mahādeva, the beloved elephant-faced Deity honoured by Hindus of every sect. He is the Lord of Obstacles (*Vighneśvara*), revered for His great wisdom and invoked first before any undertaking, for He knows all intricacies of each soul's *karma* and the perfect path of *dharma* that makes action successful. He sits on the *mūlādhāra chakra* and is easy of access. Lord Gaṇeśa is sometimes identified with the Ṛg Vedic God Brihaspati ('Lord of Prayer, the Holy Word).' *Ṛg Veda* 2.23.1

Kārttikeya: Child of the Pleiades, from *Krittikā*, 'Pleiades.' A son of Śiva. A great Mahādeva worshipped in all parts of India and the world. Also known as Murugan, Kumara, Skanda, Shanmukhanatha, Subramanya and more. He is the God who guides that part of evolution which is religion, the transformation of the instinctive into a divine wisdom through the practice of *yoga*. He holds the holy *vel* of *jñāna śakti*, which is His Power to vanquish darkness or ignorance.[12]

III

God's relationship to the world is not limited to the transcendent (*para*) form which is endowed with the six auspicious qualities, of which the six cultic divinities constitute a radiant reflection. In fact, the Vaiṣṇava Tantras or cultic scriptures speak of five forms of God:

(1) *Para* or the Transcendent;
(2) *Vyūha* or the Grouped;
(3) *Vibhava* or the Incarnated;
(4) *Antaryāmī* or the Immanent; and
(5) *Arcā* or the Idol.[13]

The Para form has already been alluded to. The Grouped form involves the process of creation and redemption and consists of three other forms along with Para, who is here identified with Vāsudeva (Kṛṣṇa), and the other three with his elder brother, son and grandson. In the process of evolution creation first assumes an

12. Satguru Sivaya Subramaniam, *Dancing With Śiva: Hinduism's Contemporary Catechism* (Concord, Cambridge: Himalayan Academy, 1993), pp. 722, 747, 803–4, 818, 831, 857. For more details, see T.M.P. Mahadevan, *Outlines of Hinduism*, Chapter 8. Cited with permission.

13. Bharatan Kumarappa, *The Hindu Conception of the Deity as Culminating in Rāmānuja* (London: Luzac & Co., 1934), pp. 311ff.

embryonic form, which subsequently manifests the male and female cosmic principles and then body and soul. The Vibhava form consists of the Incarnations, as of Rāma celebrated in the epic *Rāmāyana* and of Kṛṣṇa celebrated in the *Mahābhārata* and the *Bhāgavata Purāṇa*. In the Immanent form, God is present within us as the Indwelling Self[14] while the Idol

> is the most concrete of God's forms. It is called *arcāvatāra*; and the belief is that God descends into the idol and makes it divinely alive, so that he may be easily accessible to his devotees. The idols such as those installed in the shrines ... are regarded as permanent incarnations, and reservoirs of the redemptive mercy of God. Śrī Pillailokācārya, a Vaiṣṇava teacher of South India, makes the following comparisons: the attempt to comprehend the transcendent form is like getting water from the other world for quenching thirst; the *Vyūha* form is like the legendary ocean of milk which also is not easy of access; the immanent form is like subterranean water which is not readily available to a thirsty man although it is right underneath his feet; the incarnated forms are like the floods that inundate the country for a while but do not last long; and the *acrā* is like the [calm] pool from which anyone anytime could slake his thirst.[15]

God's relationship to the cosmos as a whole, rather than to our world as such, may be related to the three modes which must invariably accompany its appearance: (1) it must come into existence (*sṛṣṭi*); (2) it must remain in existence for a given duration (*sthiti*): and (3) it must pass out of existence (*saṁhāra*). When God is thus brought into relationship with the universe then it is clear that Bhagavān or Īśvara, as God or Lord stands not only by itself but can now be brought into relationship with the three gods of Hinduism, the widely known if not widely employed trinity or *trimūrti*, namely Brahmā, Viṣṇu and Śiva.[16] 'It may, however, be noted that, whereas the Trinity is presented in Scholastic Philosophy as a mystery, it is a fundamental definition of Hindu's religious philosophy.'[17]

14. It may be worth noting that 'the whole system of caste and untouchability is undermined by the perception of the Indwelling Self in all' (S. Radhakrishnan, ed., *The Principal Upaniṣads* [London: George Allen & Unwin, 1953], p. 445).

15. T.M.P. Mahadevan, *Outlines of Hinduism*, pp. 193–4.

16. Vettam Mani, *Purāṇic Encyclopedia* (Delhi: Motilal Banarsidass, 1974), p. 147.

17. Alain Daniélou, *Hindu Polytheism* (New York: Bollingen Foundation, Series LXXIII; Pantheon Books, 1964), p. 24, note 7.

CHAPTER V

Devī

Once the ultimate reality is visualized in personal rather than impersonal terms, then this 'persona' could be either male or female. The ultimate reality, when viewed as a male 'person', is called Īśvara. When the same ultimate reality is viewed as a female person, it is called Devī. This is the most common way the ultimate reality is referred to when conceptualized as a feminine principle; other names such as *ādyā* (the original one) and *śakti* (energy) are also employed, though less often.

Hinduism possesses a full-blown feminine theology. One strand within it completely and unequivocally identifies the ultimate reality with the Goddess, and she is supreme in her own right and not on account of association with any God. Her supreme and independent status is most clearly spelled out in the *Devīmāhātmya*, which constitutes a section of the *Mārkaṇḍeya Purāṇa*, one of the eighteen Purāṇas or texts which deal with the life and deeds of divine beings.

In this particular account the gods are terrorized by the demon in the form of a water buffalo called Mahiṣa and none of the great gods such as Brahmā, Viṣṇu and Śiva can save them. What the gods could not achieve singly they decided to accomplish collectively:

> Their intense powers poured forth as fire from their mouths. Vishnu, Shiva, and all gods sent forth their energies, each according to his nature, in the form of sheets and streams of flame. These fires rushed together, combining into a flaming cloud which grew and grew, and meanwhile gradually condensed. Eventually it assumed the shape of the Goddess.[1]

1. Heinrich Zimmer, *Myths and Symbols in Indian Art and Civilization* (edited by Joseph Campbell) (New York and Evanston: Harper & Row, 1946), p. 190.

It should not be thought, however, that the goddess was a product of the powers of the male gods. Rather, 'by a gesture of perfect surrender and fully willed abdication they had *returned their energies to the primeval* shakti*, the one force, the fountain head, whence originally all had stemmed*.'[2]

The Devī, thus, is the supreme divinity and in *theology* the gods of creation, preservation and destruction, namely Brahmā, Viṣṇu and Śiva, are subordinate to her and act in accordance with her will.

Several levels can be detected in the operation of the feminine principle in Hinduism. The one just described is the supreme one, when she is the counterpart of Īśvara, supreme by herself. At another level, she is shown as the spouse of Śiva, who, incidentally, more than any other god is referred to as Īśvara when the word is used to denote not the supreme god but one member of the trinity. As the spouse of Śiva, she plays a dual role—dominant and docile. As Śakti, she is the one who 'wears the pants' and even assumes the superior position in amorous encounters; as Pārvatī she is the homely housewife. In the androgynous depiction known as the 'form in which Īśvara (Śiva) is half female', she appears as Śiva's equal.

In its androcentric adaptation, the feminine principle also appears as the wives of the various gods, but in its gynocentric version the feminine principle holds supreme sway. Her conquest of the buffalo demon in this respect represents the triumph of the female principle over all negative forces. Religious art may be pressed into service to prove this point. Heinrich Zimmer draws on the depiction in an illustrated manuscript and a seventh-century relief to dramatize the impact of the representation of the ultimate reality as an active feminine principle. The manuscript depicts the acquisition of the various weapons from the various gods, weapons which she brandishes in her multiple hands.

> Into the hands of the Supreme Goddess ... [the gods] deliver their various weapons, utensils, ornaments, and emblems, these containing their particularized energies and traits. Into the all-comprehending source out of which they themselves originally evolved, they now merge their disparate natures and disparate powers of action. Shiva, the ascetic, is shown in the upper left hand corner, handing over the trident. Facing him, in the upper right, is the four-headed Brahmā, giving up his alms bowl and the manuscript of the magic wisdom of the Vedas. In the central foreground is Kāla, the God of Time,

2. Ibid., emphasis added.

extending to the Goddess a sword and a shield. At his right stands the legendary father of the Goddess, the mountain king Himālaya, with the lion that she is to ride.[3]

Thus equipped she engaged the protean and deadly demon. This depiction in sculpture celebrating her victory over the demon has been thus described:

First annihilating the army of the titan, the Goddess roped the mighty buffalo-form with a noose. The demon escaped, however, emerging from the buffalo body in the form of a lion. Immediately, the Goddess beheaded the lion, whereupon Mahisha, by virtue of his Māyā—energy of self-transformation, escaped again, now in the form of a hero with a sword. Ruthlessly the Goddess riddled this new embodiment with a shower of arrows. But then the demon stood before her as an elephant, and with his trunk reached out and seized her. He dragged her towards him, but she severed the trunk with the stroke of a sword. The demon returned, now, to his favorite shape—that of the giant buffalo shaking the universe with the stamping of its hoofs. But the Goddess scornfully laughed, and again roared with a loud voice of laughter at all his tricks and devices. Pausing a moment, in full wrath, she lifted to her lips, serenely, a bowl filled with the inebriating, invigorating, liquor of the divine life-force, and while she sipped the matchless drink, her eyes turned red. The buffalo-demon, uprooting mountains with his horns, was flinging them against her, shouting defiantly at her the while, but with her arrows she was shattering them to dust. She called out to the shouting monster: 'Shout on! Go on shouting one moment more, you fool, while I sip my fill of this delicious brew. The gods soon will be crying out for joy, and you should lie murdered at my feet.'

Even while she spoke, the Goddess leapt into the air, and from above came down on the demon's neck. She dashed him to the earth, and sent the trident through his neck. The adversary attempted once again to abandon the buffalo-body, issuing from its mouth in the shape of a hero with a sword; but he had only half emerged when he was caught. He was half inside the buffalo and half outside, when the Goddess, with a swift and terrific stroke, beheaded him, and he died.[4]

Thus the goddess represents (1) supremacy, (2) superiority, (3) equality as well as (4) inferiority in relation to the gods. The Devī, as Mahādevī or the Great Goddess, represents the first aspect, for

Ultimately Devī becomes associated with the *trimūrti*, and homage paid to her is counted as homage to the three deities comprising it, since they are believed to have been born from her qualities. Thus when the joint power of Brahmā, Viṣṇu and Śiva is combined in the form of Īśvara 'it becomes the Supreme-

3. Ibid., p. 191.
4. Ibid., p. 192.

Goddess (Bhagavatī), the Resplendent-One (Devī)'. Devī is all things, as is indicated by her numerous epithets. Thus she is Ambikā (the Mother), Kanyā (the Virgin), Satī (Virtuous), Kāmākṣī (Wanton-eyed), etc.[5]

The aspect of her superiority comes into play in the role of Śakti, as demonstrated earlier. The aspect of equality is apparent in the androgynous form, of which the following account is significant, as towards the end, when the female form becomes free of the male, the subsequent development of supremacy and 'subordination' as wife are all comprised within it.

Śiva sprung forth, half male, half female—an awesome sight. It seemed to hold a promise, but one that could not be fulfilled. The right half, male, the left half, female—both facing forward in superhuman beauty from their common vertical axis-could not mate. The divine androgyne, Ardhanārīśvara, the Lord Whose Half Is Woman, perfect and fulfilled within its own wholeness, was beyond desire. No progeny, divine or human, could be expected from this integrity. Brahmā commanded Śiva to divide himself: the right half was Śiva, the left half became the Great Goddess. She sent forth a goddess like herself to be born in order to become Śiva's wife. Her name was Satī. She was born as a daughter of Dakṣa, the Patriarch and Sacrificer, himself a son of Brahmā. Satī became Śiva's wife.[6]

The trimūrti was mentioned several times in the discussion of the Devī[7] and we must now turn to a consideration of this doctrine.

5. Margaret and James Stutley, *A Dictionary of Hinduism* (London: Routledge & Kegan Paul, 1977), p. 75.

6. Stella Kramrisch, *Manifestations of Shiva* (Philadelphia Museum of Art, 1981), pp. xvi–xvii. For another context, see William P. Harman, *The Sacred Marriage of a Hindu Goddess* (Bloomington and Indianapolis: Indiana University Press, 1989).

7. For more on the subject see Tracy Pintchman, *The Rise of the Goddess in the Hindu Tradition* (Albany, NY: State University of New York Press, 1994).

CHAPTER VI

The Hindu Trinity (Trimūrti)

A.L. Basham points out that

As early as Gupta times a holy trinity of Hinduism, the *Trimūrti* or triple form, was evolved, of Brahmā the creator, Viṣṇu the preserver, and Śiva the destroyer. The doctrine of the Trimūrti was occasionally popular in some circles, and is proclaimed in the fine hymn of Kālidāsa, which inspired a once well-known poem of Emerson:

> Praise to you, O Trinity,
> one before creation,
> afterwards divided
> in your three qualities! ...
> You, the one cause
> of death and life and birth,
> in your three forms
> proclaim your own glory....
> In the cycle of your day and night
> all things live and all things die.
> When you wake we live,
> when you sleep we perish....
> Hard and soft, large and small,
> heavy and light, you are all things.
> You are both substance and form,
> ineffable in power....
> You are the knower and the known,
> you are the eater and the food,
> you are the priest and the oblation,
> you are the worshipper and the prayer.[1]

1. A.L. Basham, *The Wonder That Was India* (London: Sidgwick & Jackson, 1988), p. 310.

Indeed, the idea can be seen as already emerging at the time of the *Maitrī*, a late Upaniṣad (*c.* 200 BC–AD 200)[2] wherein Kautsya's Hymn of Praise begins as follows: 'Thou art Brahmā and verily thou art Viṣṇu and thou art Rudra ...' and proceeds to enumerate other gods. S. Radhakrishnan remarks: 'The relation of the three forms (*mūrti-traya*), to the supreme is here indicated. The three, Brahmā, Viṣṇu and Śiva are not to be conceived as independent persons, they are the threefold manifestations of the one Supreme'.[3] For, although the names of several gods are mentioned in the hymn, the next passage restricts itself to identifying the three gods of the trimūrti with the three guṇas or qualities:

Brahmā — *Rajas*
Viṣṇu — *Sattva*
Rudra — *Tamas*

These three guṇas, depending on the context, signify the constituents of the universe or the qualities of the subjects which they describe. Their natural order of enumeration is sattva, rajas and tamas, just as the natural order of enumeration of the trimūrti is Brahmā, Viṣṇu and Śiva. The two orders of enumeration, however, do not coincide: rajas denotes activity: sattva, stability, goodness and purity, and tamas, darkness, inertia and dullness. As the process of creation requires activity, rajas must be associated with Brahmā; preservation requires stability, hence the association of Viṣṇu with sattva; and, as destruction consigns things to darkness, tamas is associated with Śiva. Thus, the three cosmic functions of creation, preservation and destruction, the three gods and the three gunas are all correlated.

There are three aspects of the doctrine which call for caution: (1) that it was not popular;[4] (2) that it represents the influence of

2. Thomas J. Hopkins, *The Hindu Religious Tradition* (Belmont, California: Dickenson Publishing Co., Inc., 1971), p. 141.

3. S. Radhakrishnan, ed., *The Principal Upaniṣads* (London: George Allen & Unwin, 1953), p. 815.

4. A.L. Basham, *The Wonder That Was India*, pp. 310–11: 'Early western students of Hinduism were impressed by the parallel between the Hindu trinity and that of Christianity. In fact the parallel is not very close, and the Hindu trinity, unlike the Holy Trinity of Christianity, never really "caught on". All Hindu trinitarianism tended to favour one god of the three; thus, from the context it is clear that Kālidāsa's hymn to the Trimūrti is really addressed to Brahmā, here looked on as the high god. The Trimūrti was in fact an artificial growth, and had little real influence.'

monistic philosophy[5]; and (3) that it represents three modalities of each god such as Viṣṇu or Śiva as creator, preserver and destroyer rather than the recognition of each distinct modality as a distinct divinity.[6]

The statement that the trinity was not popular is true in the sense that it is not as integral to Hindu theology as the doctrine of trinity is to the Christian, but it is not true in the sense that the idea was not widely diffused or did not play an important role in the evolution of Hindu thought, for

> The Upaniṣad presentation of Brahmā as a mental image of the abstract *brahman* temporarily solved one problem of the monotheistic theory, but raised another, represented by the cults of Viṣṇu and Śiva, which necessitated further theological adjustment. This was accomplished by the introduction of a triad (*trimūrti*) in which Brahmā, Viṣṇu and Śiva constituted in one form the three aspects of *brahman*. But this too conflicted with the notion of an eternal universe of which continuity, not creativity, was the dominant characteristic, and thus Brahmā had to be given a new role. He became the equilibrium (*rajas*) between two opposing principles (the centripetal and centrifugal), represented by Viṣṇu and Śiva respectively, the former representing preservation and renewal, the latter elimination or destruction.[7]

5. M. Hiriyanna, *The Essentials of Indian Philosophy*, p. 176: 'At one stage in their history, probably after they had triumphed over their common rivals of Jainism and Buddhism, these theistic creeds which were sectarian from the beginning seem to have developed a sharp antagonism. As a reaction against it arose the belief, doubtless under the influence of monistic philosophy, that the distinction of the three Gods is but an abstraction and that all of them are but phases of the one supreme God (Īśvara).'

6. Klaus K. Klostermaier, *A Survey of Hinduism* (Albany, NY: State University of New York Press, 1989), pp. 132–3: 'The exclusive association of the title *Lord* with one particular name has led to the development of mutually exclusive religions whose worship and mythology centred around the One God, dismissing in this process the gods of the others as minor beings. Later attempts to unify different sects, at least theoretically, and to consider their rival Lords as equal sharers of one divine power in the *trimūrti* have sometimes led to wrong conclusions among Western students of Hinduism. Hindu texts do indeed speak of the triad of Brahmā as creator, Viṣṇu as preserver, and Śiva as destroyer, fulfilling the functions of the One God, but all those texts belong to one of the traditions in which the Supreme is identical with one of those names and the three separate names are but different aspects of the same being. Some of the famous *trimūrtis* are quite clearly recognizable as artistic expressions of different modalities of one and the same *Īśvara*.'

7. Margaret and James Stutley, *A Dictionary of Hinduism* (London: Routledge & Kegan Paul, 1977), p. 48.

Similarly, although it is tempting to assume that monistic philosophy may underlie this development, this need not necessarily have been the case for two reasons: one theistic and the other universalistic. The move from the early polytheism of the Mantra period to the monotheism or, rather, henotheism, of the Brāhmaṇa period is associated with the 'search for a power which worked behind' the gods or 'the principle immanent in them'. However, when the search culminates in some form of monotheism, then the identification of the functions immanent in such a principle at the cosmic level represents a logical progression of the same trend and would naturally lead in the direction of trimūrti. Moreover, in Hindu thought, the gods are not always represented as depicting a monistic principle—the monistic principle itself is mentioned as one aspect of the ultimate principle. Thus Manu (XII. 123): 'Some call him Agni, others Manu, others Vital Breath, and again others eternal Brahman.'

The last point is significant inasmuch as the trimūrti in the Elephanta caves near Bombay was earlier mistaken as representing the three gods Brahmā, Viṣṇu and Śiva but, on further investigation has been identified as *Maheśa-mūrti*, that is a trinity of Śiva.[8] 'This means that none of the faces are really representations of Vishnu or Brahmā as such but aspects of Shiva himself.'[9] However, this does not negate the fact that the other trimūrti of Brahmā, Viṣṇu and Śiva does exist. The trimūrti has functioned both as the three forms of God, and as the three forms of one particular God.

8. Jitendra Nath Banerjea, *The Development of Hindu Iconography* (Delhi: Munshiram Manoharlal, 1974), pp. 476–7.

9. See Heinrich Zimmer, *Myths and Symbols in Indian Art and Civilization* (edited by Joseph Campbell) (New York: Harper & Row, 1946), p. 134, note.

CHAPTER VII

Brahmā

The first member of the Hindu trinity, as it were, is Brahmā. The name has usually been explained as the masculinization of Brahman, which designates the ultimate reality in the neuter,[1] but it is also plausible that the god arose as a divinization of Brahmā, a word which originally designated a supervisory priest.[2]

Brahmā is closely associated with the Vedas and to see how this association is connected with creation, one has to take into account certain characteristic Hindu ideas. One of them is that the universe undergoes periodic cycles of appearance and dissolution, on a rather spectacular scale. The following account must suffice to give us some idea of the temporal dimensions involved, before which even computation in light years begins to appear rather dim.

> According to this system the cosmos passes through cycles within cycles for all eternity. The basic cycle is the *kalpa*, a 'day of Brahmā', or 4,320 million earthly years. His night is of equal length. 360 such days and nights constitute a 'year of Brahmā' and his life is 100 such years long. The largest cycle is therefore 311,040,000 million years long, after which the whole universe returns to the ineffable world-spirit, until another creator god is evolved.[3]

So, there is really no creation as such which takes place, in the sense of *creatio ex nihilo*. Rather, what happens is more properly described as manifestation. According to Hindu thought, such manifestation involves the Hindu revelatory scriptures, the Vedas. This

1. A.L. Basham, *The Wonder That Was India* (London: Sidgwick & Jackson, 1988), p. 240.

2. Greg Bailey, *The Mythology of Brahmā* (Delhi: Oxford University Press, 1983), p. 6.

3. A.L. Basham, *The Wonder That Was India*, p. 320.

is one reason why Brahmā, the so-called creator-god, is associated with them. The process of creation, in its more popular if less accurate depiction, is described as follows:

> When anyone wants to make a thing, he first recollects the word signifying it, and then makes it. ... This is evident to us in experience, and the creation of the world was similar. The words in the Veda (as they were in the past world-cycle) manifested themselves in the mind of Prajāpati, the creator, before creation, and then he created things accordingly. Thus, for instance, from the word '*bhūr*' (earth) which occurred in his mind he created the terrestrial world.[4]

Along with the creation of the universe Brahmā also imparts knowledge of the Vedic text to inspired human beings or seers. The basic idea involved here is that 'sages and gods who excel in knowledge and action by virtue of their actions in the past aeon, are able to recollect the Veda by God's grace as it was in the past aeon, just as a man waking from sleep is able to recollect and continue his previous waking experience.'[5] Sometimes it is said that sages 'see' the Vedas at the beginning of creation. This is taken to mean that 'God makes the Vedic propositions flash in the minds of the sages in the same linguistic form in which they are now available.'[6]

The Sanskrit word used to denote revelation is *śabda*, and the same word has to serve 'for both "idea" and articulate speech',[7] which may explain some of the confusion that surrounds accounts of creation in Hinduism. Moreover, in general, the idea of creation—so significant for Judaism, Christianity and Islam—does not excite Hindu thinkers to the same extent, perhaps because here it involves repetition to the point of boredom!

The significant points that emerge from the foregoing discussion are (1) a realization of the close connection between Brahmā and the Vedas, a connection which is implied in both the possible derivations of the word Brahmā; and (2) a similarly close connection between the two and the process of creation.

In view of this, it is hardly surprising that iconic depictions of Brahmā always involve the association of Brahmā with the Vedas. For instance, Brahmā is often depicted as possessing four heads.

4. K. Satchidananda Murty, *Revelation and Reason in Advaita Vedānta* (New York: Columbia University Press, 1959), p. 35.

5. Ibid., p. 50.

6. Ibid.

7. Ibid., p. 36.

According to one explanation, these depict the four Vedas. Similarly, Brahmā is often shown as holding a sheaf or a book in one hand. This, again, is said to represent the Vedas, although the Vedas were meant to have been transmitted orally without being committed to writing. In one of the hands he holds a ladle, which is employed in sacrificial rituals as laid down in the Vedas. In the mythology of Brahmā, the goddess Sarasvatī is sometimes represented as his wife and sometimes as his daughter. Some scholars see in this a picturesque representation of the fact that originally Vedic studies and rituals were conducted around a river of that name, which subsequently changed course and dried up. Perhaps the racial memory of the sacred river[8] reappears in the myths. Sometimes the most famous mantra or chant of the *Ṛg Veda*, called 'Gāyatrī' after the metre, is 'personified as a goddess, the wife of Brahmā and mother of the four Vedas'.[9]

It might not be out of place to say a few words about the vicissitudes of Brahmā as a god. He is a particularly significant god in the age of the Brāhmaṇas and later Vedic hymns. While the hymns of the Mantra period are addressed to different gods, in the Brāhmaṇa period the 'belief in many gods of the early hymns now becomes more or less definite monotheism'.[10] However, M. Hiriyanna points out that, in contradistinction from 'monotheism in the ordinary acceptation of the term',[11] the monotheism of the Brāhmaṇas aimed 'rather at the discovery, not of one god who is above other gods, but of the common power that works behind them all or, as we might otherwise put it, the principle immanent in all of them'.[12] He goes on to observe:

> This attempt to derive a general, and virtually impersonal, conception of the supreme God from the common characteristics of deities is, with a remarkable freedom of speculation, made again, and again, so that we have, in the period, a number of such conceptions which succeed and replace one another.[13]

In this henotheistic musical chairs:

8. See A.L. Basham, *The Wonder That Was India*, p. 316.
9. Margaret and James Stutley, *A Dictionary of Hinduism* (London: Routledge & Kegan Paul, 1977), p. 97.
10. M. Hiriyanna, *The Essentials of Indian Philosophy* (London: George Allen & Unwin, 1948), p. 14.
11. Ibid.
12. Ibid.
13. Ibid.

The most prominent among the conceptions of the supreme God, so enthroned and dethroned afterwards, is that of Prajāpati or 'Father-god', whose name implies that all created beings are his children. This title is found used first in its literal sense of 'lord of creatures' as an attribute of various gods. But later it ceases to represent merely an aspect of divinity, and acquires an independent status. Thus in an oft-recited hymn of the Ṛgveda, to a question repeated nine times, 'Who is the God to whom we are to offer sacrifice?' the answer is given that it is Prajāpati 'who is the one lord of all created things'. He is described elsewhere as born of *ṛta*, the principle of righteousness which rules the world; and the description shows that, though the deity is abstract, being the result of elevating a mere epithet to the rank of the Almighty, it does not lack the moral exaltation characterizing the earlier and more concrete gods. Indeed, he is often regarded as an ethical authority. Prajāpati represents the highest conception of unitary godhead in the later Mantras and Brāhmaṇas, taken as a whole. But even that is replaced, in course of time, by others; and still later, as for example in some of the Upanishads, the deity is reduced to a clearly secondary rank under the designation of Brahmā (*masc.*).[14]

This reduction in rank which Brahmā underwent, with brief intervals of resuscitation, continued through the period of Vedic and classical Hinduism. Brahmā's later history may be briefly summarized before we tackle the intriguing issue it raises.[15]

It seems that

the theory of periodic creation or re-creation and the subsequent recognition of Śiva and Viṣṇu as the media for the mystical realization of *brahman*, made Brahmā philosophically irrelevant, and by the nineteenth century his cult had virtually ceased to exist, so that of all the temples of India, there remained only two dedicated solely to Brahmā.[16]

The virtual extinction of the worship of Brahmā has long puzzled scholars and there seem to be virtually as many explanations of it as there are scholars offering them. There is the mythological explanation which takes at least three forms: (1) that he was demoted because he developed incestuous inclinations towards his daughter;[17] (2) that, being no longer needed, he 'died' after completing the task of creation;[18] or (3) because he lied in the following context. Once, while the superiority of the gods was in dispute, a massive column

14. Ibid., p. 15.

15. Margaret and James Stutley, *A Dictionary of Hinduism*, p. 48.

16. Ibid.

17. Jitendra Nath Banerjea, *The Development of Hindu Iconography* (Delhi: Munshiram Manoharlal, 1974), p. 513, note 1.

18. Tarapada Bhattacharya, *The Cult of Brahmā* (Varanasi: Chowkhamba Sanskrit Series Office, 1969), p. 118.

of fire emerged, emblematic of Śiva. Viṣṇu and Brahmā set out to see if its bottom or top could be found. Viṣṇu admitted his failure to find the bottom but Brahmā lied that he had reached the top. Thereupon, 'Brahmā was cursed by Śiva for telling a lie not to have a cult of his own'.[19]

This Śaivite account that 'Brahmā was deprived of worship because of a lie may be understood as a blackmail of the Brahmins, whose special lord he must have been and who did not recognize the Śaivites as orthodox'.[20] That the other sects organized around Viṣṇu and Śiva capitalized on Brahmā's falling on bad days is not in doubt. In a Vaiṣṇava myth for instance, 'Bhṛgu is deputed to visit the three "gods" of the *trimūrti* to ascertain which one of them was most worthy of worship'. He found Brahmā 'too wrapped up in himself', and Śiva too engrossed in his wife Pārvatī. Viṣṇu alone proved to be worthy.[21]

The question that this raises is of distinguishing between cause and effect. Did such accounts cause the occultation of Brahmā or do they merely offer mythological explanations of what had already occurred? The same question must be asked of the following explanation in terms of mythic times: 'Brahmā was adorable in the Satya Yuga; in the Tretā Yuga "sacrifice" is said to be so; in the Dvāpara Yuga, Viṣṇu is worshipped. I ... [Śiva] am worshipped in all the four (yugas).'[22] Similarly, Margaret and James Stutley's suggestion that Brahmā became otiose because his role as creator was taken over by Viṣṇu and Śiva begs the question. It has been observed that 'Brahmā's popularity declined before temple-building became a respectable Hindu activity and there are remarkably few temples dedicated to him.'[23] Could it then be that the reason for Brahmā's eclipse lay in the fact that Brahmā was the patron-deity of Vedic worship and Vedic worship was aniconic? A late but popular Sanskrit text accounts for the decline in the worship of Brahmā thus:

19. Jitendra Nath Banerjea, *The Development of Hindu Iconography*, p. 514. For more details, see Heinrich Zimmer, *Myths and Symbols in Indian Art and Civilization* (edited by Joseph Campbell) (New York: Harper & Row), 1946, pp. 128–30.

20. Klaus K. Klostermaier, *A Survey of Hinduism* (Albany: State University of New York Press, 1989), p. 133.

21. Margaret and James Stutley, *A Dictionary of Hinduism*, p. 48.

22. Tarapada Bhattacharya, *The Cult of Brahmā*, p. 119.

23. K.M. Sen, *Hinduism* (Harmondsworth: Penguin Books, 1961), p. 59, note 1.

Long ago Brahmā and Viṣṇu went to see Śiva near Himavān. They saw a shining phallus there in front of them. It was of immense size. One of them went downwards and the other upwards to find out the end of it. Both returned without reaching the top or the bottom and by penance they pleased Śiva who appeared before them and asked them what boon they desired. Brahmā asked Śiva to take birth as his son. Śiva did not like this and said that nobody would worship Brahmā because of his extravagant desire (namely, to have Śiva as his son). Viṣṇu requested that he should be made a servant at Śiva's feet. So Viṣṇu incarnated as Śiva's Śakti (power). That Śakti is Pārvatī. So Viṣṇu and Pārvatī are one and the same in a sense.[24]

It is possible that the decline in the worship of Brahmā has something to do with the disappearance of Buddhism from India. It should not be forgotten that it was Brahmā who induced Buddha to go out and preach his message to everyone when Buddha was uncertain about the course of action to follow. Moreover, Brahmā and Indra are both important gods in Buddhism and both may have suffered eclipse along with it. In any event, the idea deserves some consideration.

Mythological and historical speculation apart, some philosophical reasons have also been put forward. From an axiological standpoint it has been suggested that, while 'Brahmā is one of the most enduring symbols of *pravṛtti* values that can be found in Indian literature', the mythology of Viṣṇu and Śiva 'is symbolic of both sets of values, *pravṛtti* and *nivṛtti*'.[25] Since it is the tension between these two and the attempts at its resolution that are characteristic of Hinduism,[26] it could be argued that Brahmā gradually became less relevant. Or, alternatively, it could be argued that religious pursuit is to be associated with nivṛtti, while 'all creations arise out of Vikshepa (disturbance). This vikshepa-śakti is Lord Brahma—the total mind-intellect equipment. Man, being essentially constituted of his mind and intellect, has already invoked his vikshepa-śakti and realized Brahmā. Hence worship and invocation of Brahmā is not undertaken by anyone.'[27]

24. Vettam Mani, *Purāṇic Encyclopedia* (Delhi: Motilal Banarsidass, 1974), p. 150.

25. Greg Bailey, *The Mythology of Brahmā*, p. xiv.

26. Ibid., Chapter 2.

27. A. Parthasarathy, 'Brahma', in R.S. Nathan, compiler, *Symbolism in Hinduism* (Bombay: Central Chinmaya Mission Trust, 1983), p. 112.

CHAPTER VIII

Viṣṇu

If Brahmā is the otiose God then Viṣṇu is the supreme, syncretic and living god. Of course, all the gods of the trinity, including Brahmā, have laid claim to supremacy, but the claim seems to have been most effective in the case of Viṣṇu and perhaps a little less so in the case of Śiva. This claim of Viṣṇu is particularly staked out in the *Viṣṇu* and *Bhāgavata Purāṇas.*

The first takes the form of a dialogue between a teacher (Parāśara) and his disciple (Maitreya). The teaching of the *Purāṇa* is summed up by Parāśara as: 'The world originated from Vishṇu; it is in Him that the world exists as a harmonious system; He is the sole sustainer and controller of the world, and in truth, the world is He' (*Vishṇu Purāṇa* I, i, 35). It is explained that God is called by different names by different people, but He of course is one, and the only one. The world is His playful manifestation (*līlā*). The One without attributes (*nirguṇa*) joyfully expresses Himself as the world full of colour, sound, touch, and other qualities (*saguṇa*).[1]

However, as already noted, in later and in what, for the purposes of this book, has been considered standard Hindu mythology, the 'three Gods, Brahmā, Vishṇu and Śiva form a triad representing three aspects of the Supreme. Brahmā is the creator, Vishṇu the preserver, and Śiva the destroyer of the world, the last being necessary for further creation.'[2]

How does Viṣṇu perform his role as a member of the trinity? Before trying to answer that question it might be worthwhile to say a few words about how he came into being, because that too has some bearing on it. The key word here is syncretic. Many scholars

1. K.M. Sen, *Hinduism* (Harmondsworth: Penguin Books, 1961), p. 76.
2. Ibid., p. 59, note 1.

think that 'three streams of thought mingle to form Vaiṣṇavism'[3], the 'creed in which Viṣṇu is worshipped as the supreme God'[4]: (1) Viṣṇu proper, who is already mentioned in the *Ṛg Veda* where he

is represented in the mantras as one of the solar deities and, as such, is associated with light and life. His essential feature, as depicted in the hymns, is his taking three strides (*tri-vikrama*) which in all probability refer to the rising, culmination, and setting of the sun. It was this worship of the sun, 'the swift-moving luminary,' that gradually transformed itself into the worship of Viṣṇu ('the pervading') as the supreme God. He had already attained supremacy in the time of the Brāhmaṇas; and in one of the older Upanishads, the goal of human life is represented as reaching the supreme abode of Viṣṇu.[5]

(2) The conception of Nārāyaṇa, whose origin too may

be traced in the Ṛg Veda, and which appears in a well-developed form in the Brāhmaṇas. The name signifies 'the abode or resting place of men' or, more generally, 'the goal of all beings.' One of the Brāhmaṇas states that Nārāyaṇa placed himself in all the world and in all the gods, and that they were all placed in him. In a relatively later Upanishad, the Mahānārāyana, in which this God occupies the position which Śiva does in the Śvetāśvatara Upanishad, his cosmic character is thus described: 'Whatever in this universe is seen or heard, pervading all that—both inside and outside—Nārāyaṇa stands.' He is called in the epic 'the son of *dharma*,' implying that the conception is not cosmic alone, but also pre-eminently ethical in its character.[6]

(3) The cult of the worship of Bhagavān ('the worshipful'), associated with Kṛṣṇa, who may have preached theism the way Buddha preached his doctrines and Mahāvīra preached Jainism in the age of religious ferment which followed the Brāhmaṇa period of the Vedas.

It soon assumed a sectarian complexion in the form of Bhāgavata religion; and one stage of it is found taught in the famous Bhagavadgītā, so far as it is theistic ... It was largely prevalent when Megasthenes visited India, so that the religion must have originated some considerable time before. This monotheistic creed came, in course of time, to be combined with the Vedic cult of Viṣṇu-Nārāyaṇa; and it was this combination that chiefly contributed to make the God of Vaiṣṇavism even more personal than that of Śaivism. Somewhat later Śrī Krishna, the prophet of the Bhāgavata religion, was deified and identified with Viṣṇu-Nārāyaṇa as an incarnation of him.[7]

3. M. Hiriyanna, *The Essentials of Indian Philosophy* (London: George Allen & Unwin, 1948), p. 35.

4. Ibid., p. 34.

5. Ibid.

6. Ibid., p. 34.

7. Ibid., p. 35.

One special feature of Vaiṣṇavism is the doctrine of avatāra or divine descent to save the world from *premature* dissolution. 'According to Hinduism generally, progress in the world is not continuous. Things grow worse and worse at times, when God intervenes catastrophically to inaugurate a reign of justice and happiness. This theory of *avatārs* helps what has all along been a noteworthy feature of Hinduism, viz. its absorption of other creeds into itself.'[8] Thus Vaiṣṇavism is syncretic in a dual sense: it emerged as a synthesis of different streams of thoughts and beliefs and tends to merge different streams of thoughts and beliefs into itself. This provides the historical background for a consideration of the theological role of Viṣṇu as the 'preserver', as a member of the trimūrti. In keeping with the cyclical cosmology of Hinduism, the universe will undergo dissolution at the appointed hour and it is the duty of Śiva, the third member of the trinity, to preside over this. However, should the universe be threatened with destruction before the appointed hour, especially as a result of the activity of demons, it is the duty of Viṣṇu to rescue it, a duty he typically performs by intervening as an incarnation. Such incarnations are said to be numerous but ten of them are considered particularly memorable.

(1) The Fish (*Matsya*): When the earth was overwhelmed by a universal flood Viṣṇu took the form of a fish and warned Manu (the first man in the present cycle) of the impending danger and then carried him to safety along with his family, in a ship attached to a horn on his head. Manu thus combined in himself the role of both Adam and Noah. In this incarnation Viṣṇu is also said to have saved the Vedas, which is curious since the Vedas are transmitted orally. Were they *also* reduced to writing, and much earlier than we think?

(2) The Tortoise (*Kūrma*): The ambrosia of the gods was also lost in the Flood and had to be recovered. This was accomplished by the gods and the non-gods acting in concert by churning the ocean. Viṣṇu then assumed the form of a tortoise to provide a firm footing for the mountain Mandara which served as the rod, with the serpent Vāsuki serving as the rope.

(3) The Boar (*Varāha*): In this incarnation Viṣṇu recovered the earth

8. M. Hiriyanna, *The Essentials of Indian Philosophy*, pp. 35–6.

from the abysmal depths into which it had been cast in anger by the demon Hiraṇyākṣa. There is a sculptural depiction of this scene from the Gupta period (fourth–fifth century).

(4) The Man-Lion (*Narasiṁha*): Hiraṇyākṣa was succeeded by his brother Hiraṇyakaśipu, whose son Prahlāda, to the chagrin of his father, became a great devotee of Viṣṇu. When Prahlāda called for Viṣṇu's help while being persecuted by his father, Viṣṇu emerged from a pillar in the form of a man-lion and ripped Hiraṇyakaśipu apart after placing him on his thigh. Hiraṇyakaśipu's death had to be stage-managed in this way to circumvent the boon Hiraṇyakaśipu had won that he could not be killed at day or night, on land or in the sky, by man or animal.

(5) The Dwarf (*Vāmana*): The pious demon-king Bali, noted for his liberality, posed a threat to the gods by his austerities. Viṣṇu neutralized him by appearing as a dwarf and was granted his request for a piece of land covered by his three strides. The dwarf assumed a gigantic form, covered the earth and sky with his two strides and relegated Bali to the nether regions with the third.

(6) Paraśurāma (Rāma with the Axe): Viṣṇu incarnated himself as the son of Jamadagni, who was oppressed by King Kārtavīrya. Thereupon Jamadagni's son, Paraśurāma, killed the king. The sons of the king retaliated by killing the Brāhmaṇa Jamadagni. To avenge his death Paraśurāma wiped out all the male members of the warrior class (kṣatriyas) twenty-one times. After each extinction the surviving women regenerated the class by bringing forth progeny through brāhmaṇas. This is curious because traditionally the varṇa of the father takes precedence in determining the varṇa of the child over that of the mother.

(7) Rāmacandra (Rāma with the Bow): Viṣṇu incarnated himself as Rāma, the son of King Daśaratha, to save the world from the depredations of the demon Rāvaṇa, who abducted Rāma's wife Sītā. Rāvaṇa was killed by Rāma and Sītā was rescued.

Rāvaṇa was a brāhmaṇa in terms of his varṇa and Rāma a kṣatriya. Thus the incarnation of Rama represents an incarnational role-reversal, when compared with that of Paraśurāma.

Rāma is an extremely popular divinity in the Hindu world and his reign on earth parallels the Western concept of the Kingdom of God.

(8) Kṛṣṇa: Viṣṇu's incarnation as Kṛṣṇa is at least as popular as Viṣṇu's incarnation as Rāma, perhaps even more. In this incarnation, which Hindu tradition places in the fourth millennium BCE, Viṣṇu incarnated himself to save the earth from the oppressive rule of King Kaṁsa, who was finally killed by Kṛṣṇa after Kaṁsa's several attempts to get Kṛṣṇa killed were unsuccessful. Kṛṣṇa performed this feat as a child. In his youth he sided with the Pāṇḍavas in the Mahābhārata war and guided them to victory, after which he moved back to his kingdom in Western India, where in due course he and his kinsmen came to a tragic end.

(9) Buddha: Different texts assign different motives for this incarnation of Viṣṇu. According to one set of accounts, Viṣṇu assumed this form to lead the wicked astray. According to another, Viṣṇu took this incarnation out of compassion to bring the bloody sacrifices of animals to an end.

(10) Kalkin: This is the name given to the incarnation yet to come, when Viṣṇu will incarnate himself to bring the dark age to a catastrophic end and inaugurate a new era of peace.[9]

These traditional accounts are regarded by historians as combining several diverse elements and hence being syncretic in nature. For instance, the incarnation of Kṛṣṇa is said to combine three distinct dimensions—that of a hero god; a pastoral god; and a child-god. It is as a hero figure that Kṛṣṇa appears in the *Mahābhārata*, just as Rāma appears as the hero in *Rāmāyaṇa*. Kṛṣṇa's famous dialogue urging Arjuna to carry on the righteous struggle when Arjuna loses nerve, known as the *Bhagavadgītā*, forms part of the *Mahābhārata*. In the epic, Kṛṣṇa guides the Pāṇḍavas, who have been ousted by the Kauravas from the kingdom which rightly belongs to them, to victory over the Kauravas. The two other dimensions of the composite personality of Kṛṣṇa are celebrated in the *Bhāgavata Purāṇa* wherein his dalliance with the milkmaids as a pastoral god and his naughty pranks as a child-god are narrated.[10]

9. A.L. Basham, *The Wonder That Was India* (London: Sidgwick & Jackson, 1988), pp. 302–3; 306–7.

10. Ibid., pp. 304–6.

CHAPTER IX

Śiva

Śiva is the third God of the trinity, responsible for destruction. In order to understand his role properly we must shed the negative emotional reaction we associate with the word *destruction.* There is nothing perverse in the process of destruction associated with Śiva. First of all, the process is a natural one. At its appointed time the universe must dissolve into its subtle form, from which it will manifest again. Perhaps the use of the word *consummation* or *transformation* rather than *destruction* is more conducive to generating the right perspective. Just as a game, a play or a TV programme runs its course and comes to an end, so does the cosmos, and it is Śiva who then folds the tent, as it were.

Moreover, not only does destruction possess a natural aspect, it may also possess a beneficial one. Thus, not only can evil be destroyed, but illness, misfortune, even radical metaphysical ignorance and the cycle of births and rebirths to which it leads can be destroyed. So, Śiva is far from being just a horrific god, he is a salvific god too. He can also destroy destruction!

We noticed earlier that each of the gods of the Hindu trinity can function in a dual way—as an aspect of God *per se* and as God in their own right, thereby appropriating the triple role of creation, preservation and destruction. In Śaivite theology these functions are usually identified as creation (*sṛṣṭi*), preservation (*sthiti*), destruction (*saṁhāra*), concealment (*tirobhāva*) and grace (*anugraha*).[1]

Just as the figure of Viṣṇu is syncretic in nature, that of Śiva, by contrast, often displays antithetical elements. This feature is traceable

1. T.M.P. Mahadevan, *Outlines of Hinduism* (Bombay: Chetana Ltd, 1971), p. 169.

early in the development of the divinity. It has been suggested that the deity combines Vedic with the pre-Vedic elements found at Harappa and Mohenjo-Daro, cities of the Indus Valley culture of the third millennium BCE. However, although

> Images of this God and of the emblems of his divinity are found among the relics of Mohenjo-Daro ... the precise relation between the creed to which it points and the Vedic faith in Rudra-Śiva is not yet known. Here is one point on which the unravelling of the true nature of the Indus valley civilization, as it is now styled, is likely to throw fresh light. It is, however, clear that there is a certain blending of antithetical features in this conception; and it may in part be alien in its nature, the alien features being later assimilated to the Aryan conception. There are various indications pointing to its mixed character. The story, narrated in more than one old work, of Dakṣa's sacrifice to which Śiva was not invited as being a 'low god', is one of them. Another indication is that Śiva worship is largely based upon Āgamas (literally 'tradition') which are not, according to some thinkers like Saṁkara, entirely in agreement with the teaching of revelation or the Vedas.[2]

These antithetical elements, however, are identifiable not merely historically but also structurally. The mythology of Śiva contains both erotic and ascetic elements,[3] and even in his role of Naṭarāja, or Lord of Dance, these elements are present. The Indian danseuse Mrinalini V. Sarabhai has remarked:

> What is perhaps most significant of all in the image is the combination of this God ascetic, the solitary One, master of meditation, with the frenzied dance of the Yogi and the artist. A dancer becomes the being that he impersonates on the stage. In the dance are aroused the entire energy of body, mind, intellect and soul. It is a complete surrender to God. Thus, a dancer is similar to the Yogi, who gives his all to the Lord.[4]

This is true not only of the image of Naṭarāja but also of some of his dances, like the *Tāṇḍava* dance which encompasses both creation and destruction.[5]

Śiva is most visibly identified with his *liṅgam*, the mark of his

2. M. Hiriyanna, *The Essentials of Indian Philosophy* (London: George Allen & Unwin, 1948), p. 34.

3. Wendy Doniger O'Flaherty, *Asceticism and Eroticism in the Mythology of Śiva* (London: Oxford University Press, 1973), *passim.*

4. R.S. Nathan, compiler, *Symbolism in Hinduism* (Bombay: Central Chinmaya Mission Trust, 1983), p. 169.

5. Margaret and James Stutley, *A Dictionary of Hinduism* (London: Routledge & Kegan Paul, 1977), p. 206.

presence. It is phallic in shape and perhaps in origin as well.[6] Even in this form it combines antithetical elements, for this 'ithyphallic condition is not priapic', for several reasons. From a Tantrika point of view it is not so because it 'represents precisely what the tantric aims to master, i.e. seminal retention in the laboratory setting of Tantric ritualistic copulation'.[7] For, after all, Śiva as the Yogin 'stands for complete control of the senses, and for supreme carnal renunciation. His phallic condition would seem to be an inane paradox unless we take into account the Tantric ideological background of this symbolism, which is truly profound'.[8] Again, even from a Tantrika point of view copulation may not be involved.

Śiva is the great ascetic god, the Great Yogi, Lord of Yogis, teacher of yoga, the ancient discipline practised in the days of the Harappa civilization (third millennium BC). Carved on some of its diminutive reliefs is a main figure in yoga posture, unmistakable in the most elaborate of these anthropomorphic representations. The discipline of yoga is practised to one end: self-mastery that comprises mind and body and readies the living being for the realization of ultimate reality. The striving for ultimate reality guided by yoga is carried out within the living being and entails the control of the breath, a control that frees the yogi from worldly attachments and concerns of the 'ego'. The control, not the rejection, of the passionate self—comprising sex—is the function of yoga.[9]

The phallic interpretation of the liṅgam is not the only one. It has been known to represent a post[10] or symbolize the pillar of light which Śiva appeared as in an account mentioned earlier. The significance of this symbol of Śiva is best brought home in a religious context as interpreted by Stella Kramrisch:

In the world of Śiva, the significance of the *liṅga* is comparable to that of the Cross in the Christian world, and that of Śiva with the *liṅga*, or of the faces of Śiva together with the shape of the *liṅga*, to the figure of the Savior on the Cross. The essential myths of the *liṅga* are those of the ascetic god who, at the command of Brahmā to procreate, castrates himself or becomes a post (*sthāṇu*).[11]

6. Jitendra Nath Banerjea, *The Development of Hindu Iconography* (Delhi: Munshiram Manoharlal, 1974), pp. 454–7.

7. Agehananda Bharati, *The Tantric Tradition* (London: Rider & Co., 1965), p. 296.

8. Ibid.

9. Stella Kramrisch, *The Presence of Śiva* (Princeton, NJ: Princeton University Press, 1981), p. xv.

10. Ibid.

11. Ibid., p. xvi.

CHAPTER X

Jīva

The *jīva* or the living being is explained in two ways in standard Hindu thought: either as possessing three bodies or as possessing five sheaths.

I

The doctrine of the three bodies was alluded to earlier. According to this view a human being possesses: (1) a physical body (*sthūla śarīra*), (2) a subtle body (*sūksma śarīra*), and (3) a causal body (*kāraṇa śarīra*).

The physical body does not require much comment; the subtle body is the most important from our point of view because it constitutes the transmigrating self. However, at the root of this individuality of the jīva lies *avidyā* or radical metaphysical ignorance about its true nature. This is the first and fundamental 'body', comprising avidyā and the ontological basis of the fact that jīva regards itself as the jīva and not ātman and is also therefore regularly referred to as jīvātman and called jīva for the sake of brevity. The state of the jīva as embodying ignorance may be described thus, when it is subject to the limitations (*upādhis*) at the root of which lies ignorance, for

> the soul does not know that this is so, because it has not the proper knowledge of its own Self, in that its own nature is hidden from it. What prevents this self-knowledge, in which the soul is at once the perceiving subject and perceived object, is *Avidyā*; Avidyā puts itself between the soul as subject and the soul as object; and is sometimes characterized subjectively as defective intellectual force, sometimes objectively as defective perceptibility. The soul is from the subjective point of view compared to a blind man whose lost sight can only be restored

by the remedy of grace; objectively it is the *Upādhis* by which the divine nature of the soul is disguised and as it were rendered latent like fire which slumbers hidden in the wood.[1]

Thus the *sthūla śarīra* or the physical (literally, *gross* or *coarse*) body is too proximate to require explanation and the kāraṇa śarīra or causal body too remote for it. Hence, in the context of the doctrines of karma and saṁsāra, it is the transmigrating self, the sūkṣma śarīra, which becomes the focus of attention. In the context of upādhis, we get the following picture of the jīvātman:

These Upādhis which condition the individualization of the soul, are, taking these all in all, the following:

I) The coarse body (*deha, sthūla-śarīram*) consisting of the elements; the soul casts it off at death.

II) Among what accompanies the soul on its migration we distinguish:

A) a changing part: *viz.* moral determination (*karma-āśraya*) which accompanies the soul into each life as a new moment, not previously (*apūrvam*) existent, and

B) an unchanging part with which the soul was invested from eternity and remains invested until liberation; this includes:

1) the subtle body (*sūkshma-śarīram, bhūta-āśraya*) consisting of the 'subtle portions of the elements which compose the seed of the body' (*dehavījāni-bhūta-sūkshmāṇi*);

2) the life-organs, termed *Prāṇas* (in the more extended sense), i.e. vital breaths, spirits. These fall into two cases, the first includes the principles of the conscious, the second those of the unconscious life.

a) The system of the conscious life is formed by

α) five organs of sense (*buddhi-indriyāṇi*): sight, hearing, smell, taste, touch;

β) five organs of action (*karma-indriyāṇi*), including the functions of speech, of the hands, the feet, the organs of generation and evacuation;

χ) the *Manas*, the central organ of conscious life, directing the organs of perception and action.

b) The system of the unconscious life consists of the *Prāṇa* in the limited sense, more properly termed *Mukhya prāṇa*, i.e., chief breath of life. This again is divided into five single Pranas, *viz., prāṇa* (in the strictest sense), *apāna, vyāna, udāna* and *samāna,* on which depend the functions of respiration and nutrition as well as the act of dying.[2]

1. Paul Deussen, *The System of the Vedānta* (Chicago: Open Court Publishing Co., 1943), p. 325.

2. Ibid., pp. 325–6.

The foregoing might not appear so obscure if we realize that the physical body corresponds with our personality in the waking state; the subtle body to our personality in the dream state and the causal body to our personality in the state of deep sleep. This also explains why transmigration is said to take place in a dream-like sequence.[3]

II

According to the other model, we can visualize our personality as consisting of layers or sheaths rather than bodies. If now we undertook a strip-search for the ātman, then the first layer we will have to discard is the sheer physical body. This is the sheath made of food or the *annamaya kośa.* The sheath of physiological action as distinguished from mere physical action will have to go next. This is the sheath made of *prāṇas* or life-forces, such as the process of digestion, for instance, as distinguished from food itself. It is called the *prāṇamaya kośa.* With the body dispensed with, we are left with the mind in its conscious mode. This sheath, made up of the ordinary conscious mind, is called the *manomaya kośa*, but behind it lies the deeper reach of the mind of undifferentiated consciousness. This is called the *vijñānamaya kośa* or the 'sheath of consciousness'. One more sheath is left before one can reach the ātman: the 'sheath of bliss' (experienced in meditation) or the *ānandamaya kośa.* One is warned not to confuse its bliss with the bliss of knowing the ātman. The general picture may be presented as follows:

> Consciousness in the Annamaya-kośa, works in the brain and is concerned with external activities; it uses at the same time the Prāṇamaya-kośa, to carry on the life-functions of the body, and affects, by this, all the objects with which it comes into contact; these two kośas leave minute particles of themselves on all the objects they touch, and the rules of physical purity are based on this fact.
>
> Consciousness, in the waking state, also uses the Manomaya-kośa, by which it desires and thinks, and these three sheaths are active during all waking consciousness. A deep thinker, a philosopher or metaphysician, also uses the Vijñānamaya-kośa in working out his thoughts, but ordinary men do not get beyond the Manomaya-kośa.
>
> When the time of death comes, the Prāṇamaya-kośa separates from the

3. For a detailed account of this approach, see Andrew O. Fort, *The Self and Its States* (Delhi: Motilal Banarsidass, 1990).

Annamaya-kośa, and leaves the latter inert and helpless, fit only for the burning ghat.[4]

III

These two modes of analysing human personality are not at odds; they dovetail. The physical body (sthūla śarīra) corresponds to the food-sheath or annamaya kośa; the subtle body (sūkṣma śarīra) to the vital air sheath, the mind sheath and the consciousness sheath (prāṇamaya-manomaya-vijñānamaya kośa) and the causal body (kāraṇa śarīra) to the bliss-sheath (ānandamaya kośa).[5]

In the interest of the economy of exposition we shall mainly speak of the subtle body (sūkṣma śarīra) as it corresponds to the transmigrating self.

4. *Sanātana-Dharma* (Adyar, Madras: The Theosophical Publishing House, 1966), pp. 138–9.

5. Ibid., p. 144.

CHAPTER XI

Saṁsāra

The process of undergoing rebirths continuously is known as saṁsāra. In principle, the process is without a beginning and an end, unless brought to an end by religious and spiritual practices of the kind detailed later. It is easier to describe this process than to define it. In a sense it has just been defined: according to an Indologist, it is the 'indefinite transmigration of living beings'.[1]

To get a full sense of what this involves, it might be worthwhile to narrate a segment of a living being's or jīva's involvement in the process for a few lives. The *Bhāgavata Purāṇa* presents such an account:

Birth One

There was a king in ancient times. He had several sons. One of them was called Bharata and he is the subject of our narrative. After ruling over the country for several years Bharata went into retirement and repaired to a hermitage. There Bharata led an ascetic life performing daily the rites laid down in the scriptures and repeating the sacred syllables. One day a thirsty doe, who was also pregnant, came to drink water from a nearby river. While thus slaking her thirst she was scared by the roar of a lion nearby. The roar caused her to panic and as a result of the shock to the system she was delivered prematurely of the new-born deer who fell into the river. Meanwhile the doe, drained by the experience and already terrified, ran into a cave. There she collapsed, and died.

In the meantime, the new-born deer, floating down the river,

1. Louis Renou, ed., *Hinduism* (New York: George Braziller, 1962), p. 43.

caught Bharata's eye and out of compassion he rescued it and began to take care of it. From then onwards he became so preoccupied with taking care of the deer that his spiritual practices began to suffer. In other words, Bharata's attention was diverted from spiritual pursuits to the more mundane pursuit of looking after the young deer. 'The deer followed him wherever he went and if it did not turn up in time in the evening after grazing Bharata went out in search of it weeping. Years went by and Bharata became old and died with the name of the deer on his lips.'

Birth Two

On account of the fact that the deer was on his mind when he died, Bharata was reborn as a deer! However, because of the religious austerities he had practised, even as a deer Bharata remembered 'his previous birth and regretted that he spent the life of a man for the sake of a deer'. Even as a deer he led a pious life. He left his mother, went down to a hermitage, and bathed daily in the river. Ultimately he died on the banks of the river.

Birth Three

In his next life Bharata, the deer-departed, was born as the son of a Brahmin. The Brahmin had two wives. From the first wife he had nine sons. It was to the second that Bharata was born. In due course the Brahmin died, and upon his death his wife, Bharata's mother, mounted his funeral pyre and committed Sati. Bharata was orphaned and left to the mercy of his stepmother and stepbrothers. He was assigned the task of looking after the cattle and fields of his brothers for his living. Bharata did all he was told, patiently.

One day, while he was keeping watch at midnight, a calamitous event occurred. A child had been born to a woman among the outcastes and the event was being celebrated. Their conception of a celebration, however, was to offer human sacrifice to the goddess Kālī. Fortunately the man escaped but unfortunately they caught hold of Bharata, who was acting as a night-watchman, as a substitute. They were getting ready to sacrifice him when 'the effulgence of the Brahmin astounded Kālī and getting angry for bringing such a Brahmin for sacrifice she devoured the outcastes and 'allowed the Brahmin to go free'.

Thus, saved by this *deus ex machina*, Bharata escaped and 'reached a village, walking all the way. That village was ruled over by a king' who was on his way to see a sage on the banks of a river, to which he was being carried in a palanquin. There were not enough bearers for the palanquin and 'so the Brahmin was asked to join the team of bearers. As they were moving the palanquin shook' because Bharata was out of step. The king reprimanded Bharata and a conversation ensued in which 'Bharata then gave the king fitting replies based on the ethics of Vedānta. The erudition of Bharata greatly impressed the king and he stepped down from the palanquin and bowed to Bharata.' 'Bharata went from there to the forests singing devotional songs in praise of Viṣṇu and at last attained salvation.'[2]

This popular Purāṇic story about Bharata and his many lives serves to illustrate several points about the process of saṁsāra.

(1) The process is continuous.

(2) The scope of rebirth includes animal life. It is said to include all forms of life.

(3) The thoughts at the time of one's death determine the next birth.

(4) Psychic dispositions, otherwise called *saṁskāras*, are of key importance in the process. Such dispositions could be conative or cognitive; emotional or moral. In fact, there is a popular aphorism in Hinduism: saṁskāra is saṁsāra.

(5) It is worth noting that in the popular understanding of the doctrine of karma actual experience is often used as a yardstick for judging the nature of karma. One would therefore have expected Bharata to be rewarded for his compassion for the deer. Perhaps he was and that is how he escaped death at the hands of the outcastes, although the text does not say so. The text instead focuses on the need for dispassion, for it was Bharata's 'passion' for the deer that led to his rebirth in that form.

(6) The story enables us to understand some aspects of the doctrine of karma, which is closely allied to that of saṁsāra. As Hiriyanna explains:

2. Adapted from Vettam Mani, *Purāṇic Encyclopedia* (Delhi: Motilal Banarsidass, 1974), p. 120.

Every deed that we do leads to a double result. It not only produces what may be termed its direct result (*phala*)—the pain or pleasure following from it according to the nature of the deed done; it also establishes in us a tendency (*saṁskāra*) to repeat the same deed in the future. The necessity involved in the karma doctrine is only in so far as the former of these results, viz. the pain or the pleasure, is concerned. As regards the latter, viz. the tendencies, they are entirely under our control; and our moral progress depends wholly upon the success with which we direct and regulate them, as they tend to express themselves in action. Nor does this double significance of karma lead to any bifurcation of life's interests or conflict in its purposes, for the ethical advance is what is intended to be made the sole aim of *all* activities. That, for example, is the explicit teaching of the *Gītā*. ... By thus adopting the betterment of one's moral nature as the goal of all endeavour, one may grow indifferent to what happens in the present as the inevitable result of past karma.[3]

However, beyond that, it enables us to see the doctrine of karma in relation to *mokṣa*[4]—for that is what Bharata was seeking to attain and is said to have attained.

(7) The story does not indicate the actual mechanism of rebirth.

The mechanism by means of which the migration is made is the *liṅga-śarīra* or the subtle body of the soul [also called *śūkṣma śarīra*]. At death only the physical dress gets disintegrated. The subtle body which is 'the vehicle of mind and character' departs and gathers unto itself a new physical body. Thus the wheel rotates, and it stops only when the goal is reached.[5]

The example of Bharata illustrates the more general pattern of saṁsāra, namely the involvement of all beings in the same process on a cosmic scale,[6] and is closely associated with the concept of karma.

3. M. Hiriyanna, *The Essentials of Indian Philosophy* (London: George Allen & Unwin, 1948), pp. 48–9.

4. M. Hiriyanna, *Popular Essays in Indian Philosophy* (Mysore: Kavyalaya Publishers, 1952), p. 46.

5. T.M.P. Mahadevan, *Outlines of Hinduism* (Bombay: Chetana Ltd, 1971), pp. 63–4.

6. See David R. Kinsley, *Hinduism: A Cultural Perspective* (second edition) (Englewood Cliffs, NJ: Prentice-Hall, 1993), pp. 85–6.

CHAPTER XII

Karma

If one accepts the view, as most Hindus do, that we continually undergo reincarnation, then the question arises: what determines where we will be incarnated and what will befall us in that incarnation? The answer to this question in a word is: karma! 'This belief [in karma] has, for long, had a profound influence on the life of the Indian people'[1] and needs to be understood carefully. One way of arriving at such an understanding is to distinguish between two aspects of it, even though we will later discover that these two aspects, though 'distinguishable in thought are not separable in fact'. The first of these aspects is that 'the doctrine extends the principles of causation to the sphere of human conduct and teaches that, as every event in the physical world is determined by its antecedents, so everything that happens in the moral realm is' determined by its antecedents.[2] The second aspect follows from the first:

> whatever we knowingly do, will, sooner or later, bring us the result we merit; and there is no way of escape from it. What we sow, we must reap, that is, the karma doctrine signifies not merely that the events of our life are determined by antecedent causes, but also that there is absolute justice in the rewards and punishments that fall to our lot in life.[3]

Once these aspects of the doctrine have been grasped, we are in a position to appreciate the consolidated statement of the doctrine:

1. M. Hiriyanna, *The Essentials of Indian Philosophy* (London: George Allen & Unwin, 1948), p. 46.
2. Ibid., p. 46.
3. Ibid., p. 48.

Karma literally means action, but as every action is triple in its nature, belonging partly to the past, partly to the present, partly to the future, it has come to mean the sequence of events, the law of causes and effects, the succession in which each effect follows its own cause. The word Karma, action simply, should however remind us that what is called the consequence of an action is really not a separate thing but is a part of the action, and cannot be divided from it. The consequence is that part of the action ... belongs to the future, and is as much a part of it as the part done in the present. Thus suffering is not the consequence of a wrong act, but an actual part of it, although it may be only experienced later. A soldier is sometimes wounded in battle, and in the excitement does not feel any pain; afterwards, when he is quiet he feels the pain; so a man sins and feels no suffering, but later the suffering makes itself felt. The suffering is not separated from the wound, any more than heat from fire, though experienced as a result.

Hence all things are linked together indissolubly, woven and interwoven inseparably; nothing occurs which is not linked to the past and to the future.[4]

The doctrine of karma naturally raises the question of the nature and extent of free will and its relation to destiny. For, if what happens in this life is a consequence of actions performed in past lives, the question naturally arises whether anything can be done about it, apart from just trying to aim at a better next life. Different answers to this question have been offered within the tradition in its classical version. We shall first present the two extreme positions and then expound the more standard middle ground.

According to one extreme version, everything is predetermined. Even according to this view, however, we have freedom in the manner in which we react to these events, which then determines our future. M. Hiriyanna explains the doctrine of karma from this standpoint. After pointing out that the doctrine of karma 'is really more than retributive' because it also constitutes 'a discipline of natural consequences to educate man morally'[5], Hiriyanna adds:

This does not, however, mean that he can avoid the consequences of his past karma. His life, in this respect, is characterized by the strictest necessity; and he has to accept all the unpleasant experiences of life as willingly as he does the pleasant. They are preordained results from which he can never free himself. The *Mahabharata* says that the consequences of what a man does will seek him out later 'as surely as a calf does its mother in a herd of cows'. So far karma

4. *Sanātana-Dharma* (Adyar, Madras: The Theosophical Publishing House, 1966), p. 97.

5. M. Hiriyanna, *The Essentials of Indian Philosophy*, p. 49.

does imply necessity, but ... it implies freedom also, viz. in the matter of ethical advance.[6]

This point may be elaborated as follows: 'The implication seems to be [that] the *karma* determines the action but not the modes of action. Jyoti's *karma* may cause him to perform a specific act, but Jyoti determines whether he acts greedily, cruelly, selfishly, charitably, kindly, lovingly, etc.'[7]

The second extreme view, which represents the other end of the spectrum, is that everything is free will, in the sense that it was freely willed at the time the original action was committed. So what now appears as destiny is really disguised free will.[8]

By and large the tradition avoids these extremes and takes the more pragmatic view that our lives possess both a certain givenness and a certain openness. 'The cards in the game of life are given to us. We do not select them. They are traced to our past karma, but we can call as we please, lead what suit we will, and as we play, we gain or lose. And there is freedom.'[9]

A more formal expression to this view is given in the doctrine of the three kinds of karma.

Hindu thinkers distinguish three kinds of *karma: sañcita, prārabdha* and *āgāmi*. *Sañcita* is all the accumulated *karma* of the past. Part of it is seen in the character of the individual, his tendencies and aptitudes, inclinations and desires, etc. *Prārabdha* is that portion of the past *karma* which is responsible for the present body. *Āgāmi* is the coming *karma* which includes also the *karma* that is being gathered at present. An apt analogy is usually given to bring home to our minds the element of freedom that *karma* involves. Imagine a bowman, with a quiver of arrows, taking aim at a target. He has already sent a shaft; and another arrow he is about to shoot. The bundle of arrows in the quiver on his back is the *sañcita*; the arrow he has shot is *prārabdha*; and the one which he is about to send forth from his bow is *āgāmi*. Of these, he has perfect control over the *sañcita* and *āgāmi*; it is only the *prārabdha* that cannot but take effect. Man has the freedom to reform his character and alter his ways. Only the past which has begun to take effect he has to suffer.[10]

6. Ibid.

7. Troy Wilson Organ, *Hinduism: Its Historical Development* (Woodbury, New York: Barron's Educational Series, Inc., 1974), p. 188.

8. Satischandra Chatterjee and Dhirendramohan Datta, *An Introduction to Indian Philosophy* (Calcutta: University of Calcutta, 1950), p. 18.

9. S. Radhakrishnan, *The Hindu View of Life* (New York: Macmillan 1927), p. 54.

10. T.M.P. Mahadevan, *Outlines of Hinduism* (Bombay: Chetna Ltd, 1971), p. 60.

II

As in the case of the workings of saṁsāra, the workings of karma are also perhaps best illustrated with the help of a story:

A gentleman who lived with his wife and two sons got initiated by a monk of a high order. The elder son was given to evil ways while the younger was spiritually inclined and liked to spend his days in studying sacred scriptures. One day a learned man came to that village and it was arranged that he should give a religious discourse. All the people of the village went to hear the discourse. The elder brother, however, did not attend, though he was asked by his younger brother to avail himself of the opportunity to hear a good religious discourse. When the father returned after hearing the discourse, he found that his younger son had not returned. The elder son, however, came back and handed over a lump of gold to his father, saying that he had picked it up on his way while returning home. The father and his elder son went with the servants in search of the younger son. They found him lying unconscious under a banyan tree. He was brought home and when he regained consciousness said that while coming back from the religious discourse his foot had struck violently against the stump of a tree and he had fallen down unconscious.

The father found it strange that the son who never thought of God even once in a day had found a lump of gold whereas the boy who was deeply devoted to God had met with an accident while returning home. Next day when his Guru came he told him all that had happened and then spoke about the doubt that had entered into his mind. He said that it seemed to him useless to say his prayers and worship God if he was going to be rewarded in this fashion. The Guru sat silent for a while engaged in deep concentration and then said that the past Karma of the elder son was so good that he could have become a king but that his evil conduct in the present life had reduced the good luck to his finding a lump of gold on the previous day; while the younger boy had been fated to die at the time the accident had taken place, but through the grace of God he had survived after meeting with a trifling accident.[11]

III

How the blandishments of saṁsāra keep us trapped in the karmic cycle may also be illustrated by a story a Hindu representative of the Indian government heard while sojourning in Tibet. It pertains to a saintly Buddhist monk:

When he reached the point of death this monk said to the disciples who stood around him: 'Well, my friends and pupils, my time on earth is finished in this

11. Swami Sambuddhananda, *Vedanta Through Stories* (Bombay: Sri Ramakrishna Ashram, 1959), pp. 77–9.

form. But I am going to be born again, since I have a few sins left to expiate. I shall be born as a small pig from that sow of ours who is shortly to give birth to a litter. I shall be one of her piglets, and as soon as I am born please make sure to kill me, so that I may be released for another birth in which to travel further on the Path. Don't forget to kill me immediately.'

Having said this, he died. Three days later the sow produced her litter. The disciples were supposed to kill them all, since they could not know which was their reincarnated master. But one of the monks said: 'The little pigs are so nice. Let us keep them for a week and then kill them.' 'If we do that,' said another, 'we must truly kill them after a week. It was the order of the *guru*.'

A week later the disciples, one of them armed with a knife, gathered again at the sty. There they saw the piglets, lying peacefully in the mud and dirt. But when the executioner approached, one little pig looked up and said, in a voice which the disciples recognised, 'Don't kill me now, I like it!'[12]

Such are the temptations of saṁsāra. According to a Hindu account, God himself similarly got carried away in a porcine incarnation and had to be forcibly released from his saṁsāric captivity.

12. Apa Pant, *A Moment in Time* (London: Hodder & Stoughton, 1974), pp. 115–16.

CHAPTER XIII

Dharma

It is said that if one wishes to understand another religion or culture one should identify a word which is untranslatable in the language of that religion and culture. Such a word (or words) holds the key to unravelling the mysteries of that religion or culture. If this is so, then *dharma* could well be that word in the context of Hinduism. Klaus K. Klostermaier remarks:

> Translations can sometimes be quite revealing. If we try to find an Indian synonym for the term religion—admittedly difficult to define even within the Western tradition!—we have to choose from a variety of terms, none of which coincides precisely with our word. The most common and most general term is *dharma*, usually translated as 'religion'. Another important aspect of religion is expressed by the term *sādhana*, frequently rendered in English as 'realization'. In its sociological sense, *religion* may often have to be understood as *sampradāya*, mostly (and erroneously) translated as 'sect', which describes the great Hindu traditions like Vaiṣṇavism, Śaivism, and Śāktism and their subdivisions. The *ṣaddarśanas*, the 'six viewpoints' that have been accepted within Hindu tradition as orthodox (religious) systems, must also be included, as must the *trimārga* scheme, which organizes the entire range of religious affiliations into *karmamārga, bhaktimārga,* and *jñānamārga*, the path of works, the path of loving devotion, and the path of knowledge, respectively.[1]

1. Klaus K. Klostermaier, *A Survey of Hinduism* (Albany, NY: State University of New York Press, 1989), p. 46. The remarks of Louis Renou on the point are equally revealing. 'What is Hinduism? It is not a religion in quite the sense in which we use that word in the West; we cannot give a first definition of it in negative terms by isolating it from its non-religious background. On one side, it is inseparable from philosophy; on another, from communal and social life. Hindu society is governed by the framework of classes and castes and "stages of life", or *ashramas*; it is these social factors that determine the concept of duty, the moral imperative, which in

To grasp such a comprehensive term is difficult but history and philology provide some help. The root of the concept goes back to the Vedic word *ṛta* which 'etymologically stands for "course"' and 'originally meant "cosmic order", the maintenance of which [was] the purpose of the [Vedic] gods; and later also came to mean "right", as preserving the world not merely from physical disorder but also from moral chaos. The one idea is, in fact, implicit in the other; and there is order in the universe, because its control is in righteous hands'.[2]

The word ṛta becomes virtually obsolete in classical Hinduism, but not the idea, which re-emerged in the word dharma. G.C. Pande identifies the centrality of this concept for classical Hinduism thus:

> The notion of *dharma* embodies the tradition of the pursuit of moral values and constitutes one of the most distinct and essential aspects of Indian culture. The concept of *dharma* is not merely theoretical but intensely practical. Embodied in rules and institutions and illustrated by popular character-types from epic stories, Puranic myths and legends and folk-tales, the notion of *dharma* reaches every man, the illiterate peasant and housewife as much as the learned philosopher and minister. *Dharma* like *sadhana* is one of those golden threads which bind the elite and the common folk together and which are available at the level of every day life but reach up to the heavens.[3]

Although ṛta and dharma are etymologically distinct, they intermesh semantically, thereby imparting to the term dharma a uniquely Hindu value. This also enables dharma to be usefully compared with the Western concept of 'right', both in the sense of righteousness

---

itself is essentially religious. The important concept of *dharma*, meaning properly the "support" of creatures and objects, denotes law in the widest sense, the presiding order that runs through every Hindu normative discipline, but also and more particularly it denotes moral law and religious merit; *dharma* is the only translation for our word "religion", than which however it is in some ways narrower and in others wider. People are born into Hinduism rather than converted to it, since the Hindu mentality is a function of the general framework of Indian life. But, naturally, this is not to deny that at a very early stage the idea of *dharma* was spread by conquest or peaceful infiltration among peoples who have originally not possessed it; how else to explain the ascendancy it won over the greater part of the subcontinent?' (*The Nature of Hinduism* [trans. Patrick Evans] [New York: Walker Company, 1951] pp. 32–3).

2. M. Hiriyanna, *The Essentials of Indian Philosophy* (London: Allen & Unwin, 1949), p. 12.

3. G.C. Pande, *Dimensions of Ancient Indian Social History* (New Delhi: Books & Books, 1984), p. 126.

(as in: it is right to see one's sick mother) and entitlement (as in: one's right to vote). Thus

The conception of *dharma* in Indian thought is so all embracing that any attempt to discuss it in short compass is difficult. As is well known, the word is polysemic, meaning variously law, duty, norm of conduct, character of things, religious merit, morality, righteousness and much else. Nevertheless, the etymology of the word gives us a root meaning underlying the others. *Dharma* is that which maintains, gives cohesion and thus strength to any given thing, to reality, and ultimately to the three worlds of nature, society, and the Transcendent (*triloka*). *Dharma* is the order of the entire reality, that which both keeps the world together and maintains each thing according to its nature. It is thus the moral internalization of the cosmological notion of ṛta, the ordered course of things. The Vedic gods, for example, are portrayed as maintaining both the cosmic and the moral orders.

In the light of our preceding discussion, two features immediately stand out: (1) the two senses of right, namely righteousness and entitlement and brought together in the Indian conception in contrast to their separation in western thought, and (2) with this convergence, the primary category is not that of moral principle, but of a primordial order that is neither exclusively moral nor exclusively cosmological but both together at once.[4]

II

One typically Hindu way of understanding things is by classifying them. In the same spirit the word dharma can be classified in several ways. According to an ancient and comprehensive classification,

dharma is sixfold, viz. dharma of varṇas (injunctions based on varṇa alone such as 'a brāhmaṇa should never drink wine' or a brāhmaṇa should not be killed'), *āśramadharma* (such rules as 'begging' and 'carrying a staff' enjoined on a brahmacārī), *varṇāśrama-dharma* (rules of conduct enjoined on a man because he belongs to a particular class and is in a particular stage of life, such as 'a brāhmaṇa *brahmacārī* should carry a staff of *palāśa* tree'), *guṇadharma* (such as protection of subjects in the case of a crowned king), *naimittika dharma* (such as expiation on doing what is forbidden), *sādhāraṇa dharma* (what is common to all humanity viz., *ahiṁsā* and other virtues).[5]

4. Joseph Prabhu, 'Dharma as an Alternative to Human Rights', in S.K. Maity, Upendra Thakur and A.K. Narain, eds, *Studies in Orientology: Essays in Memory of Prof. A.L. Basham* (Agra: Y.K. Publishers, 1988), p. 178.

5. P.V. Kane, *History of Dharmaśāstra* (Poona: Bhandarkar Oriental Research Institute, 1974), vol. II, pt I, pp. 2–3.

Out of these, the varṇa and āśrama dharmas are discussed in detail later and in that context the concepts of *varṇāśrama-dharma* and *guṇa dharma* also receive attention. *Naimittika-dharma* belongs to the realm of ritualistic piety and purity, and though much discussed in law books and elsewhere, is only of limited interest. By contrast, the treatment of the concept of *sādhāraṇa-dharma* and dharma in general has been somewhat neglected in standard works on Hinduism. A modest effort will now be made to remedy this situation.

III

First, sādhāraṇa-dharma. It is best to contrast it with *viśeṣa-dharma* or specific duties. Those of varṇa and āśrama are often mentioned in this category, but concepts such as *rājadharma* (duties specific to a king), *strīdharma* (duties specific to a woman) and *yatidharma* (duties specific to ascetics) are also to be placed here. These correspond broadly to the concept of professional ethics, just as guṇadharma might resonate with situation ethics, as distinguished from ethics in general. All of these, however, on account of being specific to a time, place, person, etc. are called *viśeṣa*. As against these, *sāmānya* or sādhāraṇa dharma is universal by nature. These are usually listed as non-violence (*ahiṁsā*), truthfulness, non-stealing, purity, and restraint of the senses.[6]

The concept of sādhāraṇa or sāmānya-dharma is significant because it provides the counterpoise to *viśeṣa-dharma* and thus sets the stage for the unresolved issue of relative versus absolute or particular versus universal dharma, although it has been claimed that the 'Purāṇas have made a successful attempt at reconciling *sādhāraṇa dharma* with *svadharma*',[7] the latter being identified with one's varna dharma, on the basis of such an interpretation of the term which may be more rigid than precise.[8] The predicament is illustrated by the case of the soldier in general and, to a certain extent, of Arjuna in the *Bhagavadgītā* in particular: should a soldier perform

6. Ibid., vol. v, pt ii, p. 1637.

7. C.S. Venkateswaran, 'The Ethics of the Purāṇas', in Wendy Doniger O'Flaherty and J. Duncan M. Derrett, eds, *The Concept of Duty in South Asia* (New Delhi & Bombay: Vikas Publishing House, 1978), p. 95.

8. Joseph Prabhu, 'Dharma as an Alternative to Human rights', p. 178.

his specific duty of killing the enemy or observe the universal value of non-violence? One Hindu resolution of the dilemma allows the man of the world to resist aggression but does *not* allow the same right to a renunciant.

Its other significance stems from the fact that the sādhāraṇa-dharmas are virtually identical with the moral qualifications presupposed by almost every type of spiritual disciple or philosophical school as a precondition for liberation or *mokṣa*. The *Yogasūtras*, for instance, list truth, celibacy, non-violence, non-stealing and non-possession as constituting *yama*, the first rung on the eight-rung ladder of liberation. In other words, the overlap between the universal ethics to be practised in the world is virtually identical with the initial ethical requirements for pursuing the path to liberation. This overlap synchronizes the values of dharma and mokṣa and thus gives concrete expression to the integral vision of Hinduism. When one considers that the initial vows of Buddhism and Jainism also coincide with the yamas and overlap with the sādhāraṇa-dharmas, one comes closer to recognizing the ties which bind Hinduism to these religions and appreciating the unity underlying the various religions of Indian origin.[9]

IV

It is, however, easy to get so lost in the minutiae of dharma[10] as to not see the wood for the trees, and fall into the trap of having one's vision so obscured by details as to not see the larger picture, like looking at the highly decorated panels of a Hindu temple at the cost of overlooking its larger architectonics. Louis Renou in particular draws attention to this danger, when he warns that 'it would be a mistake to overlook the implicit presence of a general morality the lines of which emerge more or less clearly in the archaic values of ritual exactitude and purity."[11] He identifies the presence of this element in the concepts of ṛta and of ahiṁsā. In fact, 'according to Manu the practice of non-violence permits a man to escape the

9. See G.C. Pande, *Dimensions of Ancient Indian Social History*, p. 170, note 6.

10. For the related concept of *adharma*, see Ariel Glucklich, *The Sense of Adharma* (New York: Oxford University Press, 1993).

11. Louis Renou, *The Nature of Hinduism* (trans. Patrick Evans), p. 106.

cycle of *karman*',[12] another doctrine which amplifies a general morality. In fact, doing good to others becomes a heroic virtue, so much so that one of the 'heroes of Brahmanism is Prince Vipashcit, who, when he finds on going down into hell that his presence solaces the damned, offers to stay there'.[13] The *Mahābhārata* is replete with similar displays of virtue by Yudhiṣṭhira. Such a general morality suffuses even the secular tradition. It is attested to by the verses of Bhartṛhari, and the epics—the *Mahābhārata* and the *Rāmāyaṇa*—and even the Purāṇas. Regarding the latter, there is the popular saying that in the eighteen bulky tomes they consist of, their putative author Vyāsa has really made only two points: that virtue consists in bringing happiness to others and vice in acting in a contrary manner. 'It is by striking notes such as these that Indian poetry transcends religious divisions and endows the Indian sensibility with a broadly human resonance.'[14] It seems fitting to conclude the discussion of dharma as morality with the words of Renou:

> In short, a holy life without any religious exercises and without any definite religious attachment can produce the same result as devotional or mystical practice. We are told over and over again that what counts is not outward piety or the caste in which your destiny has caused you to be born, but conduct. Buddhism has no monopoly in urging this.[15]

Dharma and karma are two words which possess both rhyme and reason, for dharma without karma is lame and karma without dharma is blind.

12. Ibid., p. 106.
13. Ibid.
14. Ibid., pp. 106–7.
15. Ibid., p. 107.

CHAPTER XIV

Māyā

The first chapter of this book introduced the essentials of classical Hindu thought. These essentials were diagrammatically, perhaps even dramatically, some might say, summarized in a chart. This chart contained a line—sometimes notional and sometimes drawn—which separated the divine realm, as conceived in classical Hinduism, containing Brahman and the trimūrti and the devī, etc. from saṃsāra, karma, dharma, jīva, etc. How, one might now ask, does classical Hindu thought visualize the relationship between the two realms? This is a central issue of all religious philosophy, not just the Hindu. In classical Hindu thought the answer is given in one word: *māyā*. This term is the key to understanding the relationship between Brahman—whether saguṇa or nirguṇa—and the universe in which we live and breathe and have our existence.

In referring to the world as māyā, classical Hindu thought is suggesting that 'there is something tricky'[1] about the universe, whether it tricks us in terms of fact or value. Those who follow the path of knowledge towards the ultimate reality or prefer the absolutistic standpoint maintain that the 'trick lies in the way the world's materiality and multiplicity pass themselves off as being independently real—real apart from the stance from which we see them—whereas in reality it is undifferentiated Brahman throughout, even as a rope lying in the dust remains a rope while mistaken for a snake'.[2] It is

1. Huston Smith, *The World's Religions* (New York: Harper & Row, 1991), p. 71.
2. Ibid., p. 71.

the power of māyā which makes the rope appear as the snake. It should be borne in mind that it is not māyā which appears as the snake, it *makes* the rope appear as the snake. Even so it makes Brahman, the sole spiritual reality, appear as this universe characterized by multiplicity.

For those who follow the path of devotion or prefer the theistic standpoint, māyā is that quality of the world which distracts us from God: 'seductive in the attractiveness in which it presents the world, trapping us within it and leaving us with no desire to journey on'.[3] And thereby hangs a tale.

In fact, thereby hang several tales: tales within tales. One particular series of such tales is recounted here.

(1) Once the holy men gathered around the great sage Vyāsa and spoke to him thus: 'You understand the divine eternal order, therefore unveil to us the secret of Viṣṇu's *māyā*'. The sage replied: 'Who can apprehend the *māyā* of the highest God, except himself. Viṣṇu's *māyā* casts its spell over all of us. It is our collective dream. The best I can do is to narrate a story about how it casts its spell.'

(2) The story which Vyāsa narrated to the holy seers runs as follows. In ancient times there lived a prince, Kāmadamana by name, who spent his time in austerities. When pressed by his father to settle down and lead a married life he displayed a certain reluctance. When asked for the cause of his reluctance he confided that he was aware of his previous lives and that over and again he had 'fallen victim to the delusion of existence—and ever through the taking of a wife'. To make his point he narrated a story to his father.

(3) The prince Kāmadamana then narrated the account of his life when he was an ascetic called Sutapas in a previous existence. During this life God Viṣṇu, pleased by his austerities, appeared before him and said: 'I grant you a boon. What would you like?'

The ascetic Sutapas replied: 'If you are pleased with me, let me comprehend your *māyā*.' Viṣṇu, however, declared that no one can comprehend his *māyā*. Indeed, on a previous occasion, the holy seer Nārada has expressed the same wish and when he had persisted in

3. Ibid.

his request Viṣṇu had said to him: 'Plunge into the yonder water and you shall *experience* the secret of my *māyā*'. Nārada did so.

(4) The story of what subsequently happened runs as follows. Nārada underwent a metamorphosis as he emerged from the pool. He emerged in the form of a princess, the daughter of the king of Banaras. In due course she was married to the son of the neighbouring king, who then succeeded to the throne. They led a happy life with many sons and grandsons. In due course, however, her husband and her father fell out. In the ensuing battle, everyone was slain. She decided to mount the gigantic funeral pyre of those who had fallen in battle. 'With her own hands she laid torch to the pyre and mounting cried aloud "My son, my son!" and when the flames were roaring, threw herself into the conflagration. The blaze immediately became cool and clear; the pyre became a pond.' And amidst the waters the princess found herself—but as the holy man Nārada. And God Viṣṇu led him out of the pool by the hand and asked: 'Who is this son whose death you are bewailing?'[4]

The account in which Viṣṇu reveals his māyā ends on a similar note. It again involves the 'model devotee' Nārada.

Through prolonged austerities and devotional practices, he had won the grace of Vishnu. The god had appeared before the saint in his hermitage and granted him the fulfilment of a wish. 'Show me the magic power of your *Māyā*,' Nārada had prayed, and the god had replied, 'I will. Come with me,' but again with that ambiguous smile on his beautifully curved lips.

From the pleasant shadow of the sheltering hermit grove, Vishnu conducted Nārada across a bare stretch of land which blazed like metal under the merciless glow of a scorching sun. The two were soon very thirsty. At some distance, in the glaring light, they perceived the thatched roofs of a tiny hamlet. Vishnu asked: 'Will you go over there and fetch me some water?'

'Certainly, O Lord,' the saint replied, and he made off to the distant group of huts. The god relaxed under the shadow of a cliff to await his return.[5]

We are next told how Nārada leaves the company of Viṣṇu and approaches the hamlet to fetch a pitcher of water. As soon as he knocks at the first door, however, he forgets the purpose of his

4. Adapted from Heinrich Zimmer, *Myths and Symbols in Indian Art and Civilization* (ed. Joseph Campbell) (New York: Harper & Row, 1946), pp. 28–31.

5. Ibid., p. 32.

visit. He enjoys the hospitality of the family and falls in love with their daughter. He marries her and has three children. After the death of the father-in-law, he becomes the *paterfamilias* and leads a pleasant existence as a prosperous householder. Twelve years pass. In the twelfth year the village is hit by a flash flood; his wife and children are carried away by the strong current as he tries to save them. Finally, he is thrown on a cliff by a billow.

> Unconscious, Nārada was stranded eventually on a little cliff. When he returned to consciousness, he opened his eyes upon a vast sheet of muddy water. He could only weep.
>
> 'Child!' He heard a familiar voice, which nearly stopped his heart. 'Where is the water you went to fetch for me? I have been waiting more than half an hour.'
>
> Nārada turned around. Instead of water he beheld the brilliant desert in the midday sun. He found the god standing at his shoulder. The cruel curves of the fascinating mouth, still smiling, parted with the gentle question: 'Do you comprehend now the secret of my *māyā*?'[6]

It may be interesting to compare the predicament of Nārada with that of Job. As in the case of Job, the model devotee is put through a series of trials which result in his coming face to face with the glory of God. It is true that Nārada is on more friendly terms with Viṣṇu than Job is with Yahweh and that the Hindu term māyā conveys a sense of not merely power but magical creative power, whereas Yahweh's account of his own creative power is elemental rather than magical. But once the orientations of the tradition are taken into account and subtracted, the structural similarity between the two stories is apparent. In both cases, a series of trials and tribulations (in one case contrived by Satan, in the other by God) provide a deeper experiential understanding of the irreducible mysterious element in the relationship between God and humans.[7]

6. Ibid., pp. 33–4.

7. See Samuel Laeuchli and Arvind Sharma, 'The Problem of Job: An Eastern Response', *Arc* 22: 83–90 (1994).

CHAPTER XV

Mokṣa

Mokṣa is the quintessential concept of Hinduism. In terms of the diagram in the introductory chapter it means that the jīva has crossed over the line from the mundane to the divine by pursuing one of the yogas successfully. The form of mokṣa may be a matter of difference of opinion but all are agreed on its effect: the cessation of rebirths, of saṁsāra.

I

This goal of mokṣa is regarded as actually attainable while one is on this earth (*jīvanmukti*), or eschatologically (*karmamukti*). There are different concepts of mokṣa in different schools, as well as different concepts within the same school; what is to be borne in mind at this juncture is that it is considered actually attainable. M. Hiriyanna has made this point forcefully:

A modern thinker writes, 'The ultimate values are not of the realm of fact, but are merely ideals which should regulate our conduct.' The view of Indian philosophers, however, is that it can undoubtedly be realized—that 'ought' means 'can.' All of them, including the heterodox, believe that the evil of *saṁsāra* carries with it the seeds of its destruction, and that it is sooner or later bound to be superseded by the good. In other words, none of the Indian systems is finally pessimistic; and the common view that they are mostly 'gospels of woe' is entirely wrong. We have more than one interesting indication in the Sanskrit language of this faith of the Indians in the ultimate goodness and rationality of the world. The Sanskrit word *sat* as noticed long ago by Max Müller means not only 'real' but also 'good.' Similarly the word *bhavya* we may add, means not only 'what will happen in the future' but also 'what is auspicious,' implying that the best is yet to be. Corresponding to this belief on the practical side, there is the belief on the theoretical side that ignorance or error will also be superseded in the end by truth for which, as one old Buddhistic verse puts it, 'the human mind has a natural partiality.' If either evil or error were final the world would be irrational.[1]

II

The question of mokṣa can be pursued in various ways. For instance, it might be asked: How does one know that someone has become liberated? As mentioned earlier, there are three main ways in which liberation is usually said to be achieved: through the paths of knowledge, devotion and action. The question then reduces itself to the following: Are there any criteria by which success in the traversing of these paths may be identified?

There is some evidence to indicate that such attempts were indeed made. For instance, it is said of the follower of jñāna-yoga that one may judge whether the aspirant has perfected the path from the total absence of fear in the person. The underlying logic seems to be that jñāna emphasizes the oneness or the unity of all being and fear can only arise from someone or something other than oneself. But this is not possible for the *jñānī*, who has become identical with all.

Perfection on the path of devotion is said to be indicated by the ability to remember God's name when one is in the throes of death. The implication here seems to be that in the biological crisis that we call death it is only our deepest emotions that can grip us. Hence, unless God has penetrated to the very core of our being his name will not come to our lips. What we are most attached to involuntarily grabs our psyche at the time of our death, so if we can remember God then it means that we are truly devoted to him. Hindu devotional literature is full of regrets about or by people whom the name of God eluded at the last moment.

Total equanimity is said to characterize one who has perfected the path of action. That is to say, such a person is never overcome by dejection. Dejection results from unfulfilled desire. If, however, one has abandoned all desire for the fruit of action, then how can

1. M. Hiriyanna, *The Essentials of Indian Philosophy* (London: George Allen & Unwin, 1949), p. 51.

its non-attainment depress one; or success, for that matter, make one feel elated?

III

These empirical tests may or may not be philosophically significant but they do reflect traditional wisdom. However, let us suppose one has pursued the path successfully. What then?

The question can be answered with different degrees of philosophical sophistication—ranging from a brief statement that this indicates the cessation of rebirth, to an elaboration of the concept of salvation in various schools of Hindu thought. Let us answer it in terms of our own referents, the two modes of Brahman—nirguṇa and saguṇa. Union with Brahman is achieved in both cases—but in one case it is ontological, in the other, psychological.

Different kinds of metaphors have been used to illustrate the point. A common one is that of merger, as in the *Muṇḍaka Upaniṣad* (III.1.8): 'Just as the flowing rivers disappear in the ocean casting off name and shape, even so the knower, freed from name and form, attains to the divine person, higher than the higher.'[2]

The merger theme, however, poses problems for the purists of both the nirguṇa and saguṇa schools. For those of the nirguṇa school, if one thing merges into the other then *both* are usually regarded as real, and this contradicts the view of Brahman as the *sole* spiritual reality. Hence, many favour metaphors of recognition, as when an adopted person is told his or her real identity which he or she has always possessed. Those who favour the saguṇa view of Brahman wish to retain a sense of distinction to relish realization, a sentiment expressed by a renowned devotional mystic thus: 'I don't want to be sugar, I want to taste sugar!' The argument can get convoluted, as when a gnostic mystic responds: 'Is Brahman insentient like sugar?'

The higher reaches of mokṣa must, like the reality itself, elude us, but it seems reasonable to say that those who favour the absolutistic standpoint tend to describe mokṣa in terms of union and those who favour the theistic in terms of communion.

2. S. Radhakrishnan, ed., *The Principal Upaniṣads* (London: George Allen & Unwin, 1953), p. 691.

IV

Mokṣa may minimally be defined as freedom from rebirth. The word mokṣa means freedom or emancipation. This naturally raises the question: Freedom from what? The answer then usually given is: Freedom from saṁsāra. Perhaps this answer needs to be refined. The Hindu tradition entertains the possibility that a 'liberated being' may still voluntarily choose to stay in the world, in saṁsāra, either for the sake of others or even for the sake of continuing to experience the bliss of devotion. However, just as space = zero gravity; mokṣa = zero karma or zero saṁsāra; or if you prefer, zero tolerance of *involuntary* involvement in saṁsāra. For all practical purposes though mokṣa may be equated with the cessation of rebirth.

Beyond this point of agreement, the explanations of mokṣa branch out in different directions. One basic distinction is the attainment of mokṣa without any differences of degree or kind and an attainment which involves such differences and degrees. The former corresponds to the realization of the nirguṇa aspect of Brahman, the latter to the saguṇa. This difference needs to be understood clearly as sometimes the same word is used to refer to it. Klaus K. Klostermaier notes in the context of salvation in Hinduism that 'most books describe various types of mokṣa; very common are the following five: *sālokya, sārṣṭi, sāmīpya, sārūpya, sāyujya*'.[3]

The word *sāyujya* means union, but in the context of the absolutism it implies ontological union (which itself is a trifle misleading as the separation of jīvātman and Brahman is viewed as merely empirical), while in the theistic case it implies psychological union. The annihilation or absorption of darkness in light illustrates sāyujya of the first kind, while the candle light overwhelmed by sunlight to the point of becoming invisible in the course of the soul's union with God illustrates sāyujya of the second kind.

If one now turns from union with God or Īśvara as such to his various manifestations, especially of Brahma, Viṣṇu and Śiva, then the worshippers of each manifestation who attain salvation repair to the respective realm of their chosen god, namely Brahmaloka,

3. Klaus K. Klostermaier, *Mythologies and Philosophies of Salvation in the Theistic Traditions of India* (Published for the Canadian Corporation for Studies in Religion by Wilfred Laurier Press, 1984), p. 84.

Viṣṇuloka or Vaikuṇṭha and Śivaloka, and lead a perpetual post-mortem existence there.

This difference in the kind of salvation between absolutistic and theistic Hinduism must now be complexified on the theistic side by indicating the differences in the degrees of salvation, as represented by the different terms such as sālokya. The four (or five if sārṣṭi is included) are sometimes regarded as states of mokṣa and sometimes as *stages*, which complicates matters further. Thus P.V.Kane notes that: 'Even in the Vedānta the conception about Mokṣa on the part of different ācāryas differs. Some declared that there were four stages to Mukti—viz, *Sālokya* (place in Lord's world), *Sāmīpya* (proximity), *Sārūpya* (attaining same form as god) and *Sāyujya* (absorption).'[4] In this scheme, not only is the place of sārṣṭi variable, its meaning also varies. It has been taken to mean 'same happiness'[5] as God or same powers as God. Further complication is introduced by the claim in some texts that sāyujya is obtainable through jñāna alone, while the others are gained through karma. Perhaps jñāna here includes bhakti, the latter being capable of being described as a 'mental mode'.[6]

V

Whether mokṣa can be achieved in this life or only in a post-mortem state is also a debated point within the tradition. Among the six orthodox schools of Hindu philosophy, the generally recognized positions are as follows: mokṣa is a post-mortem state in the Nyāya and Vaiśeṣika schools. It can be achieved in this life according to Sāṅkhya and Yoga, but not according to Mīmāṁsā. In the case of Vedānta, the situation varies with the sub-schools. If one takes only the three major schools into account it is possible while living in Advaita but is essentially considered a post-mortem state in Viśiṣṭādvaita[6] and Dvaita Vedānta.[7]

4. P.V. Kane, *History of Dharmaśāstra* (Poona: Bhandarkar Oriental Research Institute, 1962), vol. v, pt ii, p. 1631.

5. Ibid.

6. M. Hiriyanna, *Outlines of Indian Philosophy* (London: George Allen & Unwin, 1932) pp. 265, 297, 333–4.

7. M. Hiriyanna, *The Essentials of Indian Philosophy*, p. 199. But see S. Radhakrishnan, ed., *The Brahma Sūtra: The Philosophy of Spiritual Life* (London: George Allen & Unwin, 1960), p. 66.

The state of the ātman in mokṣa, as also the nature of mokṣa is also a moot point among these schools. In Nyāya and Vaiśeṣika there is no joy, only absence of pain;[8] in Sāṅkhya and Yoga 'the self or spirit is left alone to enjoy its *kaivalya*'[9] or '(aloofness) from *prakṛti* (matter). It becomes completely free from all forms of pain. Although there is no positive pleasure in the state of release ... there is undisturbable peace for the spirit which has regained its nature of pure consciousness'.[10] In other schools the attainment of bliss is also associated with mokṣa.

8. T.M.P. Mahadevan, *Outlines of Hinduism* (Bombay: Chetana Ltd, 1971), p. 108.
9. Ibid., p. 129.
10. Ibid., p. 124.

CHAPTER XVI

Jñāna-yoga

One of the ways of overcoming the divide in the chart, or in life itself, between the transcendental and the empirical is through the path of knowledge or *jñāna-yoga.*

Traditionally, on the basis of a famous Upaniṣadic text, it is said to consist of three stages: *śravaṇa* or audition, *manana* or reflection, and *nididhyāsana* or *dhyāna*,that is, meditation.

I

Śravaṇa consists of hearing the doctrines about the ultimate nature of reality. Normally it is heard from a guru or read from a scripture; although tradition emphasizes the need for a competent guru to properly 'hear'—that is, understand the text.

To arrive at a proper understanding of the text, the pupil needs to fulfil certain conditions and the master needs to meet certain conditions. In the case of the disciple or pupil the qualities are moral and intellectual in nature; in the case of the guru the qualities most often emphasized are threefold: (1) the guru should be well versed in the Vedas; (2) the guru should have realized the ultimate reality himself or herself and (3) the guru should possess no ego.

Once these conditions have been met and the teachings of the Vedas imparted, the student is ready for the next stage.

II

The significance of the stage of manana or reflection may be explained as follows:

[M]erely to accept the teaching, although it may be quite true, would constitute blind faith; and it does not become philosophy until rational support is sought out. The beliefs of others are, no doubt, often of immense use to us, for we cannot know everything for ourselves. Man's advance is mostly due to his capacity for receiving and profiting by the thought and experience of others. But the matter is altogether different in the case of a subject like philosophy, whose relation to life is so peculiarly intimate. Others may teach us here the truths which they have reached as well as the method by which they did so; but, unless we successfully repeat that process and rediscover those truths for ourselves, we cannot get the depth of conviction which alone can be called 'philosophy' in the complete sense of the term. If there are facts which are beyond the reach of reason and cannot therefore be absolutely demonstrated, philosophy should at least point to the *likelihood* of their being true. This is recognized in the Upanishads, for they prescribe what is called *manana* or 'reflection' in addition to study (*śravaṇa*) in the sense of learning the truth from a preceptor. It means that philosophy, though it may begin as faith, does not end there.[1]

III

However, mere intellectual conviction is not enough and the 'training prescribed in the Upaniṣads does not stop here'.[2] It goes further:

It includes also what is called *dhyāna* or 'meditation,' which means constant dwelling upon the truth of which one has become intellectually convinced. This meditation is otherwise known as *yoga*, ... A number of sections in the Upanishads are taken up with describing modes of exercise, *upāsanās* as they are called, which prepare the disciple for contemplating the ultimate truth, by accustoming him to draw away his mind from all disturbing thoughts and fix it on one object only. The aim of the final contemplation is to enable him to grasp the unity of existence directly—as directly as he has grasped its diversity. Thus, if reflection (*manana*) is for getting intellectual conviction, meditation (*dhyāna*) is for gaining direct experience. Without the acquisition of such immediate or intuitive experience, philosophy, even if it represents a logical certainty, will be of purely academic interest. Such theoretical knowledge may be a mental accomplishment; but, being mediate, it cannot dispel the immediate conviction in the ultimacy of diversity and will not therefore become a permanent influence on life. The Upanishads base this part of their teaching on a fact of experience, viz. that a mediate knowledge of truth cannot overcome an immediate illusion—that seeing alone is believing.[3]

1. M. Hiriyanna, *The Essentials of Indian Philosophy* (London: George Allen & Unwin, 1949), p. 26.
2. Ibid., p. 26.
3. Ibid., pp. 26–7.

IV

There is a difference of opinion among those who follow the path of knowledge on the relative roles of these three steps. According to one school, the first step, śravaṇa, may suffice to bring about realization. Just as 'If a man standing in a row of people is told that he is the tenth, as soon as he hears it, he immediately knows himself to be the tenth in the row'.[4] In this case no reflection and subsequent meditation is necessary for realization. Others hold that mere audition may not suffice. The knowledge communicated by the teacher may not be 'fully convincing, especially as it is so much at variance with the verdict of common experience (*asam-bhāvanā*)'[5] and even if intellectual conviction is present, 'old habits of thought (*viparīta-sambhāvanā*) incompatible with it may now and again assert themselves'[6] so that meditation may also be required as the next step.

V

Paradoxically, the path of knowledge culminates in the realization of what one already and always was. One no doubt realizes one's identity with ātman and its identity with Brahman but, according to jñāna-yoga, such is always the case, the change brought about by the practice of this path is 'not in the realm of being but in that of thought',[7] for in jñāna-yoga 'religion is not an *ought-ness* but an *is-ness*'.[8] Thus it is explained that:

As in the other doctrines, the achievement of the goal here also means bringing about a change; only the change is, in the present doctrine, conceived to be, not in the realm of being but in that of thought. That is to say, man has to alter totally his standpoint towards himself and the world in order to become free. Final freedom does not therefore mean any actual change in the nature of the self. To give a familiar illustration: In a lunar eclipse, the moon is actually obscured by the shadow of the earth; and it remains eclipsed until this obscuration is removed by a change in the relative position of the heavenly bodies

4. K. Satchidananda Murty, *Revelation and Reason in Advaita Vedānta* (New York: Columbia University Press, 1959), p. 108.

5. M. Hiriyanna, *The Essentials of Indian Philosophy*, p. 172.

6. Ibid.

7. Ibid. p. 169.

8. T.M.P. Mahadevan, *Outlines of Hinduism* (Bombay: Chetana Ltd, 1971), pp. 94–5.

> concerned, and the sun's light again fully falls on it. Here the change is real. In a solar eclipse on the other hand, nothing at all happens to the luminary; and it continues to be, during the eclipse, as it was before. It is only the position of the observer with reference to the sun and the moon that gives rise to the wrong notion of the eclipse. When there is an appropriate shifting of that position, the eclipse perforce ceases to appear. Similarly in the present case also, the identity of the self with Brahman is not to be newly attained; it is already there and has only to be realized in one's own experience. This does not mean that there is no need, ... for undergoing any practical discipline to realize it ... [9]

Were that the case, the conclusion would have sufficed and the rest of the book been unnecessary!

VI

The precise role of meditation in jñāna-yōga is a subject of controversy,[10] as also that of yoga and the transic states associated with it, but the place assigned to the intuitive grasp of ultimate reality cannot be gainsaid.

9. M. Hiriyanna, *The Essentials of Indian Philosophy*, pp. 169–70.

10. See Jonathan Bader, *Meditation in Śaṅkara's Vedānta* (New Delhi: Aditya Prakasan, 1990). Also see Anantanand Rambachan, *Accomplishing the Accomplished: The Vedas as a Source of Valid Knowledge in Śaṅkara* (Honolulu: University of Hawaii Press, 1991).

CHAPTER XVII

Bhakti-yoga

Jñāna-yoga is directed towards the realization of nirguṇa Brahman wherein the sole spiritual reality of Brahman leaves no room for any kind of distinction, even between master–disciple, means–end, brahman–ātman, etc. *Bhakti-yoga* is directed towards the realization of saguṇa Brahman, and this kind of yoga functions within the framework of a somewhat different set of presuppositions.

A special mark of monotheistic belief, whether Śaivism or Vaiṣṇavism, is the distinction it makes between God, the individual soul, and the world of which he is the author. The soul is usually conceived as eternal, but as entirely dependent upon God; and it therefore becomes the first duty of man to make himself a conscious and willing instrument in the fulfilment of his purpose. What the conception of the goal of life according to early Indian theism is cannot be definitely stated, for it is presented in diverse forms. Generally speaking, it may be taken as reaching the presence of God or becoming godlike. The predominant means of achieving this end is, besides good conduct (*caryā*), loving devotion (*bhakti*) to God, such as will win his grace (*prasāda*)—a means whose potency, as the reader will recall, is recognized even in the oldest portions of the Veda.[1]

How these sets of presuppositions function is perhaps best explained with the help of the *Śvetāśvatara Upaniṣad*, in which 'a new metaphysical system and a new doctrine of salvation are developed' around a 'theistic focus'[2] by contrast with the 'absolutistic focus' of

1. M. Hiriyanna, *The Essentials of Indian Philosophy* (London: George Allen & Unwin, 1949), p. 36.

2. Thomas J. Hopkins, *The Hindu Religious Tradition* (Belmont, California: Dickenson Publishing Co., Inc., 1971), p. 70.

the early Upaniṣads, more in line with jñāna-yoga. To begin with, there is in the *Śvetāśvatara* not just one eternal reality of Brahman as in the early Upaniṣads, but three eternal realities. The *Śvetāśvatara* speaks of:

three 'unborn ones': the Lord, knowing and all-powerful; the individual *ātman*, unknowing and powerless; and Nature, Prakṛiti, made up of primary matter. In terms of relationships, this triad can be described as the Mover or Impeller (the Lord), the enjoyer (the individual self), and the object of enjoyment (Nature, or primary matter). Brahman, the infinite Self, encompasses these three aspects but is itself inactive.[3]

In this framework, salvation is achieved in a manner different from when there was only one eternal reality.

Salvation for the individual self occurs by a change in the relationships within the triad. The self in his true nature is immortal and unchanging, but through ignorance he is attached to changeable matter. Not knowing the Lord, the self has become bound to Nature as an enjoyer—like a bird sitting in a tree eating its sweet fruit, like a male delighting in an ever-productive female (Prakṛiti). To become free, he must break his bondage; he must give up the fruit, leave the female with whom he has had enjoyment. This can happen only if he comes to know the Lord, the ruler of both the self and changeable Nature, all-powerful but uninvolved and content:

> The Lord (*Īśa*) supports all this which has been joined together—the changeable [Nature] and the unchangeable [the self], the manifest and the unmanifest; but the self, not being the Lord [or without the Lord] is bound because he is an enjoyer. Knowing God, he is freed from all fetters. (*Śvetāśvatara* I.8)[4]

The concept of dhyāna acquires a different meaning in the context of bhakti-yoga:

Knowledge of the Lord comes through meditation (*dhyāna*). Here the *Śvetāśvatara* makes a significant shift in the Upanishadic concept of knowledge. Saving knowledge is not knowledge of the impersonal Brahman but of the personal Lord, and it is gained by coming to know Him as resident within one's self. This is explained by means of an analogy: the form (*mūrti*) of fire is present in wood, even though it is not seen; it becomes visible when the friction of the drill used to make fire brings it forth. So meditation on the sound syllable *om*, the seed mantra of the Lord, brings forth the vision of the Lord hidden in the self:

By practicing the friction of meditation, making one's own body the

3. Ibid.
4. Ibid., p. 70.

> lower friction-stick and the syllable *om* the upper friction-stick, one may see God who is, as it were, hidden [within the body]. (*Śvetāśvatara* I.14).[5]

The *Śvetāśvatara Upaniṣad* is a Śaiva Upaniṣad and it was noted earlier how in some forms of Śaivism a graded approach to God through different kinds of devotional attitudes is developed. Much of what has been said here applies to both Śaiva and Vaiṣṇava theism, except that in Vaiṣṇava theism the tendency to rank the various devotional attitudes in a fixed manner is less marked. Herein, many different attitudes to God called *bhāvas* are recognized and six are emphasized, namely *dāsya*, *sakhya*, *vātsalya*, *śānta*, *kānta* and *madhura* :

> *Dāsya-bhāva* is the attitude of a servant to his master. Hanumān is the classical example of an ideal servant of God. This type of relationship marks the beginning of love. At a later stage *bhakti* gets deepened and is comparable to the love and regard that a man has for his friend. This is *sakhya-bhāva*. The relationship between Kucela and Kṛṣṇa was of this type. Arjuna too for the most part moved with Kṛṣṇa as a friend. Still higher and more intimate is *vātsalya-bhāva*, the love of the parent to the child. Kausalyā had the Lord Himself as her child in the form of Rāma. The love of Yaśodā to Kṛṣṇa was of the nature of *vātsalya*. *Śānta-bhāva* is the converse of *vātsalya*; it is the feeling of a child to its parent. Dhruva and Prahlāda are the classical examples. They were the children of God in every sense of the term. *Kānta-bhāva* is the love of the wife to the husband. The relationship between Sītā and Rāma, and between Rukmiṇī and Kṛṣṇa was of this kind. This is a closer kinship than those we have considered so far. But the closest of all is *madhura-bhāva*, the romantic love of the lover and the beloved, as in the case of Rādhā and Kṛṣṇa.[6]

Human emotions are paradigmatic for these devotional attitudes and the scope and variety of bhāvas enable one to realize the comprehensive nature of the path of devotion, especially when one considers the number of deities one can choose from among those of Hinduism—and even those outside it. But crucial to and underlying all attitudes to God is the fundamental one of surrender to him, which is technically called *prapatti* and represents the culmination of bhakti. Such surrender is said to be of two kinds. In one a devotee clings to the Lord as the young of a monkey does to its mother. This is known as 'monkey-logic'. In the other and the more extreme form one leaves everything to the Lord, just as kittens do nothing and move entirely at the initiative of the mother-cat. This is called

5. Ibid., p. 71.
6. T.M.P. Mahadevan, *Outlines of Hinduism* (Bombay: Chetana Ltd, 1971), p. 91.

'cat-logic'. These two positions have occasionally been compared with the Pelagian and the Augustinian positions on the issue of grace.

In any case, one surrenders one's will to God and acts in accordance with His Will. Such a devotional frame of mind finds expression in the following narrative:

There was a man who was intensely devoted to Sri Rama and he believed that nothing could happen in the world without His Will and that His will was the ultimate cause for every action of his and every step that he took. Once he was passing through a forest when he found dacoits returning with booty after committing a dacoity. Seeing him they told him to carry their booty and placed a heavy load upon his head. He went with them but a party of policemen came and when the dacoits saw them coming, they ran away in different directions leaving him behind with the booty on his head. The police arrested him and brought him to the police station and after a trial he was sent to jail. When he was released after his term of imprisonment he came home in his village. The people of the village asked why he had been absent for such a long period. He said, 'Everything has happened by Rama's Will. By Rama's Will I passed by a lonely road in a forest and by Rama's Will I was seized by a band of dacoits and asked to carry their booty. By Rama's Will the police came and the dacoits ran away, leaving me behind. By Rama's Will I was arrested, tried, and sentenced and by Rama's Will, having served my term, I have been released and have come home."[7]

7. Swami Sambuddhananda, *Vedanta Through Stories* (Bombay: Sri Ramakrishna Ashram, 1959), pp. 192–3.

CHAPTER XVIII

Karma-yoga

Just as the ultimate reality can be reached through the paths of knowledge and devotion, so can it be reached through the path of action. This path consists in performing the duties of one's station in life with a spirit of detachment, that is, without hankering after the fruits of those actions. The exposition of this path is said to be one of the main contributions of the *Bhagavadgītā* to Hindu spirituality, although it is not indifferent to the paths of knowledge and devotion. Its basic teaching on this point may be summarized as follows:

> The technique of detachment taught by the Blessed Kṛṣṇa through the *Gītā* is a sort of 'middle path'. On the one hand his devotee is to avoid the extreme of clinging to the sphere of action and its fruits (the selfish pursuit of life for personal aims, out of acquisitiveness and possessiveness), while on the other hand the negative extreme of barren abstinence from every kind and phase of action is to be shunned with equal care. The first mistake is that of the normal behavior of the naïve worldly being, prone to act and eager for the results. This only leads to a continuation of the hell of the round of rebirths—our usual headlong and unhelpful participation in the unavoidable sufferings that go with being an ego. Whereas the opposite mistake is that of neurotic abstention; the mistake of the absolute ascetics—such men as the monks of the Jainas and Ājīvikas—who indulge in the vain hope that one may rid oneself of karmic influxes simply by mortifying the flesh, stopping all mental and emotional processes, and starving to death the bodily frame. Against these the *Bhagavad Gītā* brings a more modern, more spiritual, more psychological point of view. Act: for actually you act no matter which way you turn—but achieve detachment from the fruits. Dissolve thus the self-concern of your ego, and with that you will discover the Self. The Self is unconcerned with either the individuality within (*jīva, puruṣa*) or the world without (*a-jīva, prakṛti*).[1]

1. Heinrich Zimmer, *Philosophies of India* (ed. Joseph Campbell) (Princeton, NJ: Princeton University Press, 1951), pp. 403–4.

I

The path of action has also been brought in relation to the paths of knowledge and devotion in the *Bhagavadgītā*. From the point of view of the path of knowledge, associated with the absolutistic standpoint of viewing the ultimate reality, this path leads to 'subjective purification. This subjective purification ... is only the proximate end of duty, for ... it is meant to subserve, through *jñāna*, the higher and final aim of liberation.' This position is based on

> the absolutistic view ... from the standpoint of theism ... one should perform one's duties for the fulfilment of God's purpose, or to state the same in other words, for the forwarding of universal life. As in the previous view, here also the duties that a person has to perform are those of his station in life; but he should do them subordinating his will completely and wholeheartedly to the divine will. This is dedicating all work to the Lord ... and is known as *bhakti-yoga* or 'the way of devotion'.[2]

II

It has already been indicated that the duties of one's station in life are determined by the twin doctrines of varṇa and āśrama, or class and stage of life. These two doctrines are discussed in detail in separate chapters. The essence of karma-yoga is deontological—the performance of duty for duty's sake. What is one's duty? This is determined by reference to the concepts of varṇa and āśrama.

The *Bhagavadgītā* draws attention to the element of varṇa or class in determining one's duty. Arjuna is urged to act as a warrior and fight even though he is reluctant to do so, because he is a warrior and it is his duty to fight as one. The key word which occurs in this context is *sva-dharma*. We noted earlier that karma-yoga emphasizes detachment from the fruits of action; giving up or abandoning not action but the fruits of action. Indeed, this insight may amount to a major contribution to world thought. Louis Renou, for instance, remarks on this 'manner of acting which must be respected—even in the political sphere—*regardless of the attitude of others*' and adds: 'In this perhaps is to be found the most spectacular contribution which India has made to the modern world and the most worthy reply to

2. M. Hiriyanna, *The Essentials of Indian Philosophy* (London: George Allen & Unwin, 1949), p. 56.

Marxism and materialism'.[3] Be that as it may, an exposition of the concept may be cited here on account of its lucid eloquence:

If the idea of duty is thus separated from that of its consequences, it may appear that there will be no means of determining its content in any particular context in life, and that therefore the Gītā teaching, while it may tell us *how* to act, fails altogether to guide us as to *what* deeds we should do. But really there is no such lack of guidance in the teaching for, according to it, the duties which a person has to undertake are determined by the place he occupies in society. This is another important principle enunciated in the Gītā, viz. that one's own duty (*sva-dharma*), be it ever so low, is superior to another's—a principle whose knowledge has filtered down even to the lowest ranks of our society as indicated, for instance, by the words which Kālidāsa puts into the mouth of the fisherman in the Śākuntalam. The significance of this principle is to elevate the moral quality of actions above their content. What really matters is the motive inspiring their doing—how actions are done and not what they are. 'God cares', someone has stated, 'more for the adverb than for the verb'. Thus the work in which Arjuna engages himself as a result of Śri Krishna's teaching is stupendous in its magnitude, being nothing less than setting right the world which is running off the rails. The actions, which ordinary people like ourselves have to perform, bear no comparison to it. While the one, for instance, would in a historical estimate count for a great deal, the other would be nowhere. Yet in point of their moral worth, the two do not differ in the least. Such a detached carrying out of one's duties, whatever they may be, is called *karma-yoga*.[4]

III

Although the *Bhagavadgītā* focuses on the varṇa aspect of one's station in life, the *Mahābhārata*, of which it is a part, elaborates the āśrama aspect of it as well, as for instance in the account which follows. The *Bhagavadgītā* refers in its opening lines to the battle of Kurukṣetra and to the Pāṇḍavas. It is on the eve of this battle that the Gītā was 'revealed' by Kṛṣṇa to Arjuna, one of the five Pāṇḍava brothers. The present account pertains not to the commencement but the conclusion of that battle.

After the great battle of Kurukshetra the Pandavas, to celebrate their victory, performed a great sacrifice and made liberal and bounteous gifts to the poor. Every one said that such a great sacrifice had never before been performed on

3. Louis Renou, ed., *Hinduism* (New York: George Braziller, 1962), pp. 55–6.

4. M. Hiriyanna, *The Essentials of Indian Philosophy*, pp. 54–5. Śākuntalam is the abbreviated title of a Sanskrit play by Kālidāsa.

the earth. But a mongoose of strange appearance came there; half of its body was golden in colour, the other half the natural brown colour of a mongoose. After rolling on the floor of the sacrificial hall it said, much to the amazement of all present, 'You are all liars; this is no sacrifice.' 'What', they all exclaimed, 'how dare you say that this is no sacrifice? Have you any idea of the immense wealth spent on this sacrifice, the amount of gold, silver and jewels, the number of horses, elephants and cows given away, the millions who have been fed and been given gifts?' 'I know it all', said the mongoose, 'but will you please listen to what I say.'

'A poor Brahmin lived in a small village with his wife, his son and his daughter-in-law. They were extremely poor and lived on what gifts they received from the villagers for running a school and for spiritual ministration. There came a three-year famine, a lot of people died, but the Brahmin and his family just managed to hold body and soul together. After having starved for several days the father brought home one morning a small quantity of barley flour which he had been fortunate enough to obtain. A meal having been prepared from the flour it was divided into four parts and the family sat down to the meal. Just then there was a knock at the door and when it was opened they saw a man who said he was hungry.'

Now in India a guest is a sacred person, almost God for the time being, and must be treated as such. The mongoose went on: 'The Brahmin said, "Come in, Sir, you are welcome." He set before the guest his own portion of the food which the guest quickly ate and said, "Sir, what you have given has only increased my hunger." The wife then offered her share to the guest and when her husband showed some reluctance she said, "It is our duty as householders to follow your footprints and to see that our guests are properly fed." She then gave her share to the guest which he ate and then complained that his hunger was not satisfied. The son then in his turn offered his portion to him. The guest ate that portion also and still remained unsatisfied. Thereupon the son's wife also in pursuance of the principle followed by her elders gave him her portion. Having partaken of that the guest departed giving his blessings to all the inmates of the house. All of them died of starvation on the same night. I came there and rolled on the floor where a few grains of the food had fallen and then I saw that one half of my body had become golden. Ever since I have been travelling all over the world wanting to see another great sacrifice, but I have been always disappointed. Nowhere else has the other half of my body become golden. That is why I say that this was no sacrifice at all.'[5]

The moral of the story is that if one is a householder then one should fulfil one's duties as a householder even at the cost of one's life. This too is an aspect of karma-yoga.

5. Swami Sambuddhananda, *Vedanta Through Stories* (Bombay: Sri Ramakrishna Ashram, 1959), pp. 122–4.

IV

The following considerations assist in assessing the significance of the path of action. The path of knowledge was popularly interpreted as involving the renunciation of worldly activities; and even the path of devotion tended to impart an other-worldly quality to one's life as one focused more on God than on this world. The path of action, however, made the astonishing and revolutionary claim that one could approach the ultimate reality by performing one's own normal worldly duties—if this could be done in the right spirit. The Indian ethos generally tended to emphasize the road of renunciation—coupled with either knowledge or devotion—as leading to realization. In this respect the doctrine of karma-yoga is significant as endowing ordinary life in the world with salvific power.

CHAPTER XIX

Varṇa

Introduction

The Sanskrit word varṇa is usually employed as a synonym of what has become known in the West as the caste system. The caste system in this sense, however, is a misnomer, for it covers two distinct if connected concepts, one referred to by the term varṇa and the other by the term *jāti*. Serious Indologists now observe considerable caution in this respect. The dean of Indologists for several decades, Basham writes in his chapter entitled 'Society: Class, Family and Individual':

In the whole of this chapter we have hardly used the word which in most minds is most strongly connected with the Hindu social order. When the Portuguese came to India in the 16th century they found the Hindu community divided into many separate groups, which they called *castas*, meaning tribes, clans or families. The name stuck, and became the usual word for the Hindu social group. In attempting to account for the remarkable proliferation of castes in 18th- and 19th-century India, authorities credulously accepted the traditional view that by a process of intermarriage and subdivision the 3,000 or more castes of modern India had evolved from the four primitive classes, and the term 'caste' was applied indiscriminately to both *varṇa* or class, and *jāti* or caste proper. This is a false terminology; castes rise and fall in the social scale, and old castes die out and new ones are formed, but the four great classes are stable. They are never more or less than four, and for over 2,000 years their order of precedence has not altered. All ancient Indian sources make a sharp distinction between the two terms; *varṇa* is much referred to, but *jāti* very little, and when it does appear in literature it does not always imply the comparatively rigid and exclusive social groups of later times. If caste is defined as a system of groups within the class, which are normally endogamous, commensal and craft-exclusive, we have no real evidence of its existence until comparatively late times.[1]

1. A.L. Basham, *The Wonder That Was India* (London: Sidgwick & Jackson, 1988), p. 148.

Anthropological investigations have further confirmed the view that the field-reality is represented by jāti rather than varṇa, which has led some scholars to observe that Hindus, in these matters, have been more conservative than their scriptures. In theory, however, each jāti belongs to a varṇa, although the precise varṇa may be a matter of contention, as the relative ranking of jātis within the varṇa.[2]

Our sources for classical Hinduism speak more of varṇas than of jātis and the historical connection between the two is far from clear. Various views have been held in this respect: that the varṇas broke down into jātis; that the varṇa system was a way of systematizing an existing social reality characterized by jātis; that the two parallel systems never quite met; that varṇa applied the higher one was up in the hierarchy and jāti the lower down one was. The situation is not helped by occasional conflation of varṇa and jāti in the literature either.[3] However, whether we take the caste system to mean varṇa plus jāti or varṇa minus jāti or varṇa hyphen jāti or varṇa equals jāti, the current literature of the caste system is enormous but, surprisingly, fails not only to take huge chunks of evidence into consideration, but also fails to look critically at what it does cover. Hence the size of this section.

The existing discussions of the Hindu social order have fallen victim to a stereotype. According to this stereotype, Hindu society is divided into watertight compartments to which one belongs by birth called 'castes'. One can marry, dine and pursue one's vocation only within the confines of this compartment. Moreover, these compartments are characterized not only by immobility at a point in time, but immutability over time. Besides, this fixed and immutable character of the social order is believed to be divinely decreed.

The stereotype in one form or another so dominates the study of classical Hinduism that it seriously distorts its social reality. The classical Hindu concept which corresponds to this so-called stereotype dubbed the 'caste system' is that of varṇa. A considerable portion of this book has been devoted to questioning this stereotype, as its persistence constitutes a major obstacle to a proper understanding of classical Hinduism. It is demonstrated here that a stereotype has

2. David R. Kinsley, *Hinduism: A Cultural Perspective* (second edition) (Englewood Cliffs, NJ: Prentice-Hall, 1993), p. 156.

3. P.V. Kane, *History of Dharmaśāstra* (Poona: Bhandarkar Oriental Research Institute, 1962), vol. v (pt II), p. 1633.

indeed been perpetrated and that it can be perpetuated only by denying or ignoring 'a substantial part of India's religious literature'.[4]

The Vedas

The earliest literary allusion to the caste system is traceable to the *Ṛg Veda*, and in it to the *Puruṣasūkta.* The following passage offers a succinct summary statement of the hymn for our purpose:

In the Puruṣa-sūkta (RV.x.90) the Puruṣa is depicted as a cosmogonic figure, a creative source, the primeval male who envelops the whole earth and who represents totality. This hymn is the earliest account of secondary creation and is of particular interest as the earliest account of the structure of Vedic society, which its alleged composer Nārāyaṇa divides into four occupational or functional categories, each corresponding to a particular part of the sacrificed body of the Puruṣa. This sacrifice became the prototype of all future sacrifices. From the Puruṣa's severed body the *brāhmaṇa* emerged from his mouth, from his arms the *rājanya*; from his thighs the *vaiśya*, and from his feet the *śūdra.* From his mind was produced the moon; from his eye the sun; the wind from his breath; from his navel the atmosphere; from his head the sky, and so forth. Upon this purely symbolic description of the social, political and economic structure of late Vedic society, subsequent Indian 'sociologists' built a caste system, which was ultimately presented in the *Manu-smṛti* as the inviolable expression of divine law.[5]

The fundamental argument involved here is that the caste system represents a divine, sacred or natural order of things depending on how the hymn is read. If the universe—and along with it, the caste system—is created by God then it is *divine.* If it is argued that the universe and the caste system came into being through a primeval sacrificial act performed by the gods and sages, then it is *sacred.* If the caste system is seen as coming into being with the sun, the moon and the sky, etc. then it is a part of the *natural* scheme of things. In any case, it is inviolable. As P.V. Kane explains:

In the Puruṣasūkta (x.90.12) the brāhmaṇa, kṣatriya, vaiśya and śūdra are said to have sprung from the mouth, arms, thighs and feet of the supreme Puruṣa. In the very next verse the sun and the moon are said to have been born from the eye and mind of the Puruṣa. This shows that the composer of the hymn

4. K.M. Sen, *Hinduism* (Harmondsworth: Penguin Books, 1963), p. 31.

5. Margaret and James Stutley, *A Dictionary of Hinduism* (London: Routledge & Kegan Paul, 1977), pp. 237–8.

regarded the division of society into four classes to be very ancient and to be as natural and God-ordained as the sun and the moon.[6]

A closer examination of the hymn in its proper perspective reveals serious difficulties with this argument.

Philological Difficulties

The word varṇa, which designates the caste system in classical Hindu usage, does not appear in the hymn at all. The four classes which were subsequently identified as varṇas are mentioned, but the word varṇa is not mentioned in connection with them. When it is, it is mentioned as *ārya* (III.34.9) and *dāsa* (II.12.4) varṇa and Agastya is mentioned as the protector of both (I.179.6). Conflict between these two varṇas is mentioned but both ārya and dāsa enemies are also alluded to (VII.83.1). Moreover, the word kṣatriya does not occur in the hymn; the word which does occur is rājanya, which is taken to correspond to the kṣatriya of the later scheme. But as Kane remarks: 'I have not been able to find the word rājanya in the Ṛg Veda anywhere except in the Puruṣasūkta. In the Aitareya brāhmaṇa (chap. 34.2) the word "rājanya" stands for a member of the 2nd class in society, while kṣatriya means a king of whom land (for sacrifice to gods) is asked for by brāhmaṇa or vaiśya."[7] The point is not earth-shaking, as the word kṣatriya is substituted for it in subsequent statements.[8] However, this does not mean that the difference just goes away even though the two may be used synonymously. Thus Pāṇini has retained the sense of kṣatriya for rājanya in IV.2.39 'but he has used it in a new constitutional significance in sūtra VI.2.34 (*Rājanya-bahu-vacana-dvandve Andhaka-vṛṣṇīṣu*), where the *kāśikā* defines *rājanya* as a member of such families in a kṣatriya tribe as were consecrated to rulership (*abhiṣikta-vaṁśya-kṣatriya*)'.[9]

Finally, not only rājanya but the words vaiśya and sūdra also occur only in this hymn in the *Ṛg Veda.* Thus the key verse connecting the hymn with the caste system contains three hapaxes.

6. P.V. Kane, *History of Dharmaśāstra*, vol. II, pt I, p. 33.

7. Ibid., p. 32. It is not entirely correct to say, therefore, that 'In the Saṁhitas *rājanya* is a synonymous term with kshatriya' (V.S. Agrawala, *India as Known to Pāṇini* (Lucknow: Prithvi Prakashan, 1963), p. 79.

8. *Śatapatha Brāhmaṇa* XIV.4.2.23; etc.

9. V.S. Agrawala, op. cit., p. 79. Diacritics modified.

Historical Difficulties

All scholars are agreed that *Ṛg Veda* x.90 is a 'late hymn',[10] and it is this hymn alone in the entire *Ṛg Veda* which contains a mention of what are later specifically identified as the four varṇas (*Śatapatha Brāhmaṇa* 5.5.4.9), where again the word rājanya rather than kṣatriya is used, although brāhmaṇa and kṣatriya are mentioned as such in *Ṛg Veda* IV.50.8.

It is of primary consideration here that the Vedas are the foundational scriptures of Hinduism, and the *Ṛg Veda* is the earliest of them. If the caste system is attested to only in a *late* hymn of this earliest work, then it seems reasonable to assume that there may have been an earlier period in which the caste system did not exist. Thus there was a time when there was Hinduism but not the system. It seems that the racial memory of such a stage is perhaps preserved in such texts as allude to an age when caste did not exist. J. Muir has collected such references and writes that in one

> remarkable text the Mahābhārata categorically asserts that originally there was no distinction of classes, the existing distribution having arisen out of differences of character and occupation. Similarly, the Bhāgavata Purāṇa in one place informs us that in the Kṛita age there was but one caste; and this view appears also to be taken in some passages which I have adduced from the Epic poems.[11]

Muir also refers to texts in which

> men are said to be the offspring of Vivasvat; in another his son Manu is said to be their progenitor; whilst in a third they are said to be descended from a female of the same name. The passage which declares Manu to have been the father of the human race explicitly affirms that men of all the four castes were descended from him.[12]

It is as if here the puruṣa of the *Puruṣasūkta* is not a divine but a human person, namely Manu.[13] In line with this tradition, the *Bhaviṣya Purāṇa* resurrects the pristine stage of a casteless society in the idiom of the four varṇas when it declares (I.41.45): 'A father has four sons. All the sons, naturally must belong to the same caste.'[14]

10. See J. Muir, *Original Sanskrit Texts* (Delhi: Oriental Publishers, 1972, reprint) pt I, pp. 11–15; R.S. Sharma, *Śūdras in Ancient India* (Delhi: Motilal Banarsidass, 1958), p. 28.

11. J. Muir, *Original Sanskrit Texts*, pt I, p. 160.

12. Ibid.

13. Ibid., p. 117.

14. R.K. Arora, *Historical and Cultural Data from the Bhaviṣya Purāṇa* (New Delhi: Sterling Publishers (P) Ltd, 1972), p. 99.

The lateness of the hymn, even if it does not indicate the absence of castes altogether, would seem to at least indicate the absence of the śūdra varṇa in the early stages of Ṛg Vedic society, specially if the *Puruṣasūkta* is considered an interpolation in the tenth book of the *Ṛg Veda*[15] as it contains the only mention of the term in that Veda.

Sociological Difficulties

The idea of caste implies caste by birth and hence its immutability. However, it is by no means clear that such was the case in the Ṛg Vedic period on the basis of both general and specific evidence.

The general evidence relates to the fact that in one hymn the poet refers to his diverse parentage. 'I am a reciter of hymns, my father is a physician and my mother grinds (corn with stones). We desire to obtain wealth in various actions' (IX.112.3).[16] In another the poet asks Indra: 'O, Indra, fond of soma, would you make me the protector of people, or would you make me a king, would you make me a sage, that has drunk soma, would you impart to me endless wealth?' (iii.44.5).[17] These verses show both genetic and occupational variability.

Evidence of a specific nature is even more convincing. Vasiṣṭha, who did not have brāhmaṇa parents, became the *purohita* of Sudrās and 'Vasiṣṭha's appointment may have been responsible for the subsequent rule that only a *purohita* should act as the officiating *brāhmaṇ* at the sacrifice'.[18] He was born of Urvaśī, who was a nymph, and from Mitra and Varuṇa, who were gods (VII.33.11). However, there is clear recognition of the fact that at this time one's varṇa could change. Thus there are cases of brāhmaṇas becoming kṣatriyas; kṣatriyas becoming brāhmaṇas; vaiśyas becoming brāhmaṇas.

The cases of a brāhmaṇa becoming a kṣatriya and then a kṣatriya becoming a brāhmaṇa are instructive. 'The priest Vidathin Bhāradvāja became a kṣatriya as soon as he was adopted by king Bharata, and his descendants were the well-known Bharata Kṣatriyas.'[19] The

15. R.S. Sharma, *Śūdras in Ancient India*, p. 28.

16. Ibid., p. 31.

17. Ibid.

18. *Śatapatha Brāhmaṇa*: XII.6.1.41; see Margaret and James Stutley, *A Dictionary of Hinduism*, p. 325.

19. P.L. Bhargava, *India in the Vedic Age* (Lucknow: The Upper India Publishing House Pvt. Ltd, 1971), p. 239.

opposite example is of Viśvāmitra who represents the 'example of a king who renounced his kingdom to enter the spiritual order'.[20] The two cases are connected and this throws a flood of light on the situation.

If Viśvāmitra had lived when caste system had become established, he need not have renounced his kingdom to become a Brāhmaṇa, because, being a Bhārata and thus a descendant of Vidathin Bhāradvāja, he would have been recognized a Brāhmaṇa by his very birth. But in the casteless Vedic society his descent from Vidathin Bhāradvāja did not make him a Brahman. He had to renounce his kingdom and lead a spiritual life in order to become a Brahman. His family specialised in priesthood in the same way as other priestly families had done and thus gained the same status as enjoyed by them. Of the younger sons of kings becoming brahmans and founding priestly groups there are numerous examples. Thus the Vainya, Śaunaka, Maitreya, Yāska, and Veda-viśvajyoti groups among the Bhārgavas and the Kāṇva, Hārīta, Kutsa, Viṣṇuvṛddha, Gārgya, Sānkṛtya, Kāpya, Maudgalya, and Rathītara groups among the Āṅgirasas were founded by persons of royal descent. Even as late as the time of king Śantanu, his brother Devāpi became a Brahman and was admitted into the Ārṣṭiṣeṇa family of the Bhārgavas.'[21]

There are also cases of vaiśyas becoming brāhmaṇas:

Thus Nābhānediṣṭha and his son and grandson Bhalandana and Vatsapri who were viś or vaiśyas became Brahmans and were admitted into the Gaviṣṭhira family of the Ātreyas. The two brothers Vasiṣṭha and Agastya, who were contemporaries of Viśvāmitra, also founded new Brahman families, and must have been viś or commoners by descent.[22]

No specific evidence is offered in other cases but the case of Nābhāgariṣṭa is explicitly mentioned in the *Brahma Purāṇa* (vii.42): *nābhāgariṣṭa-putrau dvau vaiśyo brāhmaṇatām gatau*, as well as *Harivaṁśa* (11.9).

It is not possible to cite a specific case of a dāsa (who are subsequently said to have been identified with the śūdras) becoming a brāhmaṇa but its possibility should not be discounted. R.S. Sharma has pointed out that

sufficient evidence has been adduced from Vedic and epic traditions to show that Indra was a brahmicide, and that his chief enemy Vṛtra was a brāhmaṇa. This also confirms the hypothesis that developed priesthood was a pre-Aryan institution, and implies that all the conquered people were not reduced to the

20. Ibid.
21. Ibid.
22. Ibid., p. 240.

position of the dāsas and śūdras. And hence, though the brāhmaṇa as such was an Indo-European institution, the priestly class of the Āryan conquerors may have been largely recruited from the conquered. Though there is nothing to indicate the proportion, it seems that some of the pre-Āryan priests found their way into the new society.[23]

A similar possibility exists in the case of dāsas being accepted as kings.

Similarly it appears that some of the conquered chiefs received high status in the new society. Priestly acceptance of gifts from the Dāsa chiefs such as Balbūtha and Tarukṣa earned them unstinted praises, through which they gained in status in the new order. That the Dāsas were in a position to make gifts and were looked upon as liberal donors can be deduced from the very meaning of the root *das* from which the noun Dāsa is derived. The process of assimilation went on in later times, for the later literature records the tradition that Pratardana Dāivodāsi went to the world of Indra, who was historically the titular ruler of the Āryan invaders.[24]

Similarly, dāsas were also accepted as vaiśyas as indicated by the expression *dāsa viśas* found in the *Ṛg Veda* (II.11.4; IV.28.4; VI.25.2) and the prevailing view is that 'other survivors of earlier societies ... were reduced to what came to be known as the fourth varṇa of Āryan society',[25] namely the śūdras.

23. R.S. Sharma, *Śūdras in Ancient India* (Delhi: Motilal Banarsidass, 1958) pp. 20–1. He goes on to say:

It would be wrong to think that all the 'blacks' were reduced to the status of the śūdra helots, since there are some references to black seers. In the *Ṛg Veda* the Aśvins are described as presenting fair-skinned women to black (śyāvāya) Kaṇva, who probably is named *kṛṣṇa* 'black' at another place and is the poet of the hymns (*RV*, VIII.85 and 86) addressed to the twin gods. It is perhaps again Kaṇva who is mentioned as *kṛṣṇa ṛṣi* in the first book of the *Ṛg Veda*. Similarly Dīrghatamas, mentioned as a singer in one hymn of the *Ṛg Veda*, may have been of dark colour, if his name was given to him on account of his complexion. It is significant that in several passages of the *Ṛg Veda* he is known by his metronymic Māmateya alone, and a later legend says that he married Uśij, a slave girl and begot Kākṣīvant. Again in the first book of the *Ṛg Veda* priestly Divodāsas, whose name suggests a dāsa origin, are described as composing new hymns, while in the tenth book the Aṅgiras author of the *RV*, x.42–44 is called 'black'. Since most of the above references occur in the later portions of the *Ṛg Veda* it would appear that towards the end of the Ṛg Vedic period some of the black seers and Dāsa priests were worming their way into the newly organised Āryan community.

24. Ibid., pp. 21–2.

25. Ibid. p. 22.

Mythological Difficulties

If the *Puruṣasūkta* had been the only account of the origin of the caste system available to us then it might have appeared more plausible to link its account with the stereotype of the present caste system, howsoever tenuous the link might be. The link is tenuous, first, because many see it as allegorical in nature, Colebrooke maintaining that the 'allegory is for the most part sufficiently obvious'[26] and, second, because

> whether the writer of the hymn intended it to be understood allegorically or not, it conveys no distinct idea of the manner in which he supposed the four castes to have originated. It is, indeed, said that the Śūdra sprang from Purusha's feet; but as regards the three superior *castes* and the members with which they are respectively connected, it is not quite clear which (i.e. the castes or the members) are to be taken as the subjects and which as the predicates, and consequently, whether we are to suppose verse 12 to declare that the three castes were the three members, or, conversely, that the three members were, or became, the three castes.[27]

It should be specially noted that the śūdra is spoken of as being born out of the feet. As birth implies coming into existence after a point in time and non-existence prior to it, is one to suppose that the śūdra varṇa came into being after a point in time, while the other three varṇas had pre-existed?[28]

However, there are other accounts of the origin of the caste system. The *sūkta* itself appears in the *Atharva Veda* and its account is traceable in the *Yajur Veda* too, in the *Vājasaneyī Samhitā*,[29] but the *Atharva Veda* and the *Vājasaneyī Samhitā* both offer other accounts of the origin as well. In the *Atharva Veda* first the rājanya (XV.VIII.1) and then both brāhmaṇa and rājanya (XV.IX.1) are described as springing from the *vrātya*. Now what is meant by vrātya? In the *Atharva Veda* (XV) it appears as the supreme Brahman, but the irony is that while according 'to the Praśna Up. (2,11) Vrātya appears as a king of cosmic being', 'Śaṅkara interprets the name as uninitiated, i.e. the first-born, and hence without anyone to initiate him.'

26. See J. Muir, *Original Sanskrit Texts*, pt I, p. 14.
27. Ibid., p. 15.
28. This might lend support to Dumézil's views of an original tripartite Indo-European society. See R.N. Dandekar, *Insights Into Hinduism* (Delhi: Ajanta Publications [India], 1979), p. 111f.
29. R.S. Sharma, *Śūdras in Ancient India*, p. 28.

However, Śaṅkara may have metaphysically sublimated a social reality, for by his time vrātya had come 'to mean one who lost caste by non-observance of prescribed ceremonies or otherwise'.[30] It had acquired this sense in the age of the Brāhmaṇas, for the *Tāṇḍya Brāhmaṇa* refers to the rite of Vrātyastoma which 'shows that not only individuals but whole tribes were absorbed into Hinduism'.[31] A stereotypical interpretation of the caste system would be wholly antithetical to such an endeavour. It has even been suggested that

> the development of the caste system in a rigid form, with strictly hereditary and mutually exclusive caste-groups, did not take place till the time when the Vedic Aryans had settled down in the middle country and were already brahmanized enough to look upon the inhabitants of the North-West—the home of the *Rig Veda*—as uncivilized Vratyas because they did not follow the strict [caste] system.[32]

The *Vājasaneyī Saṁhitā* of the *Yajur Veda* (XIV. 28ff), in a passage also found in the *Taittirīya Saṁhitā*,[33] describes the emergence of a host of beings among which the four varṇas are included. Interestingly, the śūdras and vaiśyas are mentioned in that order and together: '... the śūdra and Ārya (vaiśya) were created: day and night were the rulers'.[34] And Varuṇa, Pūshan, Vāyu, Soma, etc. emerge after them. Thus the hierarchy one is accustomed to is seriously challenged. J. Muir is led to conclude that

> Even, therefore, if we should suppose that the author of the Purusha Sūkta meant to represent the four castes as having literally sprung from separate parts of Purusha's body, it is evident that the same idea was not always or even generally adopted by those who followed him, as a revealed truth in which they were bound to acquiesce. In fact, nothing is clearer than that in all these cosmogonies, the writers, while generally assuming certain prevalent ideas as

30. S. Radhakrishnan, ed., *The Principal Upaniṣads* (London: George Allen & Unwin, 1953), p. 657. Also see Margaret and James Stutley, *A Dictionary of Hinduism*, p. 339.

31. S. Radhakrishnan, *The Hindu View of Life* (New York: The Macmillan Co., 1927), p. 29. Also see Har Bilas Sarda, ed., *Dayanand Commemoration Volume* (Ajmer: 1933), pp. 169–80.

32. V.M. Apte, 'Social and Economic Conditions', in R.C. Majumdar, ed., *The Vedic Age* (London: George Allen & Unwin, 1952), p. 387.

33. J. Muir, *Original Sanskrit Texts*, pt I, p. 18.

34. Ibid., p. 18. For more on ārya, see Mahinda Palihawadana, *The Indra Cult as Ideology: A Clue to Power Struggle in an Ancient Society* (Vidyodaya J. Arts. Sci. Lett. vol. 9, nos 1 & 2, pt II), pp. 32–4.

the basis of their descriptions, gave the freest scope to their individual fancy in the invention of details. In such circumstances, perfect coincidence cannot be expected in the narratives.[35]

Indeed, serious thought must be given to two considerations at this stage. First, the śūdra as a class may not have existed as a varṇa at some stage early in the Ṛg Vedic period, as its mention appears only in the *Puruṣasūkta*. This is probably confirmed by evidence from the *Atharva Veda* (which reproduces the *Puruṣasūkta*)[36] in that when in the *Atharva Veda* (v.xvii.8-9) it is 'claimed that the Brāhmaṇa enjoys the right to become the first husband of a woman as against the rājanya and the vaiśya',[37] the śūdra is not mentioned 'probably because his varṇa did not exist at that stage'. R.S. Sharma draws attention to a verse (v.xvii.9) of the *Atharva Veda* which 'on the basis of Whitney, can be assigned to the early period of the *Atharva Veda*'[38] and which mentions only brāhmaṇa, rājanya and vaiśya, as in the reference cited earlier, leaving out the śūdra. 'It is evident then that the Śūdras appear as a social class only towards the end of the period of the *Atharva Veda*, when the *Puruṣasūkta* version of their origin may have been inserted into the tenth book of the *Ṛg Veda*.'[39]

It is clear from the discussion so far that the stereotype of the caste system does not apply to the Saṁhitā period, though there are signs that towards its end the *varṇa* system started developing, probably under priestly influence. The features which are most closely associated with it in its popular understanding, such as interdiction of interdining and intermarriage, and occupational petrification, are not in evidence. In conclusion, the interrelationships among the *varṇas* may also be considered. In this context the following verse of the *Yajur Veda* (*Vājasaneyī Saṁhitā* xxvi.2) is significant: Yathemāṁ vacāṁ kalyāṇīmāvadāni janebhyaḥ, brahmarājanyābhyāṁ śūdrāya cāryāya ca svāya cāreaṇāya ...

This verse has received a minimalist and a maximalist interpretation. R.S. Sharma favours a minimalist interpretation:

In one of the supplementary formulae of the *Vājasaneyī Saṁhitā*, to be used in connection with various seasonal and domestic sacrifices, a desire is expressed for talking *kalyāṇīvāk* to the member of all the varṇas. It is contended that this

35. J. Muir, *Original Sanskrit Texts*, pt i, p. 34.
36. R.S. Sharma, *Śūdras in Ancient India*, p. 29.
37. Ibid., p. 40.
38. Ibid., p. 30.
39. Ibid.

refers to the equal right of all classes to the study of the Veda. But the term *kalyāṇīvāk* does not stand for the Veda. The commentators are right when they take it in the sense of kind and courteous speech. It would imply that friendly words were to be used in talking to the members of all the varṇas.[40]

A number of other scholars, however, favour the maximalist interpretation that it indicates the accessibility of the Vedas to all members of society at the time.[41] The question is: are the modern scholars reading into it their liberal view or are the medieval scholars such as Uvaṭa and Mahīdhara reading into it their classical view debarring sections of Hindus from Vedic study?[42]

The Brāhmaṇas

It is in the Brāhmaṇas that one finds for a first time the clear statement of the four varṇas specifically as varṇas. The *Śatapatha Brāhmaṇa* (V.V.IV.9) declares: *catvāro vai varṇāḥ brāhmaṇo rājanyo vaiśyaḥ śūdraśca.* Moreover, during the Brāhmaṇa period, varṇa distinctions are extended to animals,[43] plants[44] and even nature[45] on the one hand and to the gods[46] and Vedic metres[47] on the other. In other words, the 'system of the four varṇas had taken deep roots in the period when the Brāhmaṇa works were composed',[48] and one would therefore expect the actual situation to conform to the stereotype of the caste system. An examination of the evidence on the point, however, does not seem to quite confirm such an impression. It does indicate a general deterioration in the condition of the śūdra,

40. Ibid., pp. 65–6.

41. B.B. Bakshi Sohanlal, 'Sri Swami Dayanand Saraswati on Untouchability and Uplift of Depressed Classes', in Har Bilas Sarda, ed., *Dayanand Commemoration Volume* (Ajmer: 1933), pp. 184–5; K. Satchidananda Murty, *Vedic Hermeneutics* (Delhi: Motilal Banarsidass, 1993), p. 14; etc.

42. For a recent discussion of varṇa along more conventional lines, see Brian K. Smith, *Classifying the Universe: The Ancient Indian Varṇa System and the Origins of Caste* (New York: Oxford University Press, 1994).

43. *Aitareya Brāhmaṇa* VI.IV.IV.12–15.

44. *Śatapatha Brāhmaṇa* I.I.I.4; *Aitareya Brāhmaṇa* viii.xxxvii.4.

45. To the natural seasons, see P.V. Kane, *History of Dharmaśāstra*, vol. II, pt I, p. 42.

46. *Śatapatha Brāhmaṇa* XIV.V.VI.23–5.

47. *Aitareya Brāhmaṇa* VII.IV.V.6

48. P.V. Kane, *History of Dharmaśāstra*, vol. II, pt I, p. 42.

specially from the point of view of Vedic sacrificial ritual,[49] but in several other respects the expectations are belied.

Etiological Considerations

It has been said that the 'origin of the caste-system has not been discussed in the Brāhmaṇas'.[50] This is not entirely true. What is true is that the *Puruṣasūkta* is *not* invoked in the context of the varṇas except in *Pañcaviṁśa Brāhmaṇa* (v.i.6–10). This in itself is an interesting fact, despite the limitations of argument by silence, for it demonstrates that the divine sanction which that hymn is supposed to accord to varṇa distinctions was not accepted as a matter of course as is the case in several sections of Smṛti literature. Moreover, this might also attest to the lateness of the hymn, and M. Hiriyanna actually discusses it in the context of the 'thought of the later hymns and the Brāhmaṇas'.[51]

The Brāhmaṇas offer other explanations of the origin of the varṇas:

(1) The *Śatapatha Brāhmaṇa* (ii.i.iv.11–12) at one point describes the first three varṇas as emerging from the utterance of *bhūḥ*, *bhuvaḥ* and *svaḥ* respectively. The suggestion is interesting as these three terms in Ṛg Vedic parlance refer to the sky, the atmospheric region and the earth respectively.[52] But in the *Puruṣasūkta* the earth is associated with the feet of the Cosmic Person *and* with the śūdra. Is the śūdra to be relegated to the nether region or are both vaiśya *and* śūdra together to be associated with the earth or is it that the varṇa had not yet emerged?

(2) The *Taittirīya Brāhmaṇa* (iii.xii.ix.2) describes the vaiśya as being born from the *Ṛg Veda*, the kṣatriya from the *Yajur* and the brāhmaṇa from the *Sāma Veda*. According to Muir: 'to complete this account of the castes from the Vedas, the author had only to add that the Śūdras had sprung from the Atharvāṅgirases (the *Atharva-veda*); but he perhaps considered that to assign such an origin to the servile

49. R.S. Sharma, *Śūdras in Ancient India*, pp. 61–2.

50. Jogiraj Basu, *India of the Age of the Brāhmaṇas* (Calcutta: Sanskrit Pustak Bhandar, 1969), p. 10.

51. M. Hiriyanna, *The Essentials of Indian Philosophy* (London: George Allen & Unwin, 1948), pp. 14, 16.

52. Monier Monier-Williams, *A Sanskrit–English Dictionary* (Oxford: Clarendon Press, 1964), p. 761.

order would have been to do it too great an honour.'[53] R.S. Sharma suggests: 'This obviously implies that the *Atharva Veda* was meant for the Śūdra—a provision which is later on vaguely repeated in the Āpastamba Dharmasūtra.'[54]

(3) The *Taittirīya Brāhmaṇa* also contains two suggestions regarding the origin of the śūdra varṇa: that the śūdra sprang from the Asuras while brāhmaṇa sprang from the gods (I.II.VI.7) and that it sprang from non-existence (*asato*) (III.II.III.9).

It is clear from the foregoing that sometimes the Brāhmaṇas offer an explanation of the origin of only two varṇas, or of three or four when the *Puruṣasūkta* is invoked. The explanations offered also differ. Another factor contributes to this fluidity, that accounts of creation in general do not take the origin of the varṇas into consideration[55] (though some do, e.g. the *Śatapatha Brāhmaṇa* II.I.IV.12), and that 'most of the Brāhmaṇa texts do not mention the Śūdra while narrating the legend of the origin of caste'[56] (though some do, e.g. the *Śatapatha Brāhmaṇa* XIV.IV.II.23).[57]

Sociological Considerations

The status of the four varṇas during this period broadly conformed to the graduated order of the brāhmaṇa, kṣatriya, vaiśya and śūdra. But on closer inspection it appears that the hierarchy in some ways was more notional than real, specially in the relationship between the brāhmaṇas and kṣatriyas. For instance, despite the brāhmaṇical insistence on social and ritual superiority in general, on occasion the superiority of the kṣatriya was acknowledged.

> There is nothing superior to the Kṣatriya. Hence the Brāhmaṇa worships Kṣatriya from a lower position in the Rājasūya.
>
> (*Śatapatha Brāhmaṇa* XIV.IV.II.23)

> The three other castes follow the Kṣatriya who goes first.
>
> (*Śatapatha Brāhmaṇa* VI.IV.IV.13)

53. J. Muir, *Original Sanskrit Texts*, pt I, pp. 17–18.
54. R.S. Sharma, *Śūdras in Ancient India*, p. 68. Good historical reasons for this are implied in the discussion on pp. 11, 22 and 38.
55. See *Taittirīya Brāhmaṇa* II.II.IX.1–10; II.III.VIII.1; *Śatapatha Brāhmaṇa* II.I.IV.12; VI.I.II.11; VII.V.II.6; X.I.III.1; XIV.IV.II.1.
56. Jogiraj Basu, *India of the Age of the Brāhmaṇas*, p. 12.
57. Also see *Śatapatha Brāhmaṇa* XIII.VI.II.10.

Whenever a king so desires he conquers a Brāhmaṇa.

(*Taittirīya Brāhmaṇa* III.IX.14)[58]

On other occasions, reciprocity is emphasized.

He quickens the Kṣatra by the Brāhmaṇa and the Brāhmaṇa by the Kṣatra; hence a Brahmin who has a Kṣatriya is superior to another Brahmin; likewise a Rājanya who has a Brahmaṇa is superior to another Kṣatriya.

(*Taittirīya Saṁhitā* V.I.X.3)

The Kṣatriya was born, i.e., the overlord of all beings was born; the employer of the commoner was born; the slayer of the enemy was born; the protector of the Brahmins was born.

(*Aitareya Brāhmaṇa* VIII.17).[59]

Similarly the śūdra, though he had limited sacrificial rights and his movements were restricted in certain parts of the sacrificial ground, had access to the sacrificial campus in general. This is clear from the *Śatapatha Brāhmaṇa* (I.I.IV.12), which prescribes modes of address for different varṇas in the soma-sacrifice in calling the *haviṣkṛt*: ' "Ehi" in the case of a Brahmana; "Agahi" and "Adrava" in the case of a Vaiśya and Rājanya, respectively; and "Ādhāva" in the case of the Śūdra'.[60]

The remarks of Weber on the existence of this passage indicate another dimension of its significance. He writes:

The entire passage is of great importance, as it shows (in opposition to what Roth says in the first vol. of this Journal) that the Śūdras were then admitted to the holy sacrifices of the Arians, and understood their speech, even if they did not speak it. The latter point cannot certainly be assumed as a necessary consequence, but it is highly probable; and I consequently incline to the view of those who regard the Sūdras as an Arian tribe which immigrated into India before the others.[61]

The soma sacrifice is generally regarded as the Vedic sacrifice *par excellence*. The *Śatapatha Brāhmaṇa* contains the following passage (V.V.IV.IX): 'For there are four castes, the Brāhmaṇa, the Rājanya, the Vaiśya, and the Śūdra; but there is not one of them that vomits Soma; but were there any one of them, then indeed there would be atonement.'[62]

58. Jogiraj Basu, *India of the Age of the Brāhmaṇas*, p. 22; last translation modified.
59. Ibid., p. 18.
60. Ibid., p. 14.
61. J. Muir, *Original Sanskrit Texts*, pt I, p. 336 fn. 164.
62. Julius Eggling, tr., *The Śatapatha-Brāhmaṇa According to the Text of the Mādhyandina School* (Delhi: Motilal Banarsidass, 1963, reprint), pt III, p. 131.

The implication, as already noted by Weber,[63] is that all the four varṇas partook of soma.

The next point to be considered here is the participation of the *niṣāda* in Vedic ritual. The niṣāda are aboriginal tribes and in a sense even lower than the śūdras, who at least may have belonged to the Aryan polity in general. In the viśvajit sacrifice, the sacrificer is asked to spend three nights with a niṣāda, along with a vaiśya and rājanya (*Jaiminīya* II.184). An interesting angle on this issue is provided by Yāska's interpretation of the term *pañca-janāḥ*, or 'five peoples', who have the right to sacrifice according to the *Ṛg Veda* (X.53–4). Yāska adds niṣāda to the four varnas to complete the pentad. This may not be historically correct for Ṛg Vedic times. R.S. Sharma points out:

> The *Nirukta* explains the term *pañcajanah* as meaning the four varnas and the *Niṣādas*. This cannot be taken as applying to the period of the *Ṛg Veda*, as is sometimes done. Neither does the word *niṣāda* occur in the *Ṛg Veda* nor is the existence of the four varṇas a well-established fact there. Obviously the term *pañcajanāḥ* refers to the five *Ṛg Vedic* tribes, whose members offered sacrifices without any distinction. Yāska's interpretation, however, shows that in his time the Śūdras as well as the Niṣādas, who came to be specified in the Dharmasūtras as a mixed caste born of a Brāhmaṇa and a Śūdra woman, could take part in the sacrifice.[64]

And, as the niṣādas would fall in the category of śūdras when compressed into the scheme of four varṇas, Yāska's interpretation further shows 'that in his opinion the whole śūdra varṇa enjoyed this right'.[65]

The question of mobility of castes may now be examined. There is evidence to show that both upward and downward mobility was possible. The *Aitareya Brāhmaṇa* instantiates the case of the grandsons of sage Viśvāmitra who became outcastes by disregarding him. The account runs as follows (VII.33.6): 'Viśvāmitra cursed them saying—"Your children shall belong to the lowest of castes" such as Āndhras, Puṇḍras, Śabaras, Pulindas and Mūtibas. Though born of Viśvāmitra's royal family they turned out to be outcastes and chiefs of Dasyus ... .'[66]

63. See. J. Muir, *Original Sanskrit Texts*, pt I, p. 367.

64. R.S. Sharma, *Śūdras in Ancient India*, p. 71.

65. Ibid., p. 72.

66. Jogiraj Basu, *India of the Age of the Brāhmaṇas*, pp. 28–9. The case of Viśvāmitra becomes particularly striking if evidence from the *Mahābhārata* is taken into account. According to chapter 40 of the Śalyaparva of the *Mahābhārata* (Citraśālā edition), Viśvāmitra was originally a kṣatriya who became a brāhmaṇa by performing *tapas* or penance. If this is taken into account in the present context, then the case of

King Janaka's case serves to illustrate the opposite—that one could rise in rank and become a brāhmaṇa from a kṣatriya. It seems that the king had a discussion with the brāhmaṇas on the rite of agnihotra and although he was pleased with Yājñavalkya's response, he implied while parting that even Yājñavalkya did not fully understand the matter.

5. They said, 'Surely, this fellow of a Rājanya has outtalked us: come, let us challenge him to a theological disputation!' Yājñavalkya said, 'We are Brāhmaṇas, and he is a Rājanya: if we were to vanquish him, whom should we say we had vanquished? But if he were to vanquish us, people would say of us that a Rājanya had vanquished Brāhmaṇas: do not think of this!' They approved of his words. But Yājñavalkya, mounting his car, drove after (the king). He overtook him, and he (the king) said, 'Is it to know the Agnihotra, Yājñavalkya?'—'The Agnihotra, O king!' he replied.[67]

After Janaka had finished explaining he was made a brāhmaṇa. 'Thus he spoke; and Yājñavalkya granted him a boon. He said, "Let mine be the (privilege of) asking questions of thee when I list, Yājñavalkya!" Thenceforth Janaka was a Brāhmaṇ.'[68]

One feature of the caste system is believed to be restriction on intermarriage but it is clear from the Brāhmaṇas that 'priests and nobles seem to have been free to intermarry with the lower classes, including the śūdra'.[69] This is indicated by the case of Vatsa and Kavaṣa. The *Pañcaviṁśa Brāhmaṇa* (XIV.VI.6) describes the case of Vatsa:

Vatsa was called a *śūdrā-putra* by his brother Medhātithi, which shows that this was probably not used as a term of abuse. It is said that Vatsa proved his Brāhmaṇahood by walking through the fire unscathed and thus wiped out this reproach. This case shows that the social rank of a person was not determined by his birth but by his worth.

The case of Kavaṣa Ailūṣa also involves the use of the epithet *dāsyāḥ putraḥ* and Sharma considers this case 'doubtful' in contrast with the previous one because the epithet may not apply literally

---

Viśvāmitra provides a *simultaneous example of upward and downward mobility.* He becomes a brāhmaṇa and his descendants become dasyus or marauders, and sink even below the śūdras in respectability.

67. Julius Eggling, tr., *The Śatapatha-Brāhmaṇa According to the Text of the Mādhyandina School*, pt v, pp. 113–14.

68. Ibid., p. 115.

69. R.S. Sharma, *Śūdras in Ancient India*, pp. 62–3.

and is 'regarded by Sāyaṇa as a term of abuse'.[70] In the text which describes the incident, Kavaṣa is also called a 'cheat' and 'no Brāhmaṇ',[71] which gives credence to the allegation that he may indeed have been born of a maid-servant. In any case, the point of the story is that ultimately status is determined by worth and not birth, as in the case of Vatsa. This incident is narrated in both the *Aitareya Brāhmaṇa* and the *Kauśītaki Brāhmaṇa* and may be presented thus.[72]

> The sages said to him (Kavaṣa), 'You are a bastard born of a maid-servant; we shall not dine with you.' Kavaṣa became angry and propitiated goddess Sarasvatī with this hymn. Then the sages considered him as shorn of sin and made obeisance to him saying, 'O seer, we bow down to you; please do not bear any malice towards us; you are superior to us, as Sarasvatī follows after thee.' Thus they appeased his wrath.

The case of Mahīdāsa, the author of the *Aitareya Brāhmaṇa*, is less clear. R.S. Sharma remarks: 'It has been pointed out that Mahīdāsa, the author of the *Aitareya Brāhmaṇa*, was a śūdra. There is nothing to support this view unless his surname *Aitareya* is interpreted as his being son of *Itarā*, which means vile, low or rejected, but this seems to be too far-fetched.'[73] Another point of view is presented by Jogiraj Basu:

> A controversy rages round his name as to whether Mahīdāsa was a Śūdra. His birth and the traditional story concerning his parentage has been stated in the introduction to this work. His mother's name was Itarā and his father had other sons by his other wives as well. The father lavished his affection on his other sons whereas Mahīdāsa was shabbily treated. From this differential treatment of the father, from the name of the mother, and the Śūdra-like name of Mahīdāsa having the word 'dasā' suffixed, many scholars headed by the erudite vedic scholar of name and fame Satyavrata Sāmaśramī arrive at the conclusion that Mahīdāsa's mother belonged to the Śūdra community. Observes Sāmaśramī: 'That he was born of a female slave (Dāsī) or maid-servant is an established fact; ... not to speak of the authorship of a Brāhmaṇa text, even vision (authorship) of Vedic hymns (mantra) is ascribed to the son of a maid-servant (Dāsīputra). He cites the anecdote of Kavaṣa to bear out his contention that bastards born of female servants are credited with the authorship of not only a Brāhmaṇa but also matra, i.e. Vedic hymn.[74]

70. Ibid., p. 63.
71. See A.B. Keith, *Rigveda Brāhmaṇas* (Cambridge: Harvard University Press, 1920), p. 148.
72. Jogiraj Basu, *India of the Age of the Brāhmaṇas*, pp. 29–30.
73. R.S. Sharma, *Śūdras in Ancient India*, p. 63.
74. Jogiraj Basu, *India of the Age of the Brāhmaṇas*, pp. 30–1.

The evidence, though not conclusive, is highly suggestive, specially if one takes the *Pañcaviṁśa Brāhmaṇa* (XIV.XI.17) into account as well. It 'provides an instance of the legal marriage of the slave girl Uśij, the mother of ṛṣi Dīrghatamas, if we may adopt her description given in the *Bṛhaddevatā*'.[75] Dīrghatamas, in turn, according to the *Vāyu Purāṇa* (II.37.67–94) had a son by a maid-servant, who became a *brahmavādin*. His name is given as Kakṣīvat and he is called Śūdrayoni in the *Mahābhārata*. P.L. Bhargava points out that this Kakṣīvat should not be confused with a royal namesake of his.

The picture that emerges is that as the Aryans settled down and moved further into India they married women belonging to the lower classes among themselves as well as the local inhabitants who were being assimilated in this class. The children of such union were not consigned to the bottom of the totem pole as a stereotypical view of the caste system would suggest. Many attained to a spiritual status regardless of birth and perhaps this historical fact found its way into Hindu myths as well.

> About a dozen ṛṣis, whose mothers belonged to what may be regarded as the one or the other section of the Śūdra varṇa, are enumerated in the *Bhaviśya Purāṇa*. With minor modifications the list recurs in several other Purāṇas and the *Mahābhārata*. It informs us that Vyāsa was born of a fisherwoman, Parāśara of a śvapāka woman, Kapiñjalada of a caṇḍāla woman, Vasiṣṭha of a prostitute (*gaṇikā*), and the best of sages (*muniśreṣṭha*) Madanapāla was the child of a boatwoman. As a justification for this kind of list, it is said at the end that the origins of the ṛṣis, rivers, pious people, great souls and of the bad character of women cannot be discovered.[76]

Thus the tradition, as the institution of caste developed, was equally aware that spirituality and virtue transcended caste.

The Āraṇyakas

The Āraṇyakas as a body of literature have not been explored as thoroughly as the Saṁhitās and the Upaniṣads, or even the Brāhmaṇas. Nevertheless, this body of literature militates against a monolithic monolatrous view of the caste system. It is true that the account of the origin of caste in the *Taittirīya Āraṇyaka* (III.XII.5–6)

75. R.S. Sharma, *Śūdras in Ancient India*, p. 63.
76. Ibid., p. 63.

follows the *Puruṣasūkta*, but *Taittirīya Āraṇyaka* I.XXIII.1–9 offers the following account of creation:

This was water, fluid. Prajāpati alone was produced on a lotus-leaf. Within, in his mind, desire arose, 'Let us create this.' Hence whatever a man aims at in his mind, he declares by speech, and performs by action. Hence this verse has been uttered, 'Desire formerly arose in it, which was the primal germ of mind, (2) (and which) sages, searching with their intellect, have discovered in the heart as the bond between the existent and the non-existent' (R.V. x.129,4). That of which he is desirous comes to the man who thus knows. He practised austere fervour. Having practised austere fervour, he shook his body. From its flesh the rishis (called) Aruṇas, Ketus, and Vātaraśanas arose. 3. His nails became the Vaikhānasas, his hairs the Bālakhilyas. The fluid (of his body became) a tortoise moving amid the waters. He said to him, 'Thou hast sprung from my skin and flesh.' 4. 'No,' replied the tortoise, 'I was here before.' In that (in his having been 'before' *pūrvam*) consists the manhood of a man (*purusha*). Becoming 'man (*purusha*) with a thousand heads, a thousand eyes, a thousand feet' (R.V. x.90,1), he ārose. Prajapati said to him, 'Thou wert produced before me: do thou first make this.' He took water from this (5) in the cavity of his two hands, and placed it on the east, repeating the text, 'so be it, o Sun.' From thence the sun arose. That was the eastern quarter. Thẹn Aruna Ketu placed (the water) to the south, saying, 'so be it, o Agni.' Thence Agni arose. That was the southern quarter. Then Aruṇa Ketu placed (the water) to the west, saying 'so be it, o Vāyu.' 6. Thence arose Vāyu. That was the western quarter. Then Aruṇa Ketu placed (the water) to the north, saying 'so be it, o Pūshan.' Thence arose Pūshan. That is this quarter. 7. Then Aruṇa Ketu placed (the water) above, saying 'so be it, o gods.' Thence arose gods, MEN, fathers, Gandharvas and Apsarases. That is the upper quarter. From the drops which fell apart arose the Asuras, Rakshases, and Piśāchas. Therefore they perished, because they were produced from drops. Hence this text has been uttered; (8) 'when the great waters became pregnant, containing wisdom, and generating Svayambhū, from them were created these creations. All this was produced from the waters. Therefore all this is Brahma Svayambhū.' Hence all this was as it were loose, as it were unsteady. Prajāpati was that. Having made himself through himself, he entered into that. Wherefore this verse has been uttered; (9) 'Having formed the world, having formed existing things and all intermediate quarters and quarters, Prajāpati, the firstborn of the ceremonial, entered into himself with himself.'[77]

It is extremely significant here that (1) although this account alludes to the first verse of the *Puruṣasūkta*, it does not refer to the origin of castes at all but rather to the origin of human beings, and that (2) although the gods and the varṇas have been connected in the

77. J. Muir, *Original Sanskrit Texts*, vol. I, pp. 32–3.

Brāhmaṇas and this account discusses the origin of the gods as well, again no reference is made to the varṇas.

The Upaniṣads

The body of literature known as the Upaniṣads or Vedānta may now be scoured for material in the light of which the stereotype of the caste system can be examined.

The *Bṛhadāraṇyaka Upaniṣad* gives an interesting account of the genesis of varṇa among the gods and human beings (I.4.11–15).

11. Verily, in the beginning this (world) was *Brahman*, one only. That, being one, did not flourish. He created further an excellent form, the *Kṣatra* power, even those who are *Kṣatras* (rulers) among the gods, Indra, Varuṇa, Soma (Moon), Rudra, Parjanya, Yama, Mṛtyu (Death), Iśāna. Therefore there is nothing higher than *Kṣatra*. Therefore at the Rājasūya sacrifice the Brāhmaṇa sits below the Kṣatriya. On Kṣatrahood alone does he confer this honour. But the Brāhmaṇa is nevertheless the source of the *Kṣatra*. Therefore even if the king attains supremacy at the end of it, he resorts to the Brāhmaṇa as his source. Therefore he who injures the Brāhmaṇa strikes at his own source. He becomes more evil as he injures one who is superior.

12. Yet he did not flourish. He created the *viś* (the commonality), these classes of gods who are designated in groups, the Vasus, Rudras, Ādityas, Viśvedevās and Maruts.

13. He did not still flourish. He created the Śūdra order, as Pūṣan. Verily, this (earth) is Pūṣan (the nourisher), for she nourishes everything that is.

14. Yet he did not flourish. He created further an excellent form, justice. This is the power of the Kṣatriya class, viz. justice. Therefore there is nothing higher than justice. So a weak man hopes (to defeat) a strong man by means of justice as one does through a king. Verily, that which is justice is truth. Therefore they say of a man who speaks the truth, he speaks justice or of a man who speaks justice that he speaks the truth. Verily, both these are the same.

15. So these (four orders were created) the Brāhmaṇa, the Kṣatriya, the Vaiśya and the Śūdra. Among the gods that Brahmā existed as Fire, among men as Brāhmaṇa, as a Kṣatriya by means of the (divine) Kṣatriya, as a Vaiśya by means of the (divine) Vaiśya, as a Śūdra by means of the (divine) Śūdra. Therefore people desire a place among the gods through fire only, and among men as the Brāhmaṇa, for by these two forms (pre-eminently) Brahmā existed. If anyone, however, departs from this world without seeing (knowing) his own world, it being unknown, does not protect him, as the Vedas unrecited or as a deed not done do not (protect him). Even if one performs a great and holy work, but without knowing this, that work of his is exhausted in the end. One should meditate only on the Self as his (true) world. The world of him who meditates

on the Self alone as his world is not exhausted for, out of that very Self he creates whatsoever he desires.[78]

The account is remarkable. There is no reference to the *Puruṣasūkta.* The four varṇas do not emerge, as it were, from primeval Man but reflect the human counterparts of the four divine varṇas. The Brāhmaṇa texts also associate both gods and men with varṇas but here the Upaniṣad has imparted a transcendental dimension to the relationship. Ian Kesarcodi-Watson has drawn pointed attention to this passage. He begins by pointing out how Hindus have been put so greatly on the defensive by attacks on the caste system (in point of fact, on the stereotype of the caste system) that they 'have chosen to claim it (is) no part of Hindu orthodoxy but rather a very much later, too deeply-foreign accretion. Rather than abandon Hinduism because of a loathing for "caste", they choose to abandon "caste" for their love of Hinduism'.[79] He goes on to say:

But this move is wholly untenable, if orthodoxy is what you wish to preserve (and you may not); as unmistakable references to this teaching are, though few, nonetheless to be found in the earliest literatures, and no grounds whatever exist for holding them later accretions. Perhaps the most significant of these references is, oddly, one of the most ignored—*Bṛhadāraṇyaka* I:4:11–15. This passage expresses what I would argue unmistakably to be the orthodox Hindu understanding of *varṇa*, in a most succinct and brilliant fashion. This is the teaching that *varṇas* are 'splendoured forms' (*śreyo-rūpas*) of *Brahmā*, brought forth as archetypal principles before all visible manifestation. As such, they, unlike *jātis*, are not things that creatures *have*, or *are*.[80]

This conception of the varṇas as ideal types has received remarkably little attention and perhaps attests to the mesmerized fascination with its stereotype, to which scholarship has been addressed.

Further, the metaphysical priority of the brāhmaṇa here may also in some way be related to the historico-mythical idea that at one time caste divisions did not exist. This could work in three ways. The text says that in the beginning this world was Brahman. This is reflected in the *Mahābhārata* as well: *sarvam brāhmam idam jagat.*[81] The word Brahman here could be understood as an adjectival form of:

78. S. Radhakrishnan, ed., *The Principal Upaniṣads*, pp. 169–71.

79. Ian Kesarcodi-Watson, 'Varṇa-Jāti and Ideal Society with Reference to the Bhagavadgītā', *The Journal of Studies in the Bhagavadgītā*, II: 44 (1982).

80. Ibid.

81. S. Radhakrishnan, *The Hindu View of Life*, p. 85.

(1) the ultimate reality brạhman;
(2) the priestly class brāhmaṇa; or
(3) the creator-god Brahmā.[82]

All three interpretations can be sustained. Radhakrishnan, for instance, states on the basis of the *Mahābhārata* text: 'In the early days of the human race, it is said, there were no class distinctions, since all are born from the Supreme'.[83] This would cover the first sense. According to a commentator, in the Upaniṣadic passage when it is said Brahmā *alone was*, it is meant that Brahmā existed 'in the form of Agni and representing the Brāhmaṇ caste'.[84] On such an understanding in that age only the brāhmaṇas existed. This would cover the second sense. Finally, it could be maintained that the universe was peopled by divine beings who 'were religious, truth-speaking, and partook of Brahmā's nature.'[85] This would cover the third sense.

There is perhaps yet another way in which the transcendental idealism of the *Bṛhadāraṇyaka* surfaces in later literature—as moral idealism depicting an age in which each human varṇa functioned as an ideal type (reflecting, as it were, its divine prototype?). This is represented in a description of the Kṛta Yuga (the golden age) found in the *Mahābhārata*:

> Brāhmaṇs, Kshattriyas, Vaiśyas, and Śūdras possessed the characteristics of the Krita. In that age were born creatures devoted to their duties. They were alike in the object of their truth, in observances and in their knowledge. At that period the castes, alike in their functions, fulfilled their duties, were unceasingly devoted to one deity, and used one formula (*mantra*), one rule, and one rite. Though they had separate duties, they had but one Veda, and practised one duty. By works connected with the four orders, and dependent on conjunctures of time, but unaffected by desire, or (hope of) reward, they attained to supreme felicity. This complete and eternal righteousness of the four castes during the Kṛita was marked by the character of that age and sought after union with the supreme soul.[86]

To recapitulate: Here the varṇas represent ideal types. The idea of there being only one varṇa in the beginning should be carefully noted. The metaphysical idea of the priority of Brahman as the ultimate

82. Monier Monier-Williams, *A Sanskrit–English Dictionary*, p. 741.
83. Ibid.
84. J. Muir, *Original Sanskrit Texts*, part I, p. 20.
85. Ibid., p. 147.
86. Ibid., p. 145.

and primordial reality should not be confused with the sociological idea of there having been a time when only one caste, i.e. a casteless society, existed. It is clearly echoed in the *Mahābhārata* and accepted as such by Śaṅkara in his gloss on the passage. At the same time, while in the Upaniṣads sociologically the varna system was being provided with a supernatural and philosophical foundation (via karma), its soteriology was moving in a direction which negated caste distinctions altogether. This is analogous to Paul's assertion that in Jesus there is no distinction between Jew and Gentile, man and woman, master and slave, etc. Thus *Bṛhadāraṇyaka* IV.3.22:

22. There (in that state) a father is not a father, a mother is not a mother, the worlds are not the worlds, the gods are not the gods, the Vedas are not the Vedas. There a thief is not a thief, the murderer is not a murderer, a *caṇḍāla* is not a *caṇḍāla*, a *paulkasa* is not a *paulkasa*, mendicant is not a mendicant, an ascetic is not an ascetic. He is not followed (affected) by good, he is not followed by evil for then he has passed beyond all sorrows of the heart.[87]

Although all distinctions, not just those of caste, are eliminated in the absolutistic salvific experience which represents the *summum bonum* in the early Upaniṣads, it is also in them that one notices for the first time the mention of the outcaste—the *caṇḍāla*—and the clear linkage between Karma and Varṇa. Students of Indian history, religion and society would do well to pause and reflect that the concept of varṇa *historically* precedes that of karma, although the latter was used by Hinduism (but significantly not by Buddhism and Jainism) to justify the former. This connection can be clearly seen in the *Chāndogya Upaniṣad* (v.10.7):

7. Those whose conduct here has been good will quickly attain a good birth (literally womb), the birth of a Brahmin, the birth of a Kṣatriya or the birth of a Vaiśya. But those whose conduct here has been evil, will quickly attain an evil birth, the birth of a dog, the birth of a hog or the birth of a Caṇḍāla.[88]

However, the very Upaniṣad, the *Chāndogya Upaniṣad*, which testifies both to the philosophical integration of the caste system with Hinduism and to the emergence of the outcastes, contains two stories which, in the opinion of many scholars, downplay the role of birth in the determination of eligibility for spiritual knowledge. These are the stories of Jānaśruti and Satyakamā, although traditional explanations

87. S. Radhakrishnan, ed., *The Principal Upaniṣads*, p. 263.
88. Ibid., p. 433.

discount the view that eligibility for Vedic studies need not depend on birth.

Jānaśruti is branded a śūdra in the course of the story by Raikva, before Raikva consents to coach him in spiritual matters after concluding what seems like, euphemistically speaking, a business-like deal.[89] As for the other story:

1. Once upon a time, Satyakāma Jabālā addressed his mother Jābāla, 'Mother, I desire to live the life of a student of sacred knowledge. Of what family am I?'
2. Then she said to him: 'I do not know, my child, of what family you are. In my youth, when I went about a great deal, as a maid-servant, I got you. So I do not know of what family you are. However, I am Jābāla by name and you are Satyakāma by name. So you may speak of yourself as Satyakāma Jābāla (the son of Jābāla).'
3. Then he went to Gautama, the son of Haridrumata and said, 'I wish to become a student of sacred knowledge. May I become your pupil, Venerable Sir.'
4. He said to him 'Of what family are you, my dear?' He replied, 'I do not know this, sir, of what family I am. I asked my mother. She answered me, "In my youth, when I went about a great deal as a maid-servant, I got you. So I do not know of what family you are. I am Jabālā by name and you are Satyakāma by name." So I am Satyakāma Jābāla, Sir.'
5. He then said to him, 'None but a Brāhmaṇa could thus explain. Bring the fuel, my dear, I will receive you, as a pupil. Thou hast not departed from the truth.' Having initiated him, he separated out four hundred lean, weak cows and said, 'Go with these, my dear.' While taking them away, he said, 'I may not return without a thousand.' He lived away a number of years. When they came to be a thousand.[90]

The point to note here is that it is Satyakāma's *honesty* and not his ancestry (which is unknown) that is taken as establishing his brahminhood.

The delinking of brahminhood from birth is carried to the point of its sole association with worth or virtue in the *Vajrasūcikopaniṣad*, which bears striking resemblance to a Buddhist text attributed to Aśvaghoṣa.[91]

The Manusmṛti

Let us now examine the typical version of the caste system in the light of Smṛti literature.

89. Ibid., p. 401 ff.
90. Ibid., pp. 406–7.
91. Ibid., pp. 935–8.

The idea of inequality based on birth has been identified with the caste system. This has the support of *Manusmṛti* x.4–5:

4. The Brāhmaṇa, the Kṣatriya and the Vaiśya castes (varṇa) are the twice-born ones, but the fourth, the Śūdra, has one birth only; there is no fifth (caste).

5. In all castes (varṇa) those (children) only which are begotten in the direct order on wedded wives, equal (in caste and married as) virgins, are to be considered as belonging to the same caste (as their fathers).[92]

However, the statement that this means 'unchangeable inequality based on birth' does not take into account certain other sections of the text. According to *Manusmṛti* II.168, a brāhmaṇa can become a śūdra even in one life.

168. A twice-born man who, not having studied the Veda, applies himself to other (and worldly study), soon falls, even while living, to the condition of a Sudra and his descendants (after him).[93]

The rot can set in even earlier, according to *Manusmṛti* x.92–3:

92. By (selling) flesh, salt, and lac a Brāhmaṇa at once becomes an outcast; by selling milk he becomes (equal to) a Śūdra in three days.

93. But by willingly selling in this world other (forbidden) commodities, a Brāhmaṇa assumes after seven nights the character of a Vaiśya.[94]

A brāhmaṇa can fall, but can members of the other varṇas rise? Manu explicitly refers to the fact that Viśvāmitra, son of Gādhi, a kṣatriya, became a brāhmaṇa by humility (VII.42). Hence, caste is a matter of character not birth, or not just birth. If character determines caste then it is not possible to claim that caste perpetuates inequality based on birth. This is clear from a consideration of the status of the śūdra in Manu (x.123–8):

123. The service of Brāhmaṇas alone is declared (to be) an excellent occupation for a Śūdra; for whatever else besides this he may perform will bear him no fruit.

124. They must allot to him out of their own family (-property) a suitable maintenance, after considering his ability, his industry, and the number of those whom he is bound to support.

125. The remnants of their food must be given to him, as well as their old clothes, the refuse of their grain, and their old household furniture.

92. G. Bühler, tr., *The Laws of Manu* (Delhi: Motilal Banarsidass, 1967; first published 1886), p. 402.

93. Ibid., p. 61.

94. Ibid., p. 422.

126. A Śūdra cannot commit an offence, causing a loss of caste (pātaka), and he is not worthy to receive the sacraments; he has no right to (fulfil) the sacred law (of the Aryans, yet) there is no prohibition against (his fulfilling certain portions of) the law.

127. (Śūdras) who are desirous to gain merit, and know (their) duty, commit no sin, but gain praise, if they imitate the practice of virtuous men without reciting sacred texts.

128. The more a (Śūdra), keeping himself free from envy, imitates the behaviour of the virtuous, the more he gains, without being censured, (exaltation in) this world and the next.[95]

That such exaltation may raise a śūdra, even in this life, to parity with a brāhmaṇa is clearly implied in the *Mahābhārata* (XII.189.4.8):

... that man is known as brāhmaṇa in whom are seen truthfulness, generosity, absence of hate, absence of wickedness, shame (restraint for avoiding wrong doing), compassion and a life of austerity; if these signs are observed in a śūdra and are not found in a brāhmaṇa, then the śūdra is not a śūdra (should not be treated as a śūdra) and the brāhmaṇa is not a brāhmaṇa.[96]

The rise of śūdra to brāhminhood is even more explicitly stated elsewhere (III.216.14–15): '... that śūdra who is ever engaged in self-control, truth and righteousness, I regard him a Brahmin. One is a twice-born by conduct alone'.[97]

It is sometimes claimed on the basis of passages in *Manusmṛti* (X.2.3, etc.) that brahmins are glorified therein. But it should not be overlooked that this applies only to *virtuous* brahmins, as vicious brahmins can be killed (VIII.350). The supreme virtue of a brahmin is friendliness to all (II.87). While others are enjoined to have an attitude of respect towards brahmins, the attitude of the brahmins towards such respect and toward others also needs to be considered. A brahmin's attitude towards the respect he receives from others is thus laid down by Manu (II.162–3):

162. A Brāhmaṇa should always fear homage as if it were poison; and constantly desire (to suffer) scorn as (he would long for) nectar.

163. For he who is scorned (nevertheless may) sleep with an easy mind, awake with an easy mind, and with an easy mind walk here among men; but the scorner utterly perishes.[98]

95. Ibid., p. 429.
96. P.V. Kane, *History of Dharmaśāstra*, vol. V, pt II, pp. 1636–7.
97. Ibid., p. 1006, author's translation.
98. G. Bühler, tr., *The Laws of Manu*, p. 60.

The attitude of universal kindness, which is how a brahmin should behave toward others, has already been referred to.

Moreover, the *Manusmṛti* gives numerous instances of members of one varṇa marrying those of another and gives a list of subcastes which emerge as a result. Thus the idea that a śūdra must marry only a śūdra doesn't work either, although that is what Manu may have hoped for, nor does it work in the case of other varṇas (x.6–23).

It might be maintained that marrying outside one's caste leads to a decline in status, but over generations caste status can be raised as well. Thus *Manusmṛti* (x.63–5):

63. Abstention from injuring (creatures), veracity, abstention from unlawfully appropriating (the goods of others), purity, and control of the organs, Manu has declared to be the summary of the law for the four castes.

64. If (a female of the caste), sprung from a Brāhmaṇa and a Śūdra female, bear (children) to one of the highest caste, the inferior (tribe) attains the highest caste within the seventh generation.

65. (Thus) a Śūdra attains the rank of a Brāhmaṇa, and (in a similar manner) a Brāhmaṇa sinks to the level of a Śūdra; but know that it is the same with the offspring of a Kṣatriya or a Vaiśya.[99]

These verses are extremely important as they display the extent to which the caste system has been misrepresented:

(1) Verse x.63 mentions dharmas which are common to all *castes*. These sādhāraṇa-dharmas or universal virtues are to be practised by all. The impression that the Hindus are locked for life in their narrow caste-specific ethics is perverse.

(2) Verses x.64 and 65 refer to the phenomena known as *jātyutkarṣa* and *jātyapkarṣa* or the rise and fall in caste status. The *Yājñavalkya Smṛti* (I.96) speaks of two kinds of *jātyutkarṣa* and *jātyapkarṣa*: one through marriage, the other through vocation.

That the change can occur either through marriage or vocation is implied in Manu in the verse describing *varṇasaṅkara* or 'confusion of castes' (x.27):

224. By adultery (committed by persons) of (different) castes, by marriage with women who ought not to be married, and by the neglect of the duties and occupations (prescribed) to each, are produced (sons who owe their origin) to a confusion of the castes.[100]

99. Ibid., p. 416.
100. Ibid., p. 407.

Not only, then, can varṇa change even within a lifetime, not only have people married across varṇa lines, but occupations too can be changed. This is specially possible in times of crisis and is called *āpaddharma.* The relevant verses in the *Manusmṛti* are x.80–3, 95, 98–100.

80. Among several occupations the most commendable are, teaching the Veda for a Brāhmaṇa, protecting (the people) for a Kṣhatriya, and trade for a Vaisya.

81. But a Brāhmaṇa, unable to subsist by his peculiar occupations just mentioned, may live according to the law applicable to Kṣhatriyas; for the latter is next to him in rank.

82. If it is asked, 'How shall it be, if he cannot maintain himself by either (of these occupations)?' The answer is, he may adopt a Vaiśya's mode of life, employing himself in agriculture and rearing cattle.

83. But a Brāhmaṇa, or a Kṣhatriya, living by a Vaiśya's mode of subsistence, shall carefully avoid (the pursuit of) agriculture, (which causes) injury to many beings and depends on others.

95. A Kṣhatriya who has fallen into distress, may subsist by all these (means); but he must never arrogantly adopt the mode of life (prescribed for his) betters.

98. A Vaiśya who is unable to subsist by his own duties, may even maintain himself by a Śūdra's mode of life, avoiding (however) acts forbidden (to him), and he should give it up, when he is able (to do so).

99. But a Śūdra, being unable to find service with the twice-born and threatened with the loss of his sons and wife (through hunger), may maintain himself by handicrafts.

100. (Let him follow) those mechanical occupations and those various practical arts by following which the twice-born are (best) served.[101]

Manu (VIII.348–51) does not confine the defence of dharma to the kṣatriyas, but includes all the three higher castes in it.

348. Twice-born men may take up arms when (they are) hindered (in the fulfilment of) their duties, when destruction (threatens) the twice-born castes (varṇa) in (evil) times.

349. In their own defence, in a strife for the fees of officiating priests, and in order to protect women and Brāhmaṇas; he who (under such circumstances) kills in the cause of right, commits no sin.

350. One may slay without hesitation an assassin who approaches (with murderous intent), whether (he be one's) teacher, a child or an aged man, or a Brāhmaṇa deeply versed in the Vedas.

101. Ibid., pp. 421, 422, 423.

351. By killing an assassin the slayer incurs no guilt, whether (he does it) publicly or secretly; in that case fury recoils upon fury.[102]

In such cases, according to Manu (x.62), those who perish attain beatitude even if they do not belong to the Aryan community.

6. Dying, without the expectation of a reward, for the sake of Brāhmaṇas and of cows, or in the defence of women and children, secures beatitude to those excluded (from the Aryan community, vāhya).[103]

The *Arthaśāstra* (IX.2) even prefers an army composed of vaiśyas and śūdras.

This provision for change of occupation in times of economic crisis and joining ranks militarily in times of political crisis may account for the fact that while 'social inequality based on birth and the prohibition in regard to marriage continued in force until recently',[104] from the medieval rather than the classical period,[105] 'the attempt to confine castes to separate professions seems never to have succeeded'.[106]

The Bhagavadgītā

A popular misconception about the *Bhagavadgītā* relates to the issue of caste. It is said to support the caste system. Three verses from the *Gītā* are often cited in support: (1) verse 31 of Chapter II in which Arjuna is asked to fight because as a kṣatriya it is his duty to do so; (2) verse 13 of Chapter IV in which Kṛṣṇa says that he has created the fourfold order of the varṇas; and (3) verse 47 of Chapter XVIII which states that one should perform one's dharma even if devoid of merit and not follow another's even if well performed.

Let us now examine the context of each of these verses.

I

In verse 31 of Chapter II Arjuna is indeed asked to fight because he is a kṣatriya. Now the question is: How compelling an argument

102. Ibid., pp. 314–15.
103. Ibid., p. 416.
104. K.M. Panikkar, *Hindu Society at the Crossroads* (Bombay: Asia Publishing House, 1961), p. 34.
105. P.V. Kane, *History of Dharmaśāstra*, vol II, pt I, p. 52.
106. K.M. Panikkar, *Hindu Society at the Crossroads*, p. 35.

does Kṛṣṇa consider it and how compelling an argument does Arjuna find it to be?

How compelling an argument does Kṛṣṇa consider it? Not very compelling. He uses the particle *api* (moreover) while introducing the argument. It is an *additional* argument. And it is embedded in a whole web of *other* arguments. It is curious that the argument by duty (*svadharma*) is followed by an argument by booty—that is if you die in battle you will gain heaven, and if you win you stand to gain a kingdom.

Thus, Kṛṣṇa does not think that the argument by caste is going to clinch the issue. It is not compelling enough. Arjuna finds it even less compelling than Kṛṣṇa, for he does not respond to it. The key question here is: Why does Arjuna not respond to it?

The answer is simple. He finds that many of the key figures involved in this battle are not kṣatriyas! In verse 8 of Chapter I, Duryodhana identifies the main warriors on his side, namely Droṇa, Bhīṣma, Karṇa, Kṛpa, Aśvatthāmā, Vikarṇa, and Saumadatti. In some versions an eighth name, that of Jayadratha, is added.

Let us now examine the background of these warriors. Droṇa is a brāhmaṇa; Bhīṣma qualifies, but barely—his father was a kṣatriya but his mother is said to have been Ganga; Karna's ancestry was unknown at this point in the narrative, and, in fact, he was once faced down by Arjuna for this reason and was made a king and therefore a kṣatriya through consecration by Duryodhana (*Mahābhārata*, Ādiparva, Chapters 134–6); Kṛpa is the son of an ascetic, *brought up* as a prince; Aśvatthāma is Droṇa's son, and so a brāhmaṇa; Vikarṇa (son of Dhṛtarāṣṭra); Saumadatti (son of king Bhūriśravas) and Jayadratha (king of Sindhu) alone qualify fully as kṣatriyas by birth.

The reasons for the tentative nature of Kṛṣṇa's argument and the sceptical response of Arjuna are clear. The appeal that Arjuna should fight because he is a kṣatriya *by birth* runs into cognitive dissonances: (i) not all the warriors who have assembled to fight are kṣatriyas; (ii) not all the 'kṣatriyas' who have assembled to fight are kṣatriyas by birth. Why should the Arjuna fight just because he is a kṣatriya? There is a further paradox: Kṛṣṇa, himself a kṣatriya, has forsworn to participate in the fight and is urging Arjuna to fight on the grounds that Arjuna is a kṣatriya. It must also be remembered that Arjuna's father is said to have been Indra. Indra's divine varṇa is no doubt kṣatriya, but one should note that the varṇa boundaries between the *human and the divine* have already been crossed in his own case!

II

In Chapter IV Kṛṣṇa claims that he has created the *cāturvarṇya* (the word is important).[107] Now, two questions arise: (1) What exactly does Kṛṣṇa claim he has created? (2) On what basis has he created what he has created?

Kṛṣṇa claims that he has created *cāturvarṇya*, that is, the collectivity of four varṇas. But it can also mean 'that which is characterized by the four varṇas', namely the social universe; and not the four varṇas *themselves as such.* The statement is a semantic double-decker.

The basis of both (1) the collectivity and (2) that which is characterized by this collectivity is *guṇa*, and karma (*guṇakarmavibhāgaśaḥ*). The word *janma* is conspicuous by its absence.

Thus, even if Kṛṣṇa has created the four varṇas, they are based not on birth but on qualities and actions and if he has created that which is characterized by the 'caste-system' rather than the system itself, then that entity or society contains divisions on the basis of qualities and actions. In both cases, birth-ascription is wanting.[108]

107. For a thorough grammatical analysis, see S.K. Belvalkar, 'Two mishandled passages from the *Bhagavadgitā*', in N. Sivarama Sastry and G. Hanumantha Rao, eds, *Prof. M. Hiriyanna Commemoration Volume* (Mysore: Prof. M. Hiriyanna Commemoration Volume Committee, 1952), pp. 1–7.

108. This point has also been noted by other scholars. K.M. Panikkar remarks: 'In the Gita it is no doubt stated:

Chaturvarnyam maya srstam
Guna karma vibhagasah

and this is often quoted as proving conclusively that caste is a divinely ordained institution. But examined carefully it would be seen that Krishna's words constitute a devastating attack on caste and not its justification. Literally translated the passage means: The fourfold order was created by Me *on the basis of quality and action.* It is the most unequivocal repudiation of the divine origin of caste *based on birth*, the most categorical denial of the Brahmin claim of inherent superiority. No one denies functional differentiations based on quality and action. Even in classless societies, people have to be divided into intellectuals, soldiers, workers and peasants, on the basis of *guna* and *karma.* This is all that the Gita teaches and yet by quoting the first line alone without adding the basis on which Krishna claims to have created it, the very purpose of the text, the categorical repudiation of caste-division based on birth, is perverted and it is made to serve the object of proving to the ignorant that the Gita affirms the sanctity of caste' (*Hindu Society at the Crossroads*, pp. 40–1). Also see P.V. Kane, *History of Dharmaśāstra*, vol. V, pt II, pp. 1635–6.

III

In Chapter XVIII Kṛṣṇa lauds the performance of svadharma. If, however, svadharma is based on guṇa and not birth then the statement that it is better to perform one's own dharma, even though inferior, as compared to the superior performance of another's dharma, must be understood differently: 'Although one may *consider* one's *dharma* as inferior and *think* that one will perform another's *dharma* better than one's own ... , one should perform one's own *dharma*', because it alone truly conforms to one's nature.[109]

The question still remains: Why is Arjuna not convinced by any shade of argument based on 'caste'? To claim that the *Bhagavadgītā* supports *any* version of the varṇa system is misleading because Arjuna does not consent to fight as long as such arguments are being put forward. He resumes the fight only when Kṛṣṇa says: 'Abandon all dharmas and seek refuge in me alone'. It should be noted here that Kṛṣṇa uses the expression *sarvadharmān*, meaning all dharmas. All dharmas must include varṇa dharmas if 'all' is to retain its meaning.

IV

If it is claimed that the *Bhagavadgītā* upholds the caste system then how are we to explain the paradox that *Arjuna decides to fight precisely when the argument of caste is withdrawn*?

The Uttaragītā

The evidence from the *Uttaragītā* in this context is also of interest, but a word about the work before discussing it. The *Uttaragītā* is known primarily for being commented upon by Gauḍapāda, the famous Advaitin, and some ascribe the work itself to him. 'It is mentioned in the colophons of some of the manuscripts that it is contained in some one or other Parvans of the *Mahābhārata*, or in the Bhāgavatapurāṇa, but we do not come across the actual text in any of the extant editions or manuscripts of these works.'[110]

109. That the *Dhammapada* (XII. 166) contains a similar exhortation seems to have gone unnoticed, see F. Max Müller, tr., *The Dhammapada* (Oxford University Press, 1881), p. 46. For a Buddhist interpretation thereof, see John Ross Carter and Mahinda Palihawadana, *The Dhammapada* (New York: Oxford University Press, 1987), pp. 230–1.

110. S.V. Oka, *Uttaragītā with a Translation into English and Appendices* (Poona: Bhandarkar Oriental Research Institute, 1957), p. i.

One of the manuscripts at the Bhandarkar Oriental Research Institute, dated AD 1809, ascribes a version of the text to the Bhīṣmaparva of the *Mahābhārata*.[111] This version is particularly interesting because it shows Arjuna as specifically asking Kṛṣṇa the question *kena varnanī*[112] or how is varṇa determined? Kṛṣṇa replies as follows:

Na jātiḥ kāraṇam tāta
guṇāḥ kalyāṇakāraṇam
Vratasthampi caṇḍālam
taṁ devā brāhmaṇam viduḥ.[113]

Birth is not the cause, my friend; it is virtues which are the cause of auspiciousness. Even a caṇḍāla observing the vow is considered a brāhmaṇa by the gods.

The verse is of interest from several standpoints. First, birth is categorically rejected as the determinant of varṇa. Second, qualities are clearly, by contrast, posited as the basis of varṇa. This point is important because some scholars tend to adhere to a middle position on caste, regarding *both* birth and qualities conjointly as its determinants. This verse clearly comes out on the side of qualities alone. Third, it is claimed that a virtuous caṇḍāla is regarded as a brāhmaṇa *by the gods*. This statement seems to counter the contention that the caste system as based on birth is divinely sanctioned, for divine sanction is here claimed for the position that varṇa is based on virtue.

One final point. The possibility of Buddhist influence in this case seems particularly strong. Gauḍapāda, to whom the text owes such recognition as it possesses, is known for his familiarity with, if not indebtedness to, Buddhist thought.[114] Buddhist texts are known to insist that brahminhood is determined by virtue and not birth.[115] However, it would be a mistake to ascribe this emphasis on virtue as the determinant of caste merely to Buddhist influence. The parallel between a virtuous śūdra and brāhmaṇa is hinted at in Buddhist texts (e.g. *Sutta-nipāta*, *Vasalasutta*, verse 27, etc.) but the equation is firmly established in the *Mahābhārata*, and carried even beyond the

111. Ibid., p. v.

112. Ibid., p. 43.

113. Ibid., p. 44.

114. Eliot Deutsch and J.A.B. van Buitenen, *A Source Book of Advaita Vedānta* (Honolulu: The University Press of Hawaii, 1971), p. 119.

115. See P.V. Kane, *History of Dharmaśāstra*, vol. v, pt II, pp. 1005, 1653.

range of Buddhism when it is asserted that 'Brāhmaṇas learned in the Vedas regard a virtuous śūdra as the effulgent Viṣṇu of the universe, the foremost one in all the world'.[116] It should be remembered that Buddhas are only born as a kṣatriya or brāhmaṇa and that Maitreya will be born as a brāhmaṇa.[117] Inasmuch as the text under discussion is ascribed to the *Mahābhārata*, the fact that divine sanction is being accorded to the equation of the virtuous caṇḍāla (who is a few notches below even the śūdra) and a brāhmaṇa is therefore quite significant.

It is also useful to consider three terms: *vṛṣala* used in the Pali texts, caṇḍāla used in our text and *vaidehaka* used as an adjective of śūdra in the passage from the *Mahābhārata*, about which R.S. Sharma remarks: 'The use of the term, *vaidehaka* as an adjective of *śūdra* seems to be curious.'[118] *Vṛṣala* is translated by Kane as just śūdra[119] and is often considered a fallen kṣatriya.[120] It is more pejorative in Pali[121] but the caṇḍāla 'is the lowest of men (*Manusmṛti* x.12), beyond the pale of the religious observances prescribed for the four varṇas (sarvadharmabahiṣkṛt, as Yaj I.93 says) and often spoken of in the same breath as dogs and crows'.[122] The vaidehaka[123] seems to be just a bit better off than the caṇḍāla. It is therefore of some significance that the word caṇḍāla is used in the *Uttaragītā*.

A textual analysis of Śruti and Smṛti texts on the caste system suggests that the picture of the system as presented in current writings is so one-sided as to be seriously flawed. It is dominated by three images:

(1) The caste system is divinely sanctioned by the *Puruṣasūkta*.
(2) The caste system divides Hindu society into watertight

116. See R.S Sharma, *Śūdras in Ancient India*, p. 274.

117. Edward Conze, tr., *Buddhist Scriptures* (Harmondsworth: Penguin Books, 1959), p. 239.

118. Ibid., p. 274.

119. P.V. Kane, *History of Dharmaśāstra*, vol. v, pt II, p. 1635.

120. J. Muir, *Original Sanskrit Texts* (London: Trübner & Co., 1874), vol. II, p. 401, 422.

121. T.W. Rhys Davids and William Stede, eds, *The Pali Text Society's Pali–English Dictionary* (London: Pali Text Society, 1966), p. 605.

122. P.V. Kane, *History of Dharmaśāstra*, vol. II, pt I, p. 81.

123. Ibid., pp. 95–6.

compartments based on birth and is burdened by restrictions on marriage, dining and occupation.

(3) The Hindu social vision is totally devoid of the concept of one single organic humanity.

All three images need to be corrected.

It is not possible, even in a documentary history, to examine in detail all discussions on the origins of caste. One will have to rest content with citing the following general conclusion arrived at by J. Muir on the basis of his survey of such evidence. He points out that the *Puruṣasūkta* is *not* the only account of the origin of castes we possess:

In other passages, where a separate origin is assigned to the castes, they are variously said to have sprung from the words Bhūh, Bhuvaḥ, Svaḥ; from different Vedas; from different sets of prayers; from the gods, and the asuras; from nonentity, and from the imperishable, the perishable, and other principles (Harivaṁśa, I.1816). In the chapters of the Vishṇu, Vāyu, and Mārkaṇḍeya Purāṇas, where castes are described as coeval with the creation, and as having been naturally distinguished by different guṇas, or qualities, involving varieties of moral character, we are nevertheless allowed to infer that those qualities exerted no influence on the classes in whom they were inherent, as the condition of the whole race during the Kṛita age is described as one of uniform perfection and happiness; while the actual separation into castes did not take place, according to the Vāyu Purāṇa, until men had become deteriorated in the Tretā age.[124]

The second image is clearly untenable in view of the role of character in determining caste. In an extreme case, that is when the caste of someone whose caste is unknown needs to be determined, Manu says (x.57–60) that, in effect, character determines birth!

57. A man of impure origin, who belongs not to any caste, (varṇa, but whose character is) not known, who, (though) not an Aryan, has the appearance of an Aryan, one may discover by his acts.

58. Behaviour unworthy of an Aryan, harshness, cruelty, and habitual neglect of the prescribed duties betray in this world the man of impure origin.

59. A base-born man either resembles in character his father, or his mother, or both; he can never conceal his real nature.

124. J. Muir, *Original Sanskrit Texts* (Delhi: Oriental Publishers, 1972, reprint), pt I, p. 156.

60. Even if a man, born in a great family, sprang from criminal intercourse, he will certainly possess the faults of his (father), be they small or great.[125]

The *Mahābhārata* (III.180.31–3) asserts the same when Yudhiṣṭhira says:

It appears to me that it is very difficult to ascertain the caste of human beings on account of the confusion of all varṇas; all sorts of men are always begetting offspring from all sorts of women; speech, sexual intercourse, being born and death—these are common to all human beings; and there is scriptural authority (for this view) in the word 'We, whoever we are, offer the sacrifice.'[126]

The universal vision of one single society in its embryonic form is attested to in the following passage:

There is a curious (and perhaps significant) verse in the *Mahābhārata*, the Indian epic of the middle of the first millennium BC. Bhṛgu, in explaining the nature of castes to Bharadvāja, says: 'Brahmins are fair, *Kṣhatṛiyas* are reddish, *Vaiśyas* are yellowish, and the *Śūdras* are black' (*Mahābhārata*, Śāntiparva, 188, 5). However, even in those early days the races do not seem to have been by any measure pure, and Bharadvāja replied: 'If different colours indicate different castes, then all castes are mixed castes' (188, 6). Interestingly enough Bharadvāja felt uncomfortable about the division and went on to ask: 'We all seem to be affected by desire, anger, fear, sorrow, worry, hunger, and labour; how do we have caste differences then?' (188, 7)[127]

A theological approach produces the same result elsewhere in the *Mahābhārata* (12.188.10): ... 'there is no (real) distinction between the varnas, (since) the whole world is of Brahmā, since it was formerly created by Brahmā, and has had the system of varṇas on account of the various actions (of men).'[128]

This culminates in the following vision of the *Bhaviṣyapurāṇa* (I.41.45–6, 49–51; 140.20):

... 'A father has four sons. All the sons, naturally, must belong to the same caste. God is the father of all the people. Then where lies the difference of caste?' 'The fruit of a tree are alike in colour and shape and alike to touch and taste. Human beings are the fruits that grow in God's tree. How then can we make distinctions as between the fruit of the same tree?' 'If you call this body as that of a Brāhmaṇa, how can you ask if one part of him or all of him is a Brāhmaṇa? If one part is known as a Brāhmaṇa, then the Brāhmaṇa will end with the cutting off of that part. If the whole body be a Brāhmaṇa, then a

125. G. Bühler, tr., *The Law of Manu*, p. 4415.
126. P.V. Kane, *History of Dharmaśāstra*, vol II, pt I, p. 61.
127. K.M. Sen, *Hinduism*, p. 28.
128. P.V. Kane, *History of Dharmaśāstra*, vol V, pt II, p. 1636.

person who performs the last rites will incur the sin of killing a Brāhmaṇa.' 'A horse can be easily told apart from a herd of cows, but a Śūdra cannot be so regarded as distinct from the twice-born.'[129]

The *Bhaviṣyapurāṇa* (I.40.21) clearly proclaims: Human beings are equal (*manuṣyajāterna paro viseśaḥ*).[130]

Kāyavya

The Case of Kāyavya

According to Benjamin Walker a 'story is told in the *Mahābhārata* how Kāyavya, the son of an outcaste Nishāda woman by a barbarian, rose to the dignity of the first caste through his virtue and piety'.[131] Should this be correct, it would represent a case not even of a śūdra but a niṣāda becoming a brāhmaṇa within a lifetime.

The position of the niṣāda *vis-à-vis* the varṇas needs to be appreciated to recognize the full significance of the above claim. It is true that in the Vedic period, the niṣādas may have enjoyed ritual privileges which were suppressed in due course. The term *pañcajanāḥ* ('five peoples') etc. which occur in the *Ṛg Veda* may, according to the opinion of Aupamanyava recorded by Yāska (*Nirukta* III.8), refer to the four varṇas plus the niṣādas. Sāyaṇa, although much later, also interprets *pañcakṛṣṭayaḥ* (five tribes) in *Ṛg Veda* X.60.4 as referring to the four varṇas and the niṣādas.[132] On the basis of these and other references, R.S. Sharma has concluded that 'occasionally the Niṣāda people and generally the Niṣāda chief enjoyed the right to the Vedic sacrifice.'[133]

This situation, however, does not seem to apply to the period of classical Hinduism, though some traces of it survive, for there is a reference in the *Mahābhārata* (I.61.48 [critical text]) to the performance of a sacrifice by a *niṣādādhipati*,[134] despite the context, which deals

129. R.K. Arora, *Historical and Cultural Data from the Bhaviṣya Purāṇa*, pp. 99–100.
130. Ibid., pp. 100, 109.
131. Benjamin Walker, *Hindu World* (London: George Allen & Unwin), vol. I, p. 206.
132. See J. Muir, *Original Sanskrit Texts*, vol. I, p. 177.
133. R.S. Sharma, *Śūdras in Ancient India*, p. 71.
134. Ibid.

with the rebirth of demons in human form. According to Manu, a niṣāda is the product of a union between a brāhmaṇa male and a śūdra female (x.8), just as a caṇḍāla is the product of a union between a śūdra male and a brāhmaṇa female. It would therefore represent a case of remarkable upward mobility if a niṣāda could become a Brāhmaṇa, as is claimed in the case of Kāyavya.

The story of Kāyavya is narrated in Chapter 135 of the Śāntiparva of the *Mahābhārata* (vulgate text). It will suffice here to reproduce a summary of the chapter as found in Sörensen.

> **[Kāyavya-carita(m)]** ('the history of Kāyavya'): There was a robber *Kāyavya*, born of a *Kshatriya* father and a *Nishāda* mother. *K.* was a practiser of *kshatriya* duties, conversant with the scriptures, free from cruelty, devoted to the *brāhmaṇs*, etc. Morning and evening he went deer-hunting; he was well conversant with all the practices of the *Nishādas*, and of all animals living in the forest, etc. Alone he could vanquish many hundreds of soldiers. He worshipped his old, blind, and deaf parents in the forest every day, etc. One day many thousands of robbers made him their leader, promising not to slay women, *brāhmaṇs*, etc. By abstaining from sin they obtained great prosperity. *Kāyavya*, though a robber, still succeeded in winning felicity in heaven (XII, 135).[135]

From this account it appears that Walker's statement is erroneous in two respects: Kāyavya was not the son of a union of an outcaste niṣāda woman and a barbarian. Kāyavya's father is clearly specified as a kṣatriya (XII.135.3). In terms of Manu he was an *ugra* (x.9); more importantly, at no place in the chapter is it claimed that Kāyavya became a brāhmaṇa, only that he honoured the brahmins (XII.135.8) and when hailed by the robbers as their leader he eulogized the role of the brahmins again (XII.135.14.16–18).

Kāyavya therefore does not represent the case of a śūdra becoming a brāhmaṇa within a lifetime.

There is, however, one account in the *Mahābhārata* which clearly alludes to a śūdra attaining the status of a *sannyāsī*. The point to be borne in mind is that on strict interpretation of classical Hindu norms, a śūdra cannot become a renunciant. In the account given in Chapter 10 of the Anuśāsanaparva of the *Mahābhārata* (critical edition), a śūdra approached a *kulapati* or head of an āśrama for initiation into *pravrajyā* (XIII.10.13), but his request was declined on account of his being a śūdra, although he was allowed to serve in

135. S. Sörensen, *An Index to the Names in the Mahābhārata* (Delhi: Motilal Banarsidass, 1963: first published 1904), p. 403.

the āśrama. Thereupon, in effect, the śūdra set up his own āśrama and practised austerities and many sages began to visit his āśrama. The śūdra then asked one particular sage to help him make an offering to the manes—a typical brahmanical undertaking. And the ritual was duly performed.

The story is not without its difficulties. First, a sannyāsī is excused from the obligation of making an offering to the manes. It is pertinent, however, that the śūdra was not initiated by the kulapati and is referred to as a *tāpasa* or ascetic rather than a renunciant. Second, the moral of the rest of the story is quite different. The account continues with how both the brahmin and the śūdra ascetic are reborn—the śūdra as a king and the brahmin as his chaplain. It turns out that the king—the former śūdra—remembered his past life while his brahmin instructor did not, because he had instructed a śūdra! The pupil—the śūdra, now king—gained the full benefit of the instruction, while gain was denied to the *instructor* because he had imparted knowledge to someone not eligible for it. The tale has a rather odd moral that imparting instruction to one not eligible for it recoils on the teacher rather than the pupil!

However, the facts of the story as distinguished from the moral establish the point that a śūdra raised himself to a status where a brahmin imparted to him the knowledge of the ritual of *pitṛkārya* (XIII.10.30), the province of brahmins, thereby accepting him as an equal. It may be added that at this pitṛkārya[136] or *śrāddha*—one of the five daily sacrifices—*other* brahmins have to be fed (III.83). Hence, acceptance in the brahmanical community is clearly implied. The fact that the śūdra was instructed in śrāddha rites clearly indicates his induction into the community of brahmins.

Mātaṅga

The Case of Mātaṅga

The case of Mātaṅga deserves to be scrupulously examined in the present context. One may begin by stating the facts briefly. Mātaṅga was

> A man who was the son of a *caṇḍāla*, but who was brought up as a *brāhmaṇa.* One day when he was cruelly goading a young ass its mother said that such

136. The word *pitṛkārya* appears in *Manusmṛti* (III.252).

> conduct was only to be expected from one of his own birth. Mātaṅga angrily demanded an explanation. The ass informed him that his mother had been a drunk and his father only a barber. Then Mātaṅga determined to become a 'real' *brāhmaṇa*, and to that end practised extreme austerities (*tapas*), but Indra still refused to recognize him as a *brāhmaṇa*. For hundreds of years he continued *tapas* until Indra relented and gave him power to move like a bird, to change his shape at will and to become famous.

It is further said that 'Sītā and Rāma visited Mātaṅga in his hermitage near the Ṛṣyamūka mountain, where the trees are said to have grown from the sweat of his pupils.'[137]

What emerges clearly from the account in the *Mahābhārata* is that Mātaṅga set out to attain brahminhood. This can be established in several ways. (1) The story of Mātaṅga is narrated by Bhīṣma to Yudhiṣṭhira in response to the following question of Yudhiṣṭhira: 'Explain to me the means—whether it be intense austere—fervour, or ceremonies, or Vedic learning—whereby a Kṣatriya, a Vaiśya or a Sūdra, if he desire it, can attain to the state of a Brāhmaṇa.'[138] (2) It is when Mātaṅga discovers that he is not a pure brāhmaṇa that he sets out to acquire brahminhood. (3) The moral of the story as it is presented is that it is not possible for a caṇḍāla to gain that status.

A close reading of the story, however, reveals several curiosities. (1) The question put by Yudhiṣṭhira is not *whether* brahminhood can be attained by the other varṇas but rather *how*. (2) The optional means suggested by Yudhiṣṭhira are: *tapasā* (by austerities) or *karmaṇā* (action)[139] or *śrutena* (learning). The account of Mātaṅga, however, concentrates on austerities and actually only demonstrates that the coveted status cannot be gained by austerities. It is silent about karma and *śruta*. Are we to conclude that austerities don't work but conduct or learning might? (3) While Bhīṣma begins by saying that the status of a brahmin cannot be gained over several lives, the account deals with only *one* life of Mātaṅga, though of prodigious duration. (4) When the she-ass consoles the colt she identifies Mātaṅga as a caṇḍāla on the basis of his behaviour *first*. She says: 'This man of wicked disposition shows no pity to a tender colt, and thereby indicates his origin; for it is birth which determines character'. But that birth she infers from character, although it is true that she

137. Margaret and James Stutley, *A Dictionary of Hinduism*, pp. 184–5.
138. J. Muir, *Original Sanskrit Texts* pt I, p. 440. Some diacritics supplied.
139. Ibid. Muir translates *karma* as ceremonies.

proceeds to narrate the dubious circumstances of Mātaṅga's birth as well. (5) Indra is supposed to confer brahminhood in this account but the varṇa of Indra himself is a kṣatriya![140] (Could royal intervention alter varṇa in ancient times?) (6) In the end, Mātaṇga is given all kinds of blessings but not brahminhood. In fact, his case again raises the interesting point whether a distinction must be drawn between a ṛṣi and a brāhmaṇa. The *Ṛg Veda* would attests to ṛṣis who are not brahmins and even in the *Mahābhārata* Mātaṅga is called a *rajarṣi*[141] but not a brāhmaṇa. Similarly, in the *Rāmāyaṇa*, again, Mātaṅga is a sage but not a brahmin.[142] Thus, if it be argued that the status of a ṛṣi is in some sense even higher than that of a brāhmaṇa, then it could be said that Mātaṅga rose to a rank even higher than that of a brahmin. But the argument that Mātaṅga could not become a brahmin still holds. Although elsewhere Benjamin Walker uses the case of Mātaṅga to illustrate the point 'how a man, claiming to be a brahmin was shown to be the son of a low-caste barber',[143] in his discussion of the legend of Mātaṅga, he correctly emphasizes that even though Indra rushed forward to save him he

> still refused to change his caste. At the request of the persevering saint the God agreed to give him the power of flight and of changing his shape at will, and assured him that he will receive all the honour due to him, but declared that it was impossible for him to become a brahmin.[144]

The issue of being able to become a sage but not a brahmin can be carried further. The Vasalasutta of the *Sutta-nipāta* alludes to the legend of Mātaṅga and is reminiscent of the *Mahābhārata* story.[145] In this *sutta*, a brahmin seeks to avoid the Buddha as an outcast, whereupon Buddha explains to him what makes one an outcast. Towards the end of his explication, the Buddha says:

> 21. 'Not by birth does one become an outcast, not by birth does one become a Brāhmaṇa; by deeds one becomes an outcast, by deeds one becomes a Brāhmaṇa. (135)
>
> 22. 'Know ye this in the way that this example of mine (shows): There was a Caṇḍāla of the Sopāka caste, well known as Mātaṅga. (136)

140. J. Muir, *Original Sanskrit Texts*, part I, p. 20.
141. Ibid., p. 442.
142. Ibid.
143. Benjamin Walker, *Hindu World*, vol. I, p. 206.
144. Ibid., vol. II, p. 44.
145. R.S. Sharma does not connect the two figures (*Śūdras in Ancient India*, p. 134).

23. 'This Mātaṅga reached the highest fame, such as was very difficult to obtain, and many Khattiyas and Brāhmaṇas went to serve him. (137)

24. 'He having mounted the vehicle of the gods, (and entered) the high road (that is) free from dust, having abandoned sensual desires, went to the Brahma world. (138)

25. 'His birth did not prevent him from being re-born in the Brahma world; (on the other hand) there are Brāhmaṇas, born in the family of preceptors, friends of the hymns (of the Vedas). (139)

26. 'But they are continually caught in sinful deeds, and are to be blamed in this world, while in the coming (world) hell (awaits them); birth does not save them from hell nor from blame. (140)

27. '(Therefore) not by birth does one become an outcast, not by birth does one become a Brāhmaṇa, by deeds one becomes an outcast, by deeds one becomes a Brāhmaṇa.' (141)[146]

Here, too, it is claimed that Mātaṅga was liberated rather than that he became a brahmin.

It must be granted that the Buddhists do not set the same store by being a brahmin as do the Hindus, but it is worth noting that even here brahminhood eludes Mātaṅga.

In this context, there are two words in Sanskrit which are relevant to the station of a brahmin: *brahmaṇya* and *brāhmaṇya*.[147] According to the Sanskrit grammatical tradition, the former is more spiritual in connotation.

Pāṇini uses the Vedic term Brahman (v.1.7) and also Brāhmaṇa for the caste (*Brāhmo' jātau*, VI.4.171). He seems to find a distinction between them taking the former in a cultural reference as shown in the derivative *brahmaṇya (Brahmane hitaṁ)* to indicate what appertains to the spiritual welfare of a Brāhmana (*Brāhmaṇebhyo hitaṁ, Bhāshya,* v.1.7; II.339), and reserving the term Brāhmana for the caste based on birth (son of a Brāhmaṇ). This point is also explained by Patañjali stating that 'although the two terms Brahman and Brāhmaṇa are synonymous (*samānārthau etau ... Brahman-śabdo Brāhmaṇa-śabdascha*, II.339), yet the affix *yat* is added only to Brahman to have the form *brahmaṇya*.'[148]

146. V. Fausböll, tr., *The Sutta-Nipāta* (Sacred Books of the East Series, vol. 10: Oxford University Press, 1881; 1973, reprint), p. 23.

147. V.S. Agrawala, *India as Known to Pāṇini* (Varanasi: Prithvi Prakashan, 1963), p. 78.

148. P.K. Gode and C.G. Karve, eds, *V.S. Apte's the Practical Sanskrit–English Dictionary* (Poona: Prasad Prakashan, 1958), vol. II, pp. 1177–8.

Thus, V.S. Apte defines *brāhmaṇya* as 'befitting a Brāhmaṇa', and *brāhmaṇya* as '1. Relating to Brahma. 2. Relating to Brahman or the creator. 3. Relating to the acquisition of sacred knowledge, holy, pious. 4. Fit for a brāhmaṇa. 5. Friendly or hospitable to a brāhmaṇa.'[149] The Monier-Williams Dictionary also distinguishes between *brahmaṇya* and *brāhmaṇya*: '*Brahmaṇya*, mfn. relating to Brahma or Brahmā, devoted to sacred knowledge or friendly to Brāhmans, religious, pious; brāhmaṇya, mfn. (fr. *brāhmaṇá*), fit for brahmans.'[150] In both cases, the *Mahābhārata* is cited as the source-text.

It is significant that the account of Mātaṅga follows distinct courses in Hindu and Buddhist literature, and this is reflected in the terminology. While in the Hindu case *brahmaṇya* has led to *brāhmaṇya*, Buddhist usage is reflected in the form Mahā-brahmā. According to Pāṇini, 'a brāhmaṇa pre-eminent in his duties (dharma)' is called *Mahābrahmaḥ* (v.4.105). The Pali texts take Mahā-brahmā to mean a superbrāhmaṇa, one with realized soul. The Mātaṅga Jātaka explicitly refers to the superior position of a Mahā-brahmā.[151] But Mahā-brahmā is really the creator-god of an epoch and has passed beyond the range of ordinary mortals.

In a sense, the Buddhist position extends beyond the caste issue but not so the Hindu. The thirtieth chapter of the Anuśāsanaparva (critical text) concludes with Mātaṅga still disgusted at not being accorded brahminhood, though many other boons are conferred on him Yudhiṣṭhira asks at the very beginning of the next chapter: Although you regard brahminhood as hard (read: impossible) in the case of Mātaṅga to attain, it is said that in ancient times Viśvāmitra became a brāhmaṇa, and so did the *rājarṣi* Vīthavya; so by what action or boon or austerity did they achieve it?[152] In other words, if it cannot be achieved, how did they achieve it?[153]

149. Ibid.

150. Monier Monier-Williams, *A Sanskrit–English Dictionary*, pp. 741–2.

151. Ibid., p. 79.

152. *Mahābhārata* XIII.31.4. *Vareṇa tapasā* in verse 4 could also be translated as *excellent austerities*.

153. Muir draws a slightly different conclusion from Yudhiṣṭhira. He reacts to Indra's statement to Mātaṅga, that a kṣatriya can become a brāhmaṇa after manifold lives, with the comment: 'The assertion here made of the impossibility of a kṣatriya becoming a brāhmaṇ until he has passed through a long series of births is of course in flagrant contradiction with the stories of Viśvāmitra, Vītahavya and others' *(Original Sanskrit Texts*, part I, p. 442).

But the point persists. Viśvāmitra and Vīthavya represent cases of kṣatriyas becoming brāhmaṇas. Do we have a case of a śūdra becoming a brāhmaṇa within a lifetime?

The case comparable to Mātaṅga is that of Vatsa albeit not on all fours. 'Vatsa was called a *Śūdrā-putra* by his brother Medhātithi. ... It is said that Vatsa proved his brāhmaṇahood by walking through the fire unscathed and thus wiped out this reproach. This case shows that the social rank of a person was not determined by his birth but by his worth.'[154] Manu remarks, in the context of trial by ordeal: 'For formerly when Vatsa was accused by his younger brother, the fire, the spy of the world, burnt not even a hair (of his) by reason of his veracity.'[155]

However, in the case of Vatsa the issue was whether or not he was a caṇḍāla. In the case of Mātaṅga the issue is whether a caṇḍāla could become a brahmin. The answer given here is: No.

Caste and Muslims

From a historical point of view the Islamic position is one of direct opposition to caste. This is clearly stated by one of the first Muslim savants to study Hindu civilization seriously, namely Alberuni, who wrote in the wake of Mahmud Ghazni's invasions of India. After alluding to caste among the ancient Persians, Alberuni remarks:

> Among the Hindus institutions of this kind abound. We Muslims, of course, stand entirely on the other side of the question, considering all men as equal, except in piety; and this is the greatest obstacle which prevents any approach or understanding between Hindus and Muslims.[156]

Alberuni presents only one side of the picture. The other emerges from a perusal of the verses of *Devalasmṛti*. Verses 7–10 may be paraphrased thus:

> When a brāhmaṇa is carried off by Mlecchas and he eats or drinks forbidden food or drink or has sexual intercourse with a woman he should not have approached, he becomes purified by doing the penance of *cāndrāyana* and *parāka*,

154. R.S. Sharma, *Śūdras in Ancient India*, pp. 62–3.

155. G. Bühler, tr., *The Laws of Manu*, p. 274.

156. Ainslie T. Embree, ed., *Alberuni's India, Translated by Edward C. Sachau* (New York: W.W. Norton & Co. Inc., 1971: abridged edition), p. 100.

that a kṣatriya becomes pure by undergoing *parāka* and *pādakṛcchra*, a vaiśya by half of *parāka* and a śūdra by a penance of *parāka* of five days.[157]

Verses 17–22 are significant enough to merit translation:

When persons are forcibly made slaves by Mlecchas, caṇḍālas and robbers, are compelled to do dirty acts, such as killing cows and other animals or sweeping the leavings of the food (of Mlecchas) or eating the leavings of the food of Mlecchas or partaking of the flesh of asses, camels and village pigs, or having intercourse with their women, or are forced to dine with them, then the penance of purifying a dvijāti that has stayed for a month in this way is prajāpātya, for one who has consecrated Vedic fires (and stayed one month or less) it is cāndrāyaṇa or parāka; for one who stays a year (with Mlecchas in this condition of things) it is both cāndrāyaṇa and parāka; a śūdra who stays (in this condition) for a month becomes pure by kṛcchrapāda; a śūdra who stays a year should drink yāvaka for half a month. The appropriate prāyaścitta should be determined by learned brāhmaṇs when a person has stayed (in the above circumstances among Mlecchas) for over a year; in four years the person (who stays in the above circumstances among Mlecchas) is reduced to their condition (i.e. becomes a mleccha and there is no prāyaścitta for him).[158]

The Muslim abhorrence of caste combined with missionary zeal produced some strange results via interdining, such as the Pir Ali Brāhmaṇs described by W.J. Wilkins:

The *Pir Ali Brāhmaṇs*. To this class some of the most respectable families of Calcutta belong. Years ago one of their ancestors went to the house of a Mussulmān, where a trick was played on him. The Mussulmān had heard it said that to 'smell food was half eating it'; and wishing to convert some of the Brāhmans in his neighbourhood, he invited them to his house, and then ordered his dinner to be served. They smelt the food, and their caste was gone. Some of them became Mussulmāns; but one who preferred to remain a Hindu, became the founder of another class, called the Pir Ali, after the man who had brought this trouble upon him.[159]

The other side of the situation is represented curiously by a verse in the well-known Advaitic manual *Pañcadaśī* (Tṛptidīpa v:239) which contains the following passage:

Just as a brāhmaṇa seized by Mlecchas and afterwards undergoing the appropriate prāyaścitta does not become confounded with Mlecchas (but returns to his

157. P.V. Kane, *History of Dharmaśāstra*, vol. II, pt I, p. 390.

158. Ibid. For possible anomalies in the different provisions and their resolution, see ibid., p. 391.

159. W.J. Wilkins, *Modern Hinduism* (Allahabad: Rupat Co., 1975: first published 1887), p. 277.

original status of being a brāhmaṇa) so the Intelligent Soul is not really to be confounded with the body and other material adjuncts.[160]

That this is not a mere poetic flight of fancy but an imagery suggested by actual cases is confirmed by the following account of P.V. Kane:

One Gangadhara Ranganatha Kulkarni of Harsul was forcibly converted by the Moslems; then the Maratha king Sambhaji ordered his minister the Paṇḍitarao to restore him to his caste after giving him appropriate prāyaścitta and the Paṇḍitarao called a meeting of learned brāhmaṇas, looked into works like the Mitaksara and with the approval of the brāhmaṇas administered prāyaścitta to him and sent him on a pilgrimage. There is a similar case in which the Paṇḍitarao under orders from the king writes to the learned brāhmaṇas of Karad about the prāyaścitta to be administered to one Khandu Jadhav who had been forcibly made by the Moslems to eat their food and in which he informs the brāhmaṇas that a fee of two rupees should be taken from the man. It may be noted in passing that Raje Netaji Palkar who was one of the great commanders under Shivaji, the founder of the Maratha Empire, was made a Moslem by the Mogul Emperor Aurangzeb and was subsequently taken back into the Hindu fold by Shivaji. In another document the learned brāhmaṇas of Poona, 46 in number, write to the brāhmaṇas of Karavira about one Narasiṁha Bhaṭṭa Toro of Paithan who had engaged as a priest in a Vedic sacrifice in which he had offered the effigy of an animal made of flour, who had therefore been made outcast and who was subsequently restored to the caste after undergoing penance.[161]

The Caste System and Medieval Reformation

The other side of the coin may also be considered, specially as reflected in the reform movements in medieval Hinduism. Thus, although normally the brahmin is held superior to the śūdra, not only was Śaṅkaradeva of Assam (1486–1568) himself *kāyastha* by birth, in his movement there are instances of 'Brāhmaṇas accepting the discipleship of Śūdras'.[162] The Satnāmīs, another religious sect, 'though considered untouchables', do not 'acknowledge the superiority of Brāhmaṇa and other castes. According to them,

160. P.V. Kane, *History of Dharmaśāstra*, vol. II, pt I, p. 391.

161. Ibid., vol. II, pt II, pp. 973–4. P.V. Kane adds elsewhere, however, that this was done only in a few instances (ibid., vol. II, pt I, p. 391).

162. Kshiti Mohan Sen, 'The Medieval Mystics of North India', in Haridas Bhattacharyya, ed., *The Cultural Heritage of India* (Calcutta: Culture, 1956), vol. IV, p. 388.

superiority consists of purity of character and conduct and devotion to God.'[163] Another medieval saint, Tulsī Sāhib, who died in 1842, remarked, on seeing a brāhmaṇa bathing in the Ganges ask a śūdra to move away, 'How inconsistent are your scriptures! They ascribe great holiness to the Gaṅgā because of its issuing from the feet of Viṣṇu while they condemn as unholy the Śūdras emanating from the same source!'[164] The *Bhāgavata Purāṇa* actually invokes the paedogenesis of the śūdra in his favour.[165]

The cobbler-saint Ravidās was in strife with brahmins throughout his life for denying any connection between varṇa-birth and spiritual worth.[166] Dādū (sixteenth century) asked people to 'give up vanity and to surrender to One God and to look upon all people as one's own brothers and sisters'.[167] The Nath and Niranjan cults also did not accept the 'sanctity of any particular caste'.[168] The Alakhanāmīs similarly 'do not admit the superiority of the so-called upper castes'.[169] Palṭū (*c.* 1757–1825) taught: 'Do not make yourself known by your caste or creed, for that will lead to narrowness'.[170] Similarly, Sadnā, the butcher-saint of Sindh, 'denied that superiority can be attained through birth'.[171] It is an interesting fact, though, that association with Muslims seriously tested Hindu liberalism when the famous poet Jagannātha fell in love with a Muslim woman.[172]

The reform movements in south India in the earlier centuries have also been critical of the caste system. Soon after the Tamil Śaiva saint Sambandhar achieved enlightenment (seventh century CE), 'a devotee, who belonged to the so-called untouchable class, but who was a highly skilled musician, was granted his request that

163. Ibid., p. 390.

164. Ibid., pp. 393–4.

165. Thomas J. Hopkins, 'The Social Teaching of the *Bhāgavata Purāṇa*', in Milton Singer, ed., *Krishna: Myths, Rites and Attitudes* (Honolulu: East-West Center Press, 1966), p. 17.

166. Kshiti Mohan Sen, *Medieval Mysticism in India* (London: Luzac & Co., 1929: translated from the Bengali by Manmohan Ghosh), pp. 79–82.

167. Ibid., p. 109.

168. Ibid., p. 120.

169. Ibid., p. 129.

170. Ibid., p. 132.

171. Ibid., p. 136.

172. Ibid., p. 144.

he with his wife might be allowed to accompany him in his tours and to play his hymns on the harp'.[173] Tamil hagiography similarly records the story of the brāhmaṇa saint-scholar Umāpati, who was drawn to a saint from a different caste and, 'casting off all pride of caste and position he approached him to seek his help', an act which resulted in Umāpati's temporary excommunication.

173. S. Satchidanandam Pillai, 'The Śaiva Saints of South India', in Haridas Bhattacharyya, ed., *The Cultural Heritage of India*, vol. IV, p. 342. Also see p. 345: 'The story of another saint of low birth, Tirunīlakaṇḍa Yalpāṇār, is equally interesting. It was he who, along with his wife, accompanied Sambandhar in all his tours. We read that on two occasions, when he was rapturously singing devotional hymns outside great temples, he was by divine command taken to the holy of holies.'

CHAPTER XX

Āśrama

Two observations are in order as one proceeds from a consideration of the institution of varṇa to that of āśrama. The first is that historically the concept of varṇa seems in general to precede that of āśramas. If the concept of varṇa may not be traced to the *Ṛg Veda* (x.90) because the word varṇa does not occur therein, although the four varṇas could be said to be mentioned (even if some uncertainty surrounds the equation of rājaṇya with kṣatriya), it is explicitly mentioned in the *Śatapatha Brāhmaṇa*. According to Kane: 'Perhaps the earliest reference to the four āśramas, though somewhat obscure, occurs in *Aitareya Brāhmaṇa* 33.11' and a 'much clearer reference to the *three* āśramas occurs in *Chāndogya Upaniṣad* II.23.1'.[1] It is in the *Jābālopaniṣad* that we find the first clear-cut statement of the doctrine of the āśramas as we know it now:

> In the Jābālopaniṣad it is said that Janaka asked Yājñavalkya to expound *saṁnyāsa* and then the four āśramas are distinctly set out. After finishing the stage of student-hood, one should become a householder; after becoming a householder one should become a forest-dweller, after being a forest-dweller, one should renounce the world; or he may do otherwise viz. he may renounce the world after the stage of student-hood itself or after being an householder or from the forest. The very day on which he becomes desireless, he should renounce the world (become a saṁnyāsin).[2]

1. P.V. Kane, *History of Dharmaśāstra* (Poona: Bhandarkar Oriental Research Institute, 1974), vol. II, pt I, p. 420, emphasis added.

2. Ibid., p. 421.

Hence the concept of varṇas may be said in general to precede that of āśramas.

The second observation, by P.V. Kane, relevant in the present context, is the following:

The theory of varṇa dealt with man as a member of the Aryan society and laid down what his rights, functions, privileges, responsibilities and duties were as a member of that society. It was addressed to man in the mass. The theory of asramas addressed itself to the individual. It tells him what his spiritual goal is, how he is to order his life and what preparations are required to attain that goal. The theory of asramas was truly a sublime conception and if owing to the exigencies of the times, the conflicts of interests and distractions of life, the scheme could not even in ancient times be carried out fully by every individual and seems to have failed in modern times, the fault does not lie with the originators of this conception.[3]

II

The standard view on the doctrine of āśramas may be identified with its presentation in the *Manusmṛti*:

As stated in Manu IV. 1 the first part of man's life is brahmacarya in which he learns at his teacher's house and after he has finished his study, in the second part of his life he marries and becomes an house-holder, discharges his debts to his ancestors by begetting sons and to the gods by performing yajñas (Manu V. 169). When he sees that his head has grey hair and that there are wrinkles on his body he resorts to the forest i.e. becomes a vānaprastha (Manu VI. 1–2). After spending the third part of his life in the forest for some time he spends the rest of his life as a saṁnyāsin (Manu VI. 33).[4]

III

It is the foregoing view that is usually implied when the āśrama system is referred to. It should be borne in mind, however, that this is not the only view encountered in Hindu thinking on the subject. Some other potentially significant views must also be noted.

(1) The *samuccaya* view: This represents the standard view that one should go through all the āśramas in a co-ordinated manner.

3. Ibid., p. 423.
4. Ibid., p. 417.

(2) The *vikalpa* view: This has two versions: (i) that one may optionally take *sannyāsa* after *brahmacharya* and (ii) a more radical version that the four āśramas do not represent four different stages of life but four life-styles which one may adopt during the course of an entire life.[5]

(3) The *bādha* view: According to this view, there is really only one āśrama, that of the *gṛhastha* or householder and the rest of the āśramas are either (i) subsidiary or (ii) dispensable.[6]

(4) The Mitākṣarā view: According to this, since all the aforementioned views have scriptural sanction, any of them may be adopted.[7]

(5) Sarvajñanārāyaṇa's view: Samuccaya, vikalpa and bādha are referred to in Manu (VI. 35). Sarvajñanārāyaṇa, a commentator on Manu, suggests that the interpretation of these views is directed towards different types of people with different degrees of spiritual development. The bādha view is meant for those immersed in the world; those less engrossed in the world should follow all the stages (samuccaya); the option (vikalpa) to leapfrog to sannyāsa after brahmacarya is meant for the spiritually advanced.[8]

(6) The *atyāśrama* view: The word *atyāśramibhyaḥ* occurs in the *Śvetāśvatara Upaniṣad.* 'It is said there that the sage Śvetāśvatara proclaimed the knowledge to those who had risen above the mere observances of āśramas."[9]

It is worth noting in conclusion that although 'this scheme is normative it is based on experience. Many Indians, even in modern times, have broken all connections with the world to live their lives in renunciation; others, without abandoning their social obligations, have, it is said "transcended the *āśramas*", and achieved the status of the "absolved life".'[10]

5. See Patrick Olivelle, 'The Notion of Āśrama in the Dharmasūtras', *Weiner Zeitschrift für die Kunde-und Ostasiens*, vol. 18, pp. 27–35 (1974).

6. P.V. Kane, *History of Dharmaśāstra*, vol. II, pt I, p. 425.

7. Ibid. Mitākṣarā: A Celebrated Commentary on *Yājñavalkyasmrti.*

8. Ibid., p. 424.

9. Ibid., p. 422.

10. Louis Renou, ed., *Hinduism* (New York: George Braziller, 1962), p. 52. For a recent study of the āśrama system in detail, see Patrick Olivelle, *The Āśrama System: The History and Hermeneutics of a Religious Institution* (New York: Oxford University Press, 1993).

IV

An understanding of the concepts of *pravṛtti* and *nivṛtti* is crucial to a proper understanding of the āśrama system, and indeed to much of Hinduism itself. Śaṅkara (eighth/ninth century) states at the commencement of the Introduction to his commentary on the *Bhagavadgītā*:

The Twofold Vedic Religion

The Lord created the universe, and wishing to secure order therein He first created the Prajāpatis (Lords of creatures) such as Marīchi and caused them to adopt the Pravritti-Dharma, the Religion of Works. He then created others such as Sanaka and Sanandana and caused them to adopt the Nivritti-Dharma, the Religion of Renunciation, characterised by knowledge and indifference of worldly objects. It is the twofold Vedic Religion of Works and Renunciation that maintains order in the universe. This Religion which directly leads to liberation and worldly prosperity has long been practised by all castes and religious orders (varṇa-āśrama)—from the brāhmaṇas downwards—who sought welfare.[11]

From this point of view, the āśrama system is an attempt to reconcile these conflicting trends within Hinduism—those of participation in worldly activities as represented by pravṛtti and of renunciation of worldly activities as represented by nivṛtti. Thus, the first two stages of life—those of the student but more especially the stage of the householder—represent the phase of participation in worldly activities, and those of the hermit and the renunciant represent the phase of withdrawal from them. This is an example of the 'middle way' of Hinduism, as it were, between the ways of complete immersion in worldly activities and abject withdrawal therefrom. What, when viewed *simultaneously*, amounts to a conflict is resolved by being pursued *successively* at different stages of life.

In this context, the contribution of the *Bhagavadgītā* to the Hindu way of life can also be viewed in a fresh light. It is however, important to recall the broader Indian religious scene, characterized by the presence of not just Hinduism but Buddhism and Jainism as well. These two religions decidedly favoured nivṛtti or renunciation over

11. Alladi Mahadeva Sastry, tr., *The Bhagavadgita with the Commentary of Sri Sankaracharya* (Madras: Samata Books, 1985), p. 2.

pravṛtti or action. M. Hiriyanna refers to the 'two ways of life ...— one of action (*pravṛtti*) and the other of renunciation (*nivṛtti*)' and points out that 'each one of them was, in all probability, adopted at first to the exclusion of the other. But before the Vedic period closed ... it had become permissible to change from one to the other, after reaching a certain stage of self-discipline'.[12] The case of Yājñavalkya in the *Bṛhadāraṇyaka Upaniṣad* provides the best example here. We may also note that 'more or less the same practice obtained in the non-Vedic schools' of Buddhism and Jainism also, for there too one could disengage from worldly life, and 'it continues to prevail among them even to this day.' However, so far as Hinduism or

the orthodox schools are concerned, a profound transformation has since taken place in the view of the relation between these two ways. The positive way of life has been transformed by the incorporation in it of the essence of the negative one. It is true that *even in its earlier sense*, the path of action involved numerous checks on natural impulses and therefore implied the need for a great deal of self-restraint. But the restraint in it was only partial, because a person who followed that path was allowed to seek his own private happiness, provided he did so without resorting to wrong action. What particularly marks the later conception *of it is the total exclusion of self-interest from it.* It does not aim at merely *subordinating* the interests of the individual to those of the community, or of any other greater whole to which he may regard himself as belonging, but at their entire abnegation. The path of action accordingly comes to lay the same emphasis on *self-renunciation as the path of* samnyāsa *does*, and one acquiesces as little as the other in what is sometimes described as 'reasonable self-love' or 'enlightened self-interest'. But it does so without *reducing, in the least, the stress on the need for engaging oneself in social activity.* Consequently, the abandonment of active social life is at no stage permitted. It must throughout be pursued, but in a spirit of absolute detachment. *By thus combining asceticism and activity, the new form of discipline elevates them both.* Asceticism thereby becomes much more than self-denial, and activity is freed from all egoistic motives. *This remarkable change we owe chiefly to the teaching of the Gītā.* Even if the Gita did not initiate it, it has given wide and permanent currency to the new idea.[13]

12. M. Hiriyanna, *The Essentials of Indian Philosophy* (London: George Allen & Unwin, 1948), p. 51.

13. Ibid., p. 52, emphasis added. Śaṅkara seems to show some awareness of this point when he writes that Kṛṣṇa taught to Arjuna 'who was deeply plunged in the ocean of grief and delusion, the *twofold Vedic religion*' (Alladi Mahadeva Sastry, tr., *The Bhagavadgita with the Commentary of Sri Sankaracharya*, p. 4; emphasis added).

CHAPTER XXI

Puruṣārthas

The word *puruṣārtha* in general means human endeavour but in the present context it means the goals or ends sought through human endeavour.[1] Classical Hindu thought essentially identifies four such goals:

(1) *Dharma* Righteous living or discharge of duties
(2) *Artha* Acquisition of wealth
(3) *Kāma* Gratification of desires
(4) *Mokṣa* Attainment of spiritual liberation

I

It seems that the acceptance of all the four puruṣārthas as legitimate ends of human endeavour was gradual.

This point should be distinguished from the one made by Kane that while the first three puruṣārthas could be pursued by all, 'the 4th Puruṣārtha of ṃoksa can be obtained only by a few'.[2] Our point is not statistical but historical and follows the argument developed by N.K. Devaraja. He draws attention to its salient points: (1) that the Indian religious scene from time immemorial has been characterized by two strands—the *śramaṇa* and the *brāhmaṇa*—often hostile to each other; (2) that an important element in this hostility was the

1. For a detailed study, see Arvind Sharma, *The Puruṣārthas: A Study in Hindu Axiology* (East Lansing: Michigan State University, 1982), p. 56.

2. P.V. Kane, *History of Dharmaśāstra* (Poona: Bhandarkar Oriental Research Institute, 1962), vol. V, part II, p. 1631.

aversion of the brāhmaṇa wing to physical renunciation; and (3) that this point is further strengthened by the observation that 'while the philosophical portions of the Upanishads stressed the need and importance of renunciation, none of the Upanishadic teachers was a sannyāsin'.[3] He also draws attention to the fact that the *Baudhāyana-Dharma Sūtra* (II.6.29–30) 'attributes the origin of the fourth āśrama (Sannyāsa) to Kapila, the son of Prahlāda, an *asura* "who, wishing to compete with gods, introduced these differences (of the four stages of life)". "A man of understanding", it goes on to say, "should not show respect to these".[4] From this, several conclusions be drawn: (1) that sannyāsa as a way of life was not part of the original Vedic ideal represented by the brāhmaṇa wing; (2) that it was part of the śramaṇa tradition; (3) that it was resisted by the brāhmaṇa tradition; (4) that, however, it was ultimately accepted by 'later Hinduism as formulated by Manu'; and that (5) 'the acceptance of this ideal must have been facilitated by the emphasis on *moksha* or liberation as the final goal of life, which is already to be met within Upanishadic literature'.[5]

II

Be that as it may, if we consider dharma and mokṣa as the two spiritual values in the above list, and artha and kāma as the two material values, then 'in earlier times the first of the two spiritual values, viz. *dharma*, alone seems to have been recognized ... there are still to be found some passages in old works which indicate that belief in the ideal of *mokṣa* was not accepted by all'.[6] Indeed, opposition in this respect seemed to have come mostly from the Mīmāṁsā or the school of thought which emphasized the role of ritual, sometimes to the extent of claiming that it had 'nothing to do with *mokṣa*'.[7].

3. N.K. Devaraja, *Hinduism and the Modern Age* (New Delhi: Islam and the Modern Age Society, 1975), p. 16.

4. Ibid., p. 16.

5. Ibid., p. 17.

6. M. Hiriyanna, *The Essentials of Indian Philosophy* (London: George Allen & Unwin, 1948), p. 50.

7. Ibid., p. 148.

However, in course of time, not only all the six orthodox schools of Hindu thought, namely Nyāya, Vaiśeṣika, Sāṅkhya, Yoga, Mīmāṁsā and Vedānta, but even the non-orthodox schools, such as the Buddhist and the Jaina (with the exception of the Cārvākas) accepted mokṣa as the supreme value. Hiriyanna writes:

> The other important point of agreement among the various schools is the recognition of liberation or release (*mokṣa*) from the cycle of rebirths as the highest of human ends or values. The Indians generally speak of four values—*artha, kāma, dharma* and *mokṣa*. Of these, the first two, which respectively mean 'wealth' and 'pleasure', are secular or purely worldly values. The other two, whose general meaning has already been indicated, may in contrast, be described as spiritual. Philosophy is concerned only with the latter, but this does not mean that it discards the other two. It does acknowledge them also, but only in so far as they help or are instrumental to, *dharma* or *mokṣa*. Owing to this judgement of preference which it implies, philosophy, as conceived in India, may be described as essentially a criticism of values. Indeed, its final aim is to determine what the *ultimate* value is, and to point out how it can be realized.[8]

Mokṣa as the supreme value is treated in another section in its own right. At this point some salient features of the four puruṣārthas may be noted.

III

For the sake of clarity it is best to distinctly enumerate points worthy of remark in this respect.

(1) Dharma, artha and kāma are often described as constituting one set and are called *trivarga.*
(2) The fact that dharma is mentioned first in this tetrad is often taken to indicate that the pursuit of the other two goals should be subject to ethical norms (dharma).
(3) 'The order in which the three are usually mentioned is (1) dharma, (2) artha, (3) kāma, in order to emphasize the supreme importance of dharma; and then, in the next degree, that of artha, for the preservation and well-being of society.'[9]
(4) Dharma is said to play a foundational role in relation to mokṣa

8. Ibid., p. 50.
9. *Sanātana-Dharma* (Adyar, Madras: The Theosophical Publishing House, 1966), p. 233.

just as it is said to play a regulative role in relation to artha and kāma.

(5) The four puruṣārthas can be brought in relation with pravṛtti or action in the world and nivṛtti or renunciation of the world. The first three pertain to pravṛtti, with its goal of abhyudaya or material well-being, and the last to nivṛtti, with its goal of *niḥśreyasa* or 'greatest good' or 'than which there is no greater good'.[10]

(6) The three guṇas, mentioned earlier in the discussion of trimūrti, can also be brought in relation to the puruṣārthas on the basis of a passage in the *Mahābhārata*: 'The "triad" of dharma-artha-kāma is known as the "trivarga" ' but 'mokṣa has its own triad, that of Sattva-rajas-tamas.'[11] In terms of the guṇas it is possible to associate dharma with sattva, artha with rajas and kāma with tamas; however, the verse speaks of a triad of mokṣa in terms of these. This could either mean that they are transcended in mokṣa, which is the common view but the direct association of the triad of guṇas with mokṣa rather than its transcendence is unusual. Hence, it is reasonable to suggest, as Bhagavan Das does, that there may be 'another way of explaining this triad of mokṣa. ... The Tamas aspect of it is Bhakti, universal love; the Rajas aspect, Yogaiśvarya, yoga-siddhi-s, Yogic powers, used for the service of living beings [*karma-yoga*] and the sattva-aspect, jñāna or prajñāna ...'[12]

(7) Apart from the varṇas there is 'another classification of men, one which is purely theoretical, is based on the three phases of human activity: *dharma* or moral activity (the highest); *artha* or interested activity and *kama* or playful activity. These three ends reflect, in part at least, the three functions they are subordinate to, a fourth end: *mokṣa* or liberation.'[13]

IV

Bhagavan Das helps highlight the significance of the doctrine of the puruṣārthas:

10. Ibid., p. 233.

11. Ibid., p. 234.

12. Ibid., p. 234. In the Bhakti literature of Hinduism, kāma has been clearly connected with bhakti.

13. Louis Renou, ed., *Hinduism* (New York: George Braziller, 1962), p. 54.

The question may well be asked: What is the good of all these institutions of Āśrama-s and Varṇa-s, stages of life and caste-classes; of worship, sacrifices, Saṁskāra-s; indeed, what is the good of all these visible and invisible worlds, births and rebirths, Karma and its consequences; in short, why is there any universe, why is there any life, why do we live, what is the purpose, end, aim, object of life, what is the good of it all?

He goes on to say that:

This question is, no doubt, the question of questions. It is the final question, to which all other questions lead up; in which they are all summed up. The answer to it, therefore, is the answer of all answers: The ... understanding of that answer makes it possible to answer all questions that may arise in connection with the human being's life-work. The Scriptures therefore duly deal with the question and supply the answer.[14]

Why? To gain the four ends, of course!

14. Ibid., p. 228.

CHAPTER XXII

Vedas

Introduction

The Vedas are the sacred books of the Hindus, and one of the 'most ancient of books in the library of mankind.'[1] This section will discuss the significance of the Vedas as books.

The moment we speak of the Vedas as books, however, a problem arises: What is a book? In common parlance a book means 'any number of written or printed sheets when bound or sewed together along one edge, usually between protective covers'.[2] But the Vedas were in existence by 1500 BCE though not written out until much later[3] and they were printed only in the nineteenth century. In what sense, then, can they be called *books*? Did the Vedas qualify to be called *books* only after they were put between covers?

To say so, however, would be to ignore another aspect of the meaning of the word *book*, that is: Anything considered as a record or a setting forth of truth; as the *book* of nature.[4]

It would, therefore, be helpful not to take a 'hide-bound', 'shelf-oriented' view of the word *book*, especially in our context, for the Vedas were transmitted orally and to consider them as *books* only

1. F. Max Müller, *Vedic Hymns* (Delhi: Motilal Banarsidass, 1964: first published 1891), p. xxxi.

2. *Webster's New Twentieth Century Dictionary of the English Language* (New York: The World Publishing Company, 1968), p. 208.

3. Mann, Weber and Zacharïae, *The History of Indian Literature* (Varanasi: Chowkhamba Sanskrit Series Office, 1961: first published 1878), p. 181.

4. Funk & Wagnalls, *New Standard Dictionary of the English Language* (New York: Funk & Wagnalls Co.), p. 309.

after they were written out or printed would to a great extent distort if not destroy the perspective.

The Vedas have been called books in several senses. They have been used in the sense of the spiritual knowledge contained in the books called the Vedas: 'When the whole country is flooded, the reservoir becomes superfluous. So, to the illumined seer the Vedas are all superfluous'.[5]

The word 'Veda' has also been used in the more usual sense of a book as a physical entity. For instance, Sāyaṇa, a famous commentator of the Vedas of the fourteenth century defines Veda in the beginning of his commentary on the Black Yajur Veda as: 'a book which reveals the knowledge of supernatural methods for the achievement of the desired object and the avoidance of the undesirable'.[6]

Hence, to treat the Vedas adequately as books it is best to adopt a comprehensive approach to the question of what a book is, as Howard Woodrow Winger has done.[7] He distinguishes between three approaches to books:

1. Books have content and a study of the character and purpose of content is one obvious approach to them.
2. Books are made and distributed to people. The investigation of this process is the province of the history of printing and publishing, the history of libraries, enumerative bibliography and textual criticism.
3. Books also have physical form. Interest in this aspect of books focuses on the materials from which they are made, their format, their script or typography and their illustration and decoration.

This chapter will use these three approaches to define a 'book'[8] and apply them to the Vedas. Since the Vedas are the sacred books of the Hindus, the first approach is most relevant and will therefore be emphasized. This does not imply, however, that the other

5. *Gītā*, II, 46; see Swami Prabhavananda, *The Spiritual Heritage of India* (London: George Allen & Unwin, 1962), p. 188. The *Gītā*, usually placed in the second century BCE, has already been referred to as an important Hindu scripture.

6. *The Cultural Heritage of India* (Calcutta: Ramakrishna Mission Institute of Culture, 1958), vol. I, p. 182.

7. *Encyclopedia Britannica* (Cambridge University Press, 1968), vol. III, p. 919.

8. Ibid., p. 919. The word 'book' has also been used in the sense of a subdivision of a literary treatise in this chapter.

approaches will be neglected. Here, the sense in which the word *book* is used tends to vary with the context and with the approach appropriate to the context.

On 2 February 1785, Sir William Jones, one of the first Englishmen to take up the study of Sanskrit—the ancient language of India—read a paper on the Hindus before the Asiatic Society. In this paper, he made the suggestion that Sanskrit, Greek and Latin bear such a strong affinity to one another that 'no philologer could examine them all three without believing them to have sprung from the same common source'.[9]

This suggestion lead to the identification of what is now known as the Indo-European family of languages.[10] Sanskrit was recognized as one of the oldest members of the Indo-European family of languages[11] and the Vedas were recognized as 'the oldest monument'[12] of Aryan speech and Aryan thought. At the same time, the Vedas had always been considered the sacred books of the Hindus and hence were assessed as 'the oldest Indian and at the same time, the oldest Indo-European literary monument.'[13]

The Vedas defined as a Book

What, then, are the Vedas?

The Vedas are the sacred books of the Hindus. They are to the Hindus what Tipiṭakas are to the Buddhists, the Bible is to the Christians and the Qur'ān to the Muslims.[14] But this is a proper comparison only in so far as their sacredness is concerned, for, as books, the point of view from which we are examining the Vedas here, they are different.

9. S.N. Mukherjee, *Sir William Jones* (Cambridge University Press, 1968), p. 95.

10. Will Durant, *Our Oriental Heritage* (New York: Simon and Schuster, 1954), p. 407.

11. J.H. Voight, *Max Mueller: The Man and His Ideas* (Calcutta: Firma K.L. Mukhopadhyaya, 1967), p. 5.

12. F. Max Müller, *Collected Works*, quoted by N.N. Law, *Age of the Ṛg Veda* (Calcutta: Firma K.L. Mukhopadhyaya, 1965), p. 10.

13. M. Winternitz, *A History of Indian Literature* (Calcutta: University of Calcutta, 1962), p. 45.

14. Ibid., p. 47. See Louis Renou, *The Destiny of the Veda in India* (ed. and tr. Dev Raj Chanana) (Delhi: Motilal Banarsidass, 1965).

The word *Veda* is derived from a root 'vid' which means *to know*.[15] It is also connected with word 'video' which helps understand why its contents are regarded by tradition as having been 'seen' by the ancient sages. Hence the word by itself means revealed knowledge—'the best of all knowledge in Hindu eyes'.[16] Just as the Bible represents to many Christians the source *par excellence* of inspiration and reflection, so Veda is 'the knowledge *par excellence*, i.e. the sacred, the religious knowledge."[17]

When the word is used to refer to a body of literature, however, it has a definite connotation: 'The word Veda means knowledge; a Veda is literally a Book of Knowledge. Vedas is applied by the Hindus to all the sacred lore of their early period; like our Bible it indicates a literature rather than a book'.[18]

It is important to familiarize oneself with the terms in which this literature of wisdom is described. The Vedas are usually considered four in number.

1. The *Ṛg Veda* or the Wisdom found in the Hymns of Praise
2. The *Sāma Veda* or the Wisdom found in the Chants/Songs
3. The *Yajur Veda* or the Wisdom found in the Sacrificial Formulas
4. The *Atharva Veda* or the Wisdom found in the Magic Formulas.

Each of these Vedas is then divided into four parts:[19] (1) the Mantras or hymnic formulas; (2) the Brāhmaṇa or commentaries on ritual; (3) the Āraṇyaka or 'forest texts' reflecting an emergent hermitic ideal; and (4) the Upaniṣads[20] or philosophical texts.

This fourfold division reflects a historical (and theological)

15. The English words 'wit' and 'wisdom' are also derived from the same root.

16. Percival Spear, ed., *The Oxford History of India* (Oxford: Clarendon Press, 1964), p. 44.

17. M. Winternitz, *A History of Indian Literature*, p. 45.

18. Will Durant, *Our Oriental Heritage*, p. 407.

19. Sometimes the division is described as consisting of only three, or even two, parts; Winternitz, *A History of Indian Literature*, p. 46.

20. 'The Sanskrit word ... would mean a sitting, an instruction; the sitting at the feet of a Master. When we read in the Gospels that Jesus "went up into a mountain and when he was set, his disciples came unto him" we can imagine them sitting at the feet of their Master and the whole Sermon on the Mount might be considered an Upaniṣad.' Juan Mascaro, *The Upaniṣads* (Harmondsworth: Penguin Books, 1965), p. 7. See James A. Santucci, *Outline of Vedic Literature* (Missoula, Mont.: Scholars Press of the American Academy of Religion, 1976).

development, the Mantras being the earliest, the Upanisads the latest, attesting to a rich, evocative, growing and lively tradition during a period roughly dated 1500–300 BC.

It is important to bear in mind the distinctions among the three or four Vedas, as also among their four divisions.[21] For although we have made the above enumeration, which is the most widely accepted one, it is important to recognize when viewing the Vedas as books that sometimes the word Veda is used in a way which either falls short of or shoots beyond the above enumeration. Deviations from the foregoing description may be noted as follows:

(1) The followers of a Hindu sect called the Ārya Samāj, which originated in the nineteenth century, consider only the Mantra portion of the four Vedas as 'the Veda'.[22]
(2) One significant Hindu tradition considers only the first three Vedas as 'the Veda' and excludes the *Atharva Veda.*[23]
(3) Another Hindu tradition includes, along with the four Vedas, a fifth called Itihāsa Veda or the Knowledge of History.[24] The same may be said of numerous small sects, each one suggesting that their own sectarian scripture constitutes 'the fifth Veda'.
(4) Sometimes Hindu scholars 'include in the Vedas several collections of shorter commentaries in aphoristic form called Sūtras',[25] thus opening the term to embrace anything written in ancient Sanskrit directly related to the Vedas.

In this chapter, the term Veda shall mean the standard description of the Vedas as four in number with their fourfold division. This body of literature is referred to as Veda in the singular and Vedas in the plural.

Aspects of the Vedas as a Book

Importance of the *Ṛg Veda*

Of the four Vedas the *Ṛg Veda* is considered the most important.

21. Sometimes the Vedas are considered three rather than four in number.

22. Percival Spear, ed., *The Oxford History of India*, p. 44.

23. For a discussion, see M. Chakravorti, *A Short History of Sanskrit Literature* (Calcutta: 111 Upper Circular Road, 1936), pp. 4–7.

24. Ibid.

25. Will Durant, *Our Oriental Heritage*, p. 407. Also see *The Cultural Heritage of India*, vol. I, pp. 183, 345.

All the other Vedas draw upon the *Ṛg Veda*. The *Sāma Veda* consists mostly of stanzas taken from the *Ṛg Veda* (except 75): the *Yajur Veda* also borrows heavily from the *Ṛg Veda*.[26] The *Atharva Veda* may be a subsequent addition to Vedic literature.[27] Thus, the *Ṛg Veda* 'unquestionably is the oldest part of the literature and the most important of the Vedas from the literary point of view'.[28]

The *Ṛg Veda* text which has come down to us is of the Śākala school. It consists of a collection of 1028 hymns (Sūktas)[29] divided into ten books (Maṇḍalas). Of these, Books II–VII known as Family Books are supposed to be the oldest; the rest were added subsequently. In bulk it equals the *Iliad*.[30] The last book, the tenth, exhibits the growth of religious philosophy and contains the famous Creation Hymn. In its theme, it differs from the ninth, which is devoted exclusively to the glorification of the Soma drink.[31] The subject matter of the *Ṛg Veda*, according to modern scholarship, largely consists of hymns in praise of the powers of nature personified as gods—Agni or god of Fire, Indra or god of Thunder and battle, Varuṇa or Sky, Sūrya or Sun, etc.

Alfred Ludwig indicates the historical significance of the *Ṛg Veda* thus: 'The Ṛg Veda presupposes nothing of that which we know in Indian literature, while on the other hand, the whole of Indian literature and the whole of Indian life presupposes the Ṛg Veda'.[32]

Importance of the Upaniṣads

While the *Ṛg Veda* enjoys historical and literary pre-eminence among the Vedas, among the fourfold division of the Vedas the Upaniṣads are of major philosophical importance. The Mantra portion consists primarily of hymns in praise of gods. The Brāhmaṇas, in prose and over sixty in number, are ritualistic and full of sacrificial speculation.

26. Percival Spear, ed., *The Oxford History of India*, p. 46.

27. Ibid., p. 45. But see Vishva Bandhu, *The Vedas and Śāstras* (Hoshiarpur: Vishveshvarananda Institute, 1966), p. 6.

28. Percival Spear, ed., *The Oxford History of India*, p. 46.

29. It is possible that the Buddhist word *sutta*, as in *Sutta-Piṭaka*, which is usually connected with the Sanskrit *sūtra*, really comes from the word *sūkta* (oral communication from Professor O.H. de A.Wijesekera).

30. F. Max Müller, *Three Lectures on the Vedanta Philosophy*, 1890 (Varanasi: Chowkhamba Sanskrit Series, 1967), p. 109.

31. M. Winternitz, *A History of Indian Literature*, p. 50.

32. Ibid., p. 52.

The Āraṇyakas—treatises meant to be absorbed (or containing rituals to be performed) in the isolation of a forest—show the beginnings of philosophical richness, which reaches its acme in the Upaniṣads, also called Vedānta because in a textual sense they are the terminal category of the Vedas or, so it is claimed, of all knowledge. And though 'a system of Indian philosophy is like a strange Eastern city, of which we know neither the streets nor the names of streets',[33] for an uninitiated traveller, most of the building bricks of which this city is made have been drawn from the Upaniṣadic kiln.

According to T.M.P. Mahadevan, the Upaniṣads are the basic springs not merely of Hindu but Indian philosophy, 'not only for the orthodox system but also for the so called heterodox systems of Indian thought'[34]—those of Buddhism and Jainism. The later schools, of Madhvācarya, Rāmānuja and Śaṅkara—the Dvaita, Viśiṣṭādvaita and Advaita schools—also claim to derive their authority from the Upaniṣads.

Mahatma Gandhi said this of the opening text of the *Iśāvāsya*, believed to be one of the oldest Upaniṣads: 'If all the Upaniṣads and the other scriptures happened all of a sudden to be reduced to ashes and if only the first verse in the Isopanishad were left intact in the memory of the Hindus, Hinduism would live forever'.[35]

Comparison with Other Scriptures

We may now revert to our consideration of the Vedas as a whole and compare them with the Bible, the Qur'ān and the Tipiṭakas—this time as books.

> It (the Vedas) does not mean one single literary work, as for instance, the word Koran; nor a complete collection of a certain number of books, compiled at some particular time, as the word Bible ... or as the word Tipitaka, the Bible of the Buddhists, but a whole great literature which arose in the course of many centuries ... .[36]

Similarly, although the Veda is a scripture like the Bible and the Qur'ān, it does not represent the entire Scripture of Hinduism. Veda

33. F. Max Müller, *Three Lectures on the Vedanta Philosophy*, p. 109.
34. Chaman Lal, *Textbook of Indian Culture* (Bombay: Bharatiya Vidya Bhavan, 1968), p. 236.
35. Ibid.
36. M. Winternitz, *A History of Indian Literature*, p. 45.

is 'Śruti'—what is heard or revealed; another great class of scripture is called 'Smṛti'—what is remembered or tradition.[37] The Vedas are Śruti either because they are divinely heard or because they were transmitted by word of mouth. The traditional method of studying and memorizing them is by hearing them recited by the preceptor. Other literature—consisting of Dharmaśāstras, Itihāsa, Purāṇas, Tantras, etc., is called Smṛti, or works whose authors can be remembered. The orthodox view regards the Śruti or the Vedas as authoritative, all other literature being subordinate to it. Whenever a conflict arises, Śruti prevails over Smṛti.

Even as a revealed scripture, however, the Veda is not like the Bible or the Qur'ān. It is

> the record of truth as it was discovered by the great rishis or saints, of ancient time rather than a revelation from God. What is enjoined within the system is not belief in the teachings so much as an attempt to reduplicate the experience of these saints.[38]

The description of Vedas as Śruti is significant: 'It is significant that to the expression Holy Scripture there corresponds in the case of the Indian the expression Śruti "hearing" because the revealed texts are not written and read, but only spoken and heard.'[39]

Thus, the word śruti[40] describes the nature of the literary corpus and hints at its oral transmission.

Recensions of the Vedas

The oral transmission of the Vedas was carried out in an 'academy where, in particular, the teachers and the taught looked upon it as their Svādhyāya ... their own (sva-) Vedic text (-adhyāya) and performed its recitation.'

> The Śākhās, as the Vedic texts were designated ... grouped fourfold, under the generic name of the four Vedas differed within the sphere of each Veda, from one another, to a varying degree, in wording as well as the nature and arrangement of their contents and in the intonation as prescribed in their formal recitation.[41]

37. Ainslee T. Embree, ed., *The Hindu Tradition* (New York: The Modern Library, 1966), p. 6.
38. Ibid., p. 6.
39. M. Winternitz, *A History of Indian Literature*, p. 49.
40. These traditional interpretations of Śruti and Smṛti, however, are challenged by Vishva Bandhu, *The Vedas and Śāstras*, pp. 4–5.
41. Ibid., p. 3.

These text recensions or Śākhās thus constituted textual variations which at one time numbered 144.[42]

Of the *Ṛg Veda*	21
Of the *Yajur Veda*	101
Of the *Sāma Veda*	13
Of the *Atharva Veda*	9
	144

Out of these, only 13, to wit, 2 which between themselves are practically identical of the Ṛg Veda, 6 of the Yajur Veda, 3 of the Sāma Veda and 2 of the Atharva Veda have come down to us in script, with about one-half of them still claiming to have quite a few families that are preserving and practising their respective ancient methods of recitation.[43]

Apart from the text recension, there were innumerable ways of singing the Mantras, especially those of the *Sāma Veda.* This is perhaps what Patañjali had in mind when he described the *Sāma Veda* as having 'one thousand ways' and 'having one thousand varieties'. The number of text recensions could not exist in 'such an incredibly large number'.[44] The possibility, however, that vast sections of the Vedas themselves have been lost cannot be completely discounted.[45]

Publication of the Vedas

As indicated above, the Vedas were transmitted orally, even as late as the seventh century when I-tsing visited India.[46] The question regarding the age of writing in India is a very vexed one; yet it is clear that even after it was known, the Vedas were not committed to writing. Thus, the old text had to be restored, by resorting to old phonetic manuals of instruction and commentaries.[47] The 'manuscripts from which we obtain most of our texts reach but seldom to a great age'.[48]

42. Ibid.

43. Ibid., p. 4.

44. Ibid., p. 3.

45. According to an orthodox tradition, the Vedas originally contained 100,000 verses, vide *The Cultural Heritage of India*, vol. I, p. 182.

46. M. Winternitz, *A History of Indian Literature*, p. 31, fn.3.

47. See F. Max Müller, *Vedic Hymns*, p. lxxii; also see Preface to the first edition, *passim*; Vishva Bandhu, *Atharvaveda* (Hoshiarpur: Vishveshvarananda Vedic Research Institute, 1960), pp. VI–XI.

48. M. Winternitz, *A History of Indian Literature*, pp. 26–35.

The appearance of the Vedas in the West dates from early in the nineteenth century. The chronological progress in this direction will be clear from the following account:

1778	An alleged translation of the *Yajur Veda* appeared in French, referred to by Voltaire as Ezzour-Vedam. It was declared to be a 'pious fraud'[49] by Sonnerat in 1782.
1789	Colonel Polier collected the manuscripts of all the four Vedas from Jaipur and sent them to the British Museum.[50]
1801–2	The French scholar Anquetil du Perron translated Dārā Shukoh's Persian translation of the Upaniṣads into Latin under the title 'Oupnek'Hat'—which enthused Schopenhauer.[51]
1816-19	Rajā Rammohun Roy translated 'a considerable number of Upaniṣads into English'.[52]

Thus, some progress had been made till 1823, when the already international nature of the interest in Indian literature was recognized by Schlegel: 'Will the English perhaps claim a monopoly of Indian literature? It would be too late. Cinnamon and clove they may keep, but these mental treasures are the common property of the educated world'.[53]

1838	F. Rosen published the first fifth of the *Ṛg Veda.*
1846	Rudolph Roth wrote his book in German 'on the literature and history of the Veda'.
1861–3	Complete text of the *Ṛg Veda* brought out by Aufrecht
1849 onwards	F. Max Müller brought out the text of the *Ṛg Veda* and sections of other Vedas in the Sacred Books of the East series.

The publication of the Vedas was a major intellectual event and achievement.

49. Ibid., p. 11. Also see M. Chakravorti, *A Short History of Sanskrit Literature*, p. 19.

50. Ibid., p. 19.

51. M. Winternitz, *A History of Indian Literature*, p. 17.

52. Ibid., p. 18.

53. Quoted by Winternitz, ibid., p. 19.

Small wonder, then, that almost a century after Sir William Jones had made his suggestion, when Max Müller published sections of the Vedas in the gigantic series, Sacred Books of the East, it created a great sensation.[54]

> The Veda has two-fold interest: it belongs to the history of the world and to the history of India. In the history of the world it fills a gap which no literary work in any other languages could fill. ... As long as a man continues to take an interest in the history of his race, and as long as we collect in libraries and museums the relics of former ages, the first place in that long row of books which contains the records of the Aryan branch of mankind, will belong to the Rig-veda.[55]

If for the Indo-Aryans the Vedas are of historical and cultural interest, for India they are of tremendous religious interest. In fact, its publication produced an even greater commotion in India than in the West. Max Müller was not surprised, and wrote: 'After all it was their Bible, and had never been published before during the three or four thousand years of its existence'.[56]

It is obvious, therefore, that in dealing with the Vedas we are dealing with no ordinary book but with a book of central significance in the religious history of India and of humanity in general.

The Traditional Hindu View of the Vedas as Books

According to the traditional Hindu view of the Vedas, these books are eternal, beginningless, not made by man, and moreover, they are the source of all religion.

The orthodox interpretation of this description is that the Vedas are destroyed at the end of the Hindu version of the Deluge and are then reconstructed and that this cycle goes on endlessly.[57] Hence, they are also beginningless. The Vedas, according to one view, were even believed to have been written out by God himself upon leaves of gold 'and this is a view which cannot easily be refuted', as Will

54. J.H. Voight, *Max Mueller: The Man and His Ideas*, p. xiii.

55. See M. Krishnamachariar, *History of Classical Sanskrit Literature* (Madras: Tirumalai-Tirupali Devasthanams Press, 1937), p. vii.

56. J.H. Voight, *Max Mueller: The Man and His Ideas*, p. 41.

57. M. Krishnamachariar, *History of Classical Sanskrit Literature*, p. vii.

Durant facetiously remarks.[58] Moreover, being the revealed word of God the Vedas are the fountainhead of religion.

It is apparent that the above description has developed along highly mythologized lines. This may be due to the excessive reverence with which the more enthusiastic adherents of a religion start looking upon their holy books. A more rational approach, endorsed by many Hindu thinkers, both ancient and modern, to these descriptions of the Vedas as books is also possible. It has been argued, for instance, that the Veda is to be considered eternal in the sense that the spiritual verities enshrined in the text are eternal, not the text itself.[59] Similarly, the Vedas as books are so ancient, of such hoary antiquity, as to appear to be without a beginning in point of time. Besides, the Vedas may be treated as not made by man in the sense that they are not the work of ordinary men but of sages who were divinely inspired. Finally, there can be little doubt that the Vedas constitute the major foundation of Hinduism and that they are the primary source of the Hindu religion. Interpreted in this light, this traditional account of the Vedas as books becomes remarkably consistent with their modern Western description to which we shall now turn.

The Modern View of the Vedas as Books

Modern Western scholarship considers the following features of great significance in relation to the Vedas as books: the purity of the text; the antiquity of the text; and the importance of the text in the history of Hinduism.

Scholars marvel at the textual purity with which the Vedas have been preserved. They were not preserved in writing, which might have been introduced in India[60] around the eighth century BCE, for the Vedas go back to 1500 BCE. As mentioned earlier, they were preserved through oral transmission. 'The Vedas are still learnt by heart as they were long ago before the invasion of Alexander and could even now be restored from the lips of religious teachers if every manuscript or printed copy of them were destroyed'.[61]

58. Will Durant, *Our Oriental Heritage*, p. 408.

59. *The Cultural Heritage of India*, vol. I, p. 345.

60. A.A. Macdonell, *A History of Sanskrit Literature* (New York: Haskell House Publishers Ltd, 1968), p. 16.

61. Ibid., p. 8.

How was this achieved?

Once the text had been determined, 'extraordinary precautions soon began to be taken to guard the canonical text thus fixed against the possibility of any change or loss'.[62] 'These devices have been five in number', and are called *pāṭha* or manner of recitation. The *first* recitation represented the Vedic passages as such and as they are recited. The *second* recitation consisted of splitting up the text into words. If the words in the text are represented by a b c, then the second recitation would split it into a, b, c. Rules were framed and observed to account for the phonetic changes at the end and at the beginning of such words which were split up! The *third* recitation was formed by taking every word with the preceding and following words; symbolically, ab, bc, ca. The *fourth* method arose from the permutation of the third in three ways: ab, ba, ab, bc, cb, bc would be the symbolic representation. The *fifth* method formed combinations in five ways—ab, ba, abc, cba, abc, etc.[63] These were the methods used to preserve the text and 'the result has been its preservation with a faithfulness unique in literary history.'[64] It is interesting to compare this record of Vedic textual preservation with that of some other religious texts. Chinese culture has preserved the Confucian texts since *c.* sixth century BCE, but in writing, not through an oral tradition. The result is that although even today a Chinese can read what Confucius wrote, no one knows exactly how he pronounced the words. Thus the Chinese development contrasts with the Hindu. The Chinese text is written in the same way but pronounced differently, while the Vedic is pronounced in the same way though written differently, depending on the region of India it is preserved in.

The experience of the Pali canon of Buddhism is also instructive. It was fixed at the various Buddhist councils[65] by the turn of the Christian era; but it degenerated and the task of 'restoring canonical literature to its original purity' had to be undertaken by Buddhaghosha in the fifth century.[66] This is continued even today by the renewed

62. Ibid., p. 50.

63. V. Varadachari, *A History of Sanskrit Literature*, p. 10.

64. Ibid., p. 50.

65. A.L. Basham, *The Wonder That Was India* (New York: Grove Press Inc., 1954), p. 266.

66. P. Thomas, *Colonists and Foreign Missionaries of Ancient India* (Ernakulam: Joseph Thomasons and Co., 1963), p. 59.

dedication of Buddhist textual scholars since the Council in the late 1950s.

It is the antiquity of the Vedas, then, which renders the continuity of the oral tradition all the more remarkable. But how old are the Vedas?

It was earlier pointed out how the *Ṛg Veda* is historically the oldest. 'No comparable literature in any Indo-European language is nearly as old as the hymns of the Ṛg Veda, which stands quite by itself high up on an isolated peak of remote antiquity'.[67] But how remote is this remote antiquity? There is considerable dispute among scholars about the antiquity of the Vedas as will be clear from the following comparisons:[68]

Tilak	4000 to 2500 BCE
Jacobi	4000 BCE
Wilson	3500 BCE
Hough	2500 to 1400 BCE
R.C. Dutt	2000 to 1400 BCE
Roth	1000 BCE
Max Müller	1500 to 1200 BCE

(The single dates refer to the *Ṛg Veda,* others refer to the probable period span of Vedic literature up to the Upaniṣads).

Says Winternitz:[69] 'It is a fact, and a fact which is truly painful to have to admit that the opinions of the best scholars differ, not to the extent of centuries but to the extent of thousand of years'.

There are four possible approaches to the problem of fixing the age of the *Ṛg Veda* or/and of the Vedas.

(1) The Astronomical Approach: The time at which any astronomical observation was made can usually be determined by the position of the stars and the planets as stated in that observation. Some passages in the Vedas mention certain astronomical details,[70] but the opinions

67. Percival Spear, ed., *The Oxford History of India*, p. 44.

68. Acharya Chatursena, *Bhāratīya Saṁskṛti Kā Itihāsa* (Meerut: Rastogi & Co., 1964), p. 355; also see M. Chakravorti, *A Short History of Sanskrit Literature*, pp. 17–18.

69. M. Winternitz, *A History of Indian Literature*, p. 253.

70. *Taittirīya Brāhmaṇa* I, 52 and *Śatapatha Brāhmaṇa* II.I.3, for instance.

of scholars are divided on the interpretation of the texts which contain astronomical data.[71]

(2) The Historical Approach: The correlation of Vedic with epigraphic or archaeological evidence could provide a clue, as for instance through the Boghazköi Inscription. But here again divergent and even contradictory conclusions are possible.[72]

Most of the authors cited on the dating of the Vedas belong to a period anterior to the discovery of the Indus Valley civilization. In 1922–23, however, the Indus Valley civilization was discovered,[73] which pushed back the antiquity of Indian history to 3000 BCE.[74]

What implication does this have for the date of the Vedas? Unfortunately, the Indus script has not yet been deciphered,[75] nor have the authors of the Indus culture been identified with any certainty.[76] Sir John Marshall, among others, believes *c.*1500 BC to be the age of the Vedas and surmises that the Indus culture was destroyed by the Ṛg Vedic Aryans. There is, however, no definite proof of this.[77] On the other hand, protagonists of an earlier date have tried to identify the Indus culture with Vedic culture with some success.[78] Thus, it is 'impossible at the present state of our knowledge to come to a definite conclusion.'[79]

(3) The Linguistic Approach: The close relationship of the Zend Avesta and the Vedas led to considerable speculation about their comparative ages, but no widely accepted conclusion has emerged except that they are closely related in point of time.

(4) The Literary Approach: 'As all the external evidence fails we are compelled to rely on the evidence arising out of the history of Indian literature itself.'[80] Here, Max Müller established the Vedas as

71. Winternitz, *A History of Indian Literature*, pp. 256–61.

72. Ibid., pp. 265–71.

73. R.C. Majumdar, ed., *The Vedic Age* (Bombay: Bharatiya Vidya Bhavan, 1965), p. 70.

74. Ibid., p. 169.

75. Ibid., p. 190.

76. Ibid., p. 193.

77. Ibid., pp. 193–4.

78. Ibid., p. 193.

79. Ibid., p. 194.

80. Winternitz, *A History of Indian Literature*, pp. 270–1.

pre-Buddhist. And then, moving backwards, he surmised the following chronology for his own division of the corpus of Vedic literature into the Chandas, Mantra, Brāhmaṇa and Sūtra periods.

Chandas	1200 to 1000 BCE
Mantra	1000 to 800 BCE
Brāhmaṇa	800 to 600 BCE
Sūtra	600 to 200 BCE[81]

Winternitz suggests, in view of the wide divergence of opinion, that a 'more prudent course' would be 'to steer clear of any fixed dates and to guard against the extremes of a stupendously ancient period or a ludicrously modern epoch'.[82]

Perhaps the proper way of approaching the problem of the date of the Vedas as books is to not try and fix the earliest likely date but to settle for the time when they can reasonably be said to have been actually existing. This will give a free hand to scholarship to work out the time of their composition while enabling us, for the purposes of this section, to present a date by when they can be said to have become established as sacred books. 'The surest evidence in this respect is still the fact that Pārśva, Mahāvīra and Buddha pre-suppose the entire Veda as a literature to all intents and purposes completed and this is a limit we must not exceed.'[83]

In other words, the Vedas cannot be placed in a time after 1000 BC.[84] How far early they can be placed is a matter of dispute. It is important to bear in mind, however, that:

> We possess in the whole world no literary relics intellectually older than the oldest hymns of the Rig Veda and I doubt whether we possess any literary relics chronologically older at all events, in our own Aryan world. ...
>
> Who can deny that Veda (Rig Veda) is the oldest monument of Aryan speech and Aryan thought, which we possess? ...
>
> If now we ask how we can fix the date ... it is quite clear that we cannot hope to fix a terminum a quo. Whether the Vedic hymns were composed 1000, or 1500 or 2000 or 3000 years BC no power on earth will ever determine.[85]

81. See N.N. Law, *Age of the Ṛg Veda* (Calcutta: Firma K.L. Mukhopadhyaya, 1965), p. 1; Max Müller, *A History of Ancient Sanskrit Literature* (Varanasi: Chowkhamba Sanskrit Series, 1968), *passim.*

82. M. Winternitz, *A History of Indian Literature*, p. 271.

83. Ibid.

84. Winternitz regards this as too conservative; ibid., p. 271.

85. F. Max Müller, quoted by Dr. N.N. Law, *Age of the Ṛg Veda*, p. 10.

Whatever the differences between the traditional Hindu and the modern Western views about the Vedas as books, in some respects they are one in assigning the Vedas a key role in the religion and culture of India.

The remarkable continuity of Indian civilization, which no other country in the world except China shares, has excited the wonder of several scholars. As A.A. Macdonell points out:

> A Vedic stanza of immemorial antiquity, addressed to the sun-god Savitri is still recited in the daily worship of the Hindus. The god Vishṇu, adored more than 3000 years ago, has countless votaries in India at the present day. Fire is still produced for sacrificial purposes by means of two sticks, as it was in ages even more remote. The wedding ceremony of the modern Hindu, to single out but one social custom, is essentially the same as it was long before the Christian era.[86]

All the elements mentioned in the above passage—the worship of the sun-god and Viṣṇu and the marriage custom—go back to the Vedas. In other words, the continuity of Indian culture rests upon and goes back to the Vedas. Moreover, all the major systems of Indian philosophy are either rooted in the Vedas or have been profoundly influenced by them. All codes of law claim to be based on or profess to impart the teaching of the Vedas. Even the *Ṛg Veda*, Whitney points out, contains 'the germs of the whole after-development of Indian religion and polity'.[87] Similarly, Indian literature goes back to the Vedas and the refined poetry, the philosophical vigour, the voluptuous mysticism and the epic simplicity of later classical writers and poets would 'float before our eyes like the mirage of a desert, unless they are provided with the historical background by the Vedas'.[88]

For the West, the importance of the Vedas lies in this: that they laid the foundation for the study of philology and comparative religion. 'In the earliest ages the Indians already analysed their sacred writings with a view to philology, classified the linguistic phenomena as a scientific system, and developed their grammar so highly that even to-day modern philology can use their attainments as a foundation'.[89]

86. A.A. Macdonell, *A History of Sanskrit Literature*, p. 8.
87. Percival Spear, ed., *The Oxford History of India*, p. 45.
88. V.S. Sukthankar, *Ghate's Lectures on Rig Veda* (Poona: Oriental Book Agency, 1966), p. 6.
89. Winternitz, *A History of Indian Literature*, p. 7.

Take, for instance, the modern English word *fortune*. It came to England through the Normans who had it in the same form, *fortune*, in northern France. It derives from the Latin *Fortuna*, which was the name of an old deity in Italy, who brought good or evil and was spoken of as the daughter of Zeus, who corresponds to the Vedic *Duos*. One of the deities the Aryans worshipped was Ushas or Dawn. Ushas is also mentioned as the daughter of Duos (or Zeus) in the Vedas. It is also called *Haryat*, which connects up with *Fortuna* through the root 'ferre' which occurs as 'Hri' (to bring) in the Vedas. Thus we can link up Ushas of the Vedas with the Italian Fortuna and the modern English word *fortune*. 'It is a long journey, indeed, from the golden rays of the dawn to the bright gold coins, by which now fortune is measured.'[90]

From the point of view of comparative religion, too, the Vedas are of great significance. They are the first account of the religion of the ancient Aryans—of which Zoroastrianism, and the Greek and Hindu religions, according to the present views, are different versions. At times, the Vedas tie up in an amazing way even with Christianity. Max Müller's remarks show how the 'in the beginning there was the word' can be compared to the Vedas.[91] Further research may reveal more clues.

The Vedas have sometimes been criticized as deserving of study in the same sense in which a physician studies the twaddle of idiots or the ravings of a madman.[92] Max Müller holds it undeniable that much, if not most of it, is 'full of rubbish'.[93] H. Oldenberg sees in the *Ṛg Veda* 'the clear trace of an ever-increasing intellectual enervation.'[94]

On the other hand, the Hindus regard the Vedas as their sacred scripture which 'provide the roots of the later growth of the Hindu tradition.'[95] More especially, the Upaniṣads section of the Vedas has excited the admiration of several generations of scholars.

How are these views to be reconciled? It appears that by viewing

90. V.S. Sukthankar, *Ghate's Lectures on Rig Veda*, p. 11.

91. F. Max Müller, *Three Lectures on the Vedanta Philosophy*, pp. 146–50.

92. Professor Eggeling's opinion mentioned by M. Krishnamachariar, *History of Classical Sanskrit Literature*, p. xii.

93. Max Müller, *Three Lectures on the Vedānta Philosophy*, p. 113.

94. Ibid., p. 63.

95. Anslee Embree, ed., *The Hindu Tradition*, p. 4; M. Winternitz, *A History of Indian Literature*, p. 48.

the Vedas as a book we gain a new insight into the context of this controversy.

As a book, the Vedas appear to be the record of the spiritual experience of a race. Just as a person grows through the stages of childhood and adolescence to maturity, the religious experience of the Hindus might show its evolution through the worship of Nature and a preoccupation with philosophical refinement of a high order. From this point of view, the Vedic classificatory scheme takes on a new significance. It also seems to accommodate the concept of evolutionary growth, thereby establishing a consistency among the various aspects of the Vedas.

Conclusion

It is impossible to open any book of Indian subjects without being referred to an earlier authority, which is generally acknowledged by the Hindus as the basis of all their knowledge, whether sacred or profane. This earlier authority, which we find alluded to in theological and philosophical works, as well as in poetry, in codes of law, in astronomical, grammatical, metrical and lexicographic compositions, is called by the one comprehensive name, *the Veda.*[96]

The essence of the significance of the Vedas as books lies in the fact that the Vedas are 'the book of origins'.[97] They are not the first books in the history of the world; that honour perhaps belongs to the *Egyptian Book of the Dead*. But the Vedas are the original Indo-European work and contain the origins of later Hindu development in the religious[98] and even secular fields. Moreover, the Vedas as books are 'living books', that they continue to mould the life of the Hindus. Thus they have been a living book for perhaps as long as the Jewish Pentateuch and have been preserved and restored in a unique manner. These aspects make the study of the Vedas as books both fascinating and rewarding.[99]

96. F. Max Müller, *A History of Ancient Sanskrit Literature*, p. 9.

97. See Brian Smith, *Reflections on Resemblance, Ritual and Religion* (New York: Oxford University Press, 1989).

98. See J.C. Heesterman, *The Broken World of Sacrifice: An Essay in Ancient Indian Ritual* (Chicago: University of Chicago Press, 1993).

99. See K. Satchidananda Murty, *Vedic Hermeneutics* (Delhi: Motilal Banarsidass, 1993).

Bibliography

Bandhu, Vishva, *The Vedas and Śāstras.* Hoshiarpur: Vishveshvarananda Institute, 1966.

Basham, A.L., *The Wonder That Was India.* New York: Grove Press Inc., 1954.

Chakravorti, M., *A Short History of Sanskrit Literature.* Calcutta: 111 Upper Circular Road, 1936.

Chatterjee, Satischandra and Dhirendramohan Datta, *An Introduction to Indian Philosophy.* Calcutta: University of Calcutta, 1968.

The Cultural Heritage of India. Calcutta: The Ramakrishna Mission Institute of Culture, 1958.

Deutsch, Eliot, *Advaita Vedānta: A Philosophical Reconstruction.* Honolulu: East-West Center Press, 1969.

Deutsch, Eliot and J.A.B. van Buitenen, *A Source Book of Advaita Vedānta.* Honolulu: The University Press of Hawaii, 1971.

Devaraja, N.K., *Hinduism and Christianity.* New Delhi: Asia Publishing House, 1969.

Dumont, Louis, *Homo Hierarchicus: The Caste System and Its Implications* (complete revised English edition). Chicago: University of Chicago Press, 1980.

Durant, Will, *Our Oriental Heritage.* New York: Simon & Schuster, 1954.

Eliade, Miracea, editor-in-chief, *The Encyclopedia of Religion.* New York: Macmillan Publishing Co., 1987, 16 vols.

Embree, A.T., ed., *The Hindu Tradition.* New York: The Modern Library, 1966.

Encyclopedia Britannica, Chicago: William Benton, 1968. vol. III.

Funk and Wagnalls. *New Standard Dictionary of the English Language.* New York: Funk and Wagnalls Co.

Grimes, John, *Problems and Perspectives in Religious Discourse: Advaita Vedānta Implications.* Albany, NY: State University of New York Press, 1994.

Hiriyanna, M., *Outlines of Indian Philosophy.* London: George Allen & Unwin, 1932.

———, *The Essentials of Indian Philosophy.* London: George Allen & Unwin, 1948.

Hopkins, Thomas J. *The Hindu Religious Tradition.* Belmont, California: Dickenson Publishing Co., Inc., 1971.

Jacob, Colonel G.A., ed. *A Manual of Hindu Pantheism: The Vedāntasāra.* Varanasi: Bharat-Bharati, 1974.

Klostermaier, Klaus K. *A Survey of Hinduism.* Albany, NY: State University of New York Press, 1989.

Krishnamachariar, M. *History of Classical Sanskrit Literature.* Madras: Tirumalai-Tirupati Devasthanams Press, 1937.

Lal, Chaman. *Textbook of Indian Culture.* Bombay: Bharatiya Vidya Bhavan, 1968.

Law, N.N., *Age of the Ṛg Veda.* Calcutta: Firma K.L. Mukhopadhyaya, 1965.

Macdonell, A.A., *A History of Sanskrit Literature*. New York: Haskell House Publishers Ltd, 1968.

Mahadevan, T.M.P. *Outlines of Hinduism*. Bombay: Chetana Ltd, 1971.

Majumdar, R.C. ed., *The Vedic Age*. Bombay: Bharatiya Vidya Bhavan, 1964.

Mukherjee, S.N. *Sir William Jones*. Cambridge: Cambridge University Press, 1968.

Müller, Max F., *Vedic Hymns* (1891). Delhi: Motilal Banarsidass, 1964.

———, *Three Lectures on the Vedanta Philosophy*. Varanasi: Chowkhamba Sanskrit Series, 1967.

Murty, K. Satchidananda. *Revelation and Reason in Advaita Vedānta*. New York: Columbia University Press, 1959.

Nakamura, Hajime. *A History of Early Vedānta Philosophy*. Delhi: Motilal Banarsidass, 1983.

Radhakrishnan, S., *The Hindu View of Life*. New York: The Macmillan Co. 1927.

Renou, Louis, ed., *Hinduism*. New York: George Braziller, 1962.

Śāstrī, Chatursena Acharya, *Bhāratīya Saṁskṛti Kā Itihāsa* ('A History of Indian Culture'). Meerut: Rastogi and Co., 1964.

Sharma, Arvind, ed. *Our Religions*, San Francisco: Harper, 1993.

Smart, Ninian. *Worldviews: Crosscultural Explorations of Human Beliefs*. New York: Charles Scribner's Sons, 1983.

Spear, Percival, ed., *The Oxford History of India*. Oxford: Clarendon Press, 1964.

Sukthankar, V.S. *Ghate's Lectures on Rig Veda*. Poona: Oriental Book Agency, 1966.

Swami Prabhavananda. *The Spiritual Heritage of India*. London: George Allen & Unwin, 1962.

Swami Satguru Sivaya Subramuniya, *Dancing with Śiva: Hinduism's Contmporary Catechism*. Concord, California: Himalayan Academy, 1993.

Thomas, P., *Colonists and Foreign Missionaries of Ancient India*. Ernakulam: Joseph Thomasons and Co., 1963.

Varadachari, V., *A History of the Samskrta Literature*. Allahabad: Ram Narain Lal Beni Prasad, 1960.

Voight, J.H., *Max Mueller: The Man and His Ideas*. Calcutta: Firma K.L. Mukhopadhyaya, 1967.

Weber, Mann and Zachariae, *The History of Indian Literature* (1878) Varanasi: Chowkhamba Sanskrit Series, 1961.

Webster's *New Twentieth Century Dictionary* of the English Language. New York: The World Publishing Co., 1968.

Winternitz, M., *A History of Indian Literature*. Calcutta: University of Calcutta Press, 1965.

Name Index

Subject Index